Lifestyle Economics

Lifestyle Economics

Consumer Behavior in a Turbulent World

Peter Earl

Lecturer in Economics
University of Tasmania

ST. MARTIN'S PRESS   NEW YORK

© Peter E. Earl, 1986

All rights reserved. For information, write:
Scholarly & Reference Division,
St. Martin's Press, Inc., 175 Fifth Avenue, New York, NY10010

First published in the United States of America in 1986

Printed in Great Britain

ISBN 0-312-48585-9

Library of Congress Cataloging-in-Publication Data

Earl, Peter E.
  Lifestyle Economics

  Bibliography: p.
  Includes index.
  1. Consumers. 2. Life style. I. Title
HC79.C6E22 1986 658.8'342 86-3852
ISBN 0-312-48585-9

Contents

Preface ix

1 Introduction: Lifestyles and Economics 1
  1.1 Economics and the World of the Modern Consumer 1
  1.2 The Methodology of Behavioural Economics 5
  1.3 Outline of the Rest of the Book 21

2 Characteristics, Household Production, and Choice 24
  2.1 Introduction 24
  2.2 The Hicksian Legacy 25
  2.3 Lancaster's Approach 29
  2.4 Criticisms of Lancaster's Approach 33
  2.5 The 'Hedonic Pricing' Literature 41
  2.6 Compensatory Models in the Marketing Literature 46
  2.7 Conclusion 51

3 The Enterprising Consumer 53
  3.1 Introduction 53
  3.2 Deliberative and Routine Decisions 56
  3.3 Strategic Planning by Households 59
  3.4 Ways of Life in Increasingly Turbulent Situations:
      The Evolving Consumer (1) 68
  3.5 Households as Organisations 79
  3.6 Conclusion 83

4 The Inquisitive Consumer 85
  4.1 Introduction 85
  4.2 The Consumer as a Scientist 87
  4.3 Prediction, Control, and Choice 92
  4.4 Emotions and Rationality 96
  4.5 Confidence, Competence, and Choice:
      The Evolving Consumer (2) 101
  4.6 Conclusion 109

5	Possibilities and Potential Surprises	111
	5.1 Introduction	111
	5.2 Origins of Ideas in the Consumer's Mind	112
	5.3 Landscapes of the Future	116
	5.4 The Possibility of Probability	123
	5.5 Possible Non-Probabilistic Alternatives to Potential Surprise	129
	5.6 Conclusion	134
6	How Minds Are Made Up	136
	6.1 Introduction	136
	6.2 Rules for Thought	137
	6.3 Conflicts and Complex Hierarchies	145
	6.4 Personality and Prediction	147
	6.5 Environmental Turbulence and Mental Organisation: The Evolving Consumer (3)	154
	6.6 Resistance to Change	162
	6.7 Conclusion	170
7	Complexity and Tests of Adequacy	174
	7.1 Introduction	174
	7.2 The Choice Matrix and its Implications	175
	7.3 Compensatory Rules	179
	7.4 Non-Compensatory Rules	182
	7.5 Short cuts within Priority Systems	188
	7.6 Tie-Break techniques and the Resolution of Dilemmas	194
	7.7 Rules within Rules	201
	7.8 Conclusion: No General Rules	204
8	Rules for Evaluating Uncertain Prospects	207
	8.1 Introduction	207
	8.2 The Expected Utility Rule and Some Recent Variants	208
	8.3 'Safety First'	212
	8.4 Procedures that Compartmentalise Gains and Losses	213
	8.5 Moulds of Tolerance for Uncertain Prospects	220
	8.6 Rules for When 'We Simply do not Know'	227
	8.7 Conclusion	230

9	Non-Compensatory Choices in Retrospect and Prospect	232
	9.1 Introduction	232
	9.2 Antecedent Analyses	233
	9.3 Orthodox Reactions	238
	9.4 The Validity of the Non-Compensatory Principle	243
	9.5 Principles—At 'All Costs'	247
	9.6 Future Empirical Work	250
10	Choice Rules and the Competitive Process	254
	10.1 Introduction	254
	10.2 Overall Implications of Price and Product Changes	255
	10.3 Effects of Price Changes on Characteristic Filtering Processes	258
	10.4 Characteristic Filtering with Income and Product Changes	263
	10.5 Implications for Pricing and Product Strategies	267
	10.6 What Car?—An Analysis of some Recommendations	271
	10.7 Trade Policy with Non-Compensatory Choice Rules	280
	10.8 Incentives and Risk Taking	282
	10.9 Concluding Thoughts	284
	Bibliography	287
	Index	306

Preface

This book holds in store very many surprises for readers who have not already encountered my earlier work on decision making and who have hitherto confined themselves to the orthodox neoclassical approach to economics. For such readers, the task of getting acquainted with the analysis in this book could be seen as an exploratory exercise prior to any in-depth study of the behavioural literature to which it refers. If it fails to convince them that a more extensive intellectual retooling is in order, it may at least leave them with a better idea of the lines along which deviant economists such as myself are pursuing research into consumer behaviour. The latter outcome would of course not be ideal from my own standpoint and I would hope that their resistance to further reading in the behavioural literature arose despite, rather than because of, the efforts I have made—first impressions of an unfamiliar literature can be all-important (see Earl, 1983a). Nonetheless, I would be pleased to have played a part in increasing the awareness amongst the profession at large in respect of alternatives to the neoclassical paradigm.

Economists who are familiar with *The Economic Imagination* (hereafter *TEI*), my first book on choice, will no doubt be wondering about its relationship with this book. *TEI* has a subtitle which begins with the word 'Towards'; this choice of wording was made to suggest that the analysis in the book was not to be regarded as my final thinking on the subject. Sure enough, shortly after I finished its sequel, *The Corporate Imagination*, I turned my attention back to individual decision makers and substantially reworked *TEI* under the title 'A Behavioural Analysis of Choice'. The University of Cambridge awarded me the Degree of Doctor of Philosophy in 1984 on the basis of that analysis, but even before I submitted it for examination I realised there was much more that I should say on the subject. The present book represents a further reworking, reorientation and extension of my original thinking on the subject of consumer behaviour. Some indication of the extent of the evolution that is involved may be given by the fact that reference is made to over two hundred works that were neither discussed nor used as empirical sources, nor noted as containing related material, in *TEI*.

However, it would be inappropriate for me to represent *Lifestyle Economics* as something other than a cross between a second edition of *TEI* and an altogether new book. Many of the basic ideas and references from *TEI* are carried over, most notably those concerning satisficing, personal construct psychology, potential surprise analysis and the 'characteristic filtering' view of brand and budgeting choices. Since I cannot presume all readers know of these ideas from *TEI* or other sources, I have to reintroduce them as if from scratch before I can begin to elaborate upon them. (The lack of a widespread knowledge of the 'hard core' elements of my research programme makes it very difficult to disseminate extensions to them via the medium of the journal article.) But in reintroducing these concepts I have carried over only a handful of sentences from *TEI*, for I can now see more accessible and appealing ways of presentation. However, in some cases I refer readers back to *TEI* for elaborations of some of the arguments that underpin the new analysis. In other words, this book can be read as if it is self-contained yet it does not render *TEI* altogether obsolete; readers who have not yet done so may find it particularly helpful to investigate Chapters 1, 2 and 7 of *TEI* in order to gain a broader view of the paradigm I employ and of the interface between consumer theory and industrial economics.

The new features of *Lifestyle Economics* include the following:

(1) A more extensive critical analysis of theoretical and empirical literature conventionally associated with the analysis of demand in characteristics space.

(2) The generalisation to the household context of recent contributions to the behavioural literature on corporate behaviour that emphasise strategic and organisational methods for facing up to complex, turbulent environments and how preferred strategies evolve or are suddenly switched as perceptions of the environment change. The resulting

analysis could be called 'a behavioural approach to household production theory'.

(3) A detailed analysis of causes of flexibility and resistance to change on the part of consumers and of the patterns of choice to which these attitudes give rise. This analysis draws on the contribution of Hinkle (1965) to personal construct psychology, along with other work in this field on the extremes of obsessive and schizophrenic behaviour that I did not discuss in *TEI*. Hinkle's ideas seem to provide very important clues about why some goods or characteristics matter more than others to particular consumers, and they hence provide a possible basis for understanding demand elasticities.

(4) An attempt to integrate analyses of deliberative decision making, rule of thumb choices, and the processes whereby expectations are formed. This integration seeks to reduce these three phenomena to outcomes of the application of rules that the consumer has previously evolved, and it is very much inspired by Simon's (1976) work on the distinction between 'substantive' and 'procedural' rationality. At times the analysis may seem to veer close to the domain of cognitive scientists who conduct work on artificial intelligence, for I tend to distinguish between the consumer's mental 'hardware', with its limited ability physically to process information, and the consumer's 'software', her personal programme of procedures for coping with life.

(5) A presentation of the case for believing that consumers often use a *multiplicity* of both compensatory and non-compensatory decision making procedures in a contingent order even within a single act of choice. Coupled with (4), this leads me to the conclusion that it is much more instructive to see consumers as going through life experimenting with possible ways of deciding what they should do, rather than as choosing amongst previously evaluated goods on the basis of a prespecified set of 'preferences'.

(6) A detailed, chapter-length critical discussion of previous literature on priority-based choices and of mainstream reactions to such ideas, followed by a much more comprehensive analysis of policy implications of decision making procedures that defy the 'principle of gross substitution'.

(7) A much more detailed analysis of the basis of Shackle's 'potential surprise' approach to choice under uncertainty and of how it relates both to recent developments within orthodox literature and to Keynes' views on 'animal spirits'. Readers may also note some evolution in my own treatment of Shackle's ideas and a consideration of Ford's (1983) book on Shackle's theory, which appeared around the same time as *TEI* was published.

(8) A more extensive use of pertinent empirical work and a manifesto for much new empirical work, particularly studies involving the use of Hinkle's 'implication grid' technique.

These new features reflect not merely the directions my own thoughts and reading have taken in the three and a half years since I finished *TEI*; they also owe a lot to points of criticism raised by reviewers of *TEI*. My good fortune in receiving a wide range of reviews from around the world rather prevented me from taking up space dealing explicitly with each reaction, but I hope uncited reviewers will be able to detect evidence of a constructive reaction to their critical comments.

Once again my explicit focus is on lifestyles in affluent economies, but the analysis seems readily applicable to the study of consumer behaviour in poor countries and, in the longer term, I plan to write a further book applying ideas from the behavioural and transactions cost/property rights literature to matters of economic development. Once again, too, this is a book populated almost exclusively by female consumers. Reverse sexism is not intended by this policy; rather, I am merely trying to remind blinkered readers that women, as well as men, can take decisions of significance.

This book was partly conceived and wholly written in Tasmania, a corner of today's turbulent world that has attracted many people in search of a lifestyle 'away from it all'. Some of the ideas were tried out in departmental workshops at the University of Stirling as well as the University of Tasmania, and only a few days before I left the United Kingdom I was delighted to receive a lively response to a seminar entitled 'The Evolving Consumer' that I presented at the City of Birmingham Polytechnic. In addition to thanking members of these audiences, I also offer my thanks to the following: to my thesis examiners, Professors J. F. Pickering and R. C. O. Matthews, for some constructive comments and suggestions; to Professor G. L. S. Shackle, for encouragement and for correspondence that improved the exposition in section 5.4; to Neil Kay, whose pioneering work on corporate evolution has been a major source of inspiration (see especially Kay, 1982, p. 150); to John Eatwell, for pointing me in the direction of the neglected but relevant writings of A. G. Hart; to Michael Brooks, Tasmania's other subjectivist economist, for many hours of stimulating discussions; to Steve Cropley, editor of *Car Magazine*, for permission to use material reproduced in Chapter 10; and, finally, to Sharon Axford, not only for putting up with my obsessive concentration on finishing this book and its predecessors in rapid succession, but also for drawing my attention to work by Makhlouf-Norris and Norris (1972) and Adams-Webber (1979) which helped to crystallise my own emerging ideas concerning 'mental strategies'. I naturally must bear full responsibility for any errors, ambiguities and omissions that remain.

1 Introduction: Lifestyles and Economics

1.1 ECONOMICS AND THE WORLD OF THE MODERN CONSUMER

Being a consumer is not an easy role to play successfully, even in an affluent society. Consumers have to act in a complex, unsettled world where surprises are commonplace and not mere deviations around a trend, a world full of novelty and obsolescence, a world that is, in short, turbulent. If opportunities are not to be thrown needlessly away, the consumer must be a skilled speculator and strategist. Instability in exchange rates and inflation rates, and the unevenness with which inflationary forces feed through the system, makes it difficult to assess trends in respect of relative prices, including real wages. Technological change results in flux in the qualities and varieties of goods on offer, while the increasing complexity of modern products opens up scope for expensive errors when consumer durables are being purchased: the modern consumer cannot hope to be an expert buyer in all markets. These difficulties are compounded by question-marks caused by government policy proposals, for example concerning moves from direct to indirect taxation or regulations concerning the introduction of lead-free petrol. Increasingly, consumers may find that structural changes in the world economy are undermining expectations about employment and promotion prospects that they have long taken for granted; yet new opportunities may not instantly stand out. Added to these worries are new puzzles arising from social changes such as the rise of the Women's Movement—for example, how a couple might carve out two careers as a joint future without these jeopardising each other.

Given this, one might expect that economists would devote a good deal of attention to the ways in which consumers set about making up their minds in situations of uncertainty and complexity. Unfortunately, this has not been the case. The typical economist proceeds to analyse consumer behaviour in a way which makes the problem of choice trivial. The individual consumer is portrayed as if she already has a completely specified set of preferences and seeks to maximise her utility subject to three constraints: her accumulated human and non-human capital, the state of technology, and the prevailing set of relative prices. The consumer's prior investments in her own skills, coupled with her initial endowment of human capital, determine her employment opportunities. The latter, in turn, constrain her in respect of the commodities she will be able and inclined to purchase, given the prevailing set of prices. Having assumed that the consumer is able to rank hypothetical bundles of consumption goods and employment obligations in order of preference, it is not surprising that the typical economist comes to think of the consumer simply as if she selects the highest-ranking bundle from her feasible set. What we have is an example of what Herbert Simon (1976, p. 130) calls 'substantive rationality': the achievement of given goals within the limits imposed by given conditions. *How* the consumer works out what these 'given conditions' might be is not discussed. The economist theorises as if the consumer has defined her problem in advance in a way that makes its solution transparent, and then allows her on to the stage seemingly to solve it.

To deal with uncertainty and the fact that consumers do not finalise their purchases all at once, the analysis might be reformulated in probabilistic terms. That is to say, a conventional economist might ask us to think of the consumer as if she has assigned probabilities to future sets of relative prices, technological changes (these two sets of probabilities would very likely be interrelated) and environmental situations at points in the future. These probabilities could be imagined to be used as decision weights, complicating the analysis somewhat for the analyst, yet not for the hypothetical consumer who could be imagined as if she were perfectly able to deal with all the extra information. Whether or not this probabilistic approach actually deals with genuine uncertainty is open to question, since it does not admit the possibility of consumers being concerned that they may be surprised by events not on their lists of 'probables'. Anyway, most of the time, and particularly in the teaching of undergraduates, the conventional analysis leaves out any mention of uncertainty (for evidence, see the indexes of texts on consumer choice or microeconomic theory generally). Choices are made to seem clinical, via references to 'commodity X versus commodity Y'; or homely, via references to 'pints of beer versus loaves of bread'. They are not represented explicitly as hazardous, expensive to reverse and caught up in the march of structural and technological change.

Perhaps the orthodox economists, who seem untroubled by analyses which leave out discussions of how difficult it is to be a consumer, are themselves the kinds of consumers who are so successful that they are never disappointed and do not realise how gifted they are as strategists and speculators. Perhaps they are not the kind of consumer who gets into the housing market at the top of the boom, who always seems to manage to buy 'high-tech' products that are about to be phased out in favour of something better, who on moving overseas fails to act quickly enough to save thousands on a tariff-free luxury car import and who on her arrival ends up buying a 'lemon' instead, who turns her career into a 'dead end', who, try as she might, never manages to look fashionable, who is always 'up to her eyes in debt', and so on. Perhaps such economists are so socially detached that they do not see consumers, like firms, engaging in a competitive struggle to establish themselves in particular 'league' positions, and not always coping well enough to avoid relegation to a more lowly status in the world. But another possibility is that the orthodox approach to model building finds it difficult to accommodate interdependent choices as well as choices that are, in a significant proportion of cases, systematically or decisively wrong; the situation could be rather akin to that in the tale of the drunk who has dropped his keys in a dark alley yet is looking for them by a lamp-post, because that is where it is light.

In the midst of conventional analyses of consumer behaviour, one also fails to encounter the term 'lifestyle', which most consumers would define as meaning a 'way of life'. This is in great contrast to what one can see in the marketing literature: in almost every consumer behaviour text designed for marketing students, much space is devoted to describing the different lifestyles in terms of which people may be classified, and how these ways of life are related to consumer attitudes. Sometimes, marketeers have devoted entire books to this task—an excellent, highly readable recent example is *The Nine American Lifestyles* (Mitchell, 1985). If economists are aware of this literature, they may not feel it worth mentioning as something which might augment or qualify their work. Of course, it is not the 'done thing' for economists to associate themselves publicly with the marketing profession. But they may well reason that lifestyles are no more than patterns that result from successive, if not actually once-and-for-all, optimising exercises in which consumers pit their preferences against their constraints.

In a simple, well-patterned and surprise-free world, such a view of the lifestyles uncovered by market research might be entirely adequate for policy-making purposes. Parts of the turbulent world of today might even approximate reasonably well to the world of orthodox economics. But what of the rest: the situations that are complex, mysterious, hazardous and yet potentially rewarding? Here, I believe we have a case for trying to look at the underpinnings of observed consumer choices in a rather different manner, to see if any novel policy conclusions emerge as candidates for serious study. In this book, I am going to look at consumer lifestyles from the standpoint of a non-mainstream approach to economics, known as behavioural theory. My policy orientation will encompass marketing issues in addition to traditional concerns of the economist. Running through the analysis will be a tension between lifestyle and turbulence; I shall be depicting patterns of consumer behaviour as if they result from the use of relatively inflexible methods of trying to cope with a mobile environment to which perfect adaptation is rendered impossible by complexity and uncertainty (see Heiner, 1983). In other words, I am going to treat 'ways of life' as if they are viscous collections of procedures for dealing with fluid situations in which ambiguity is the order of the day. I shall not normally speak of consumers as having sets of preferences. Nor shall I presume that consumers necessarily develop viable—let alone foolproof—procedures for controlling their environments or surviving in them despite inherent scope for error and unpleasant surprises. To do so would seem unwise when it is commonplace to see households disintegrating; lives overshadowed by feelings of regret concerning missed opportunities; people seeking different worlds via drink, drugs and other escapist activities;

extensive use of tranquillisers, social workers and psychiatrists; and finance companies inviting tenders for repossessed consumer durables. But it would be heartening to think that some consumers might find that what I have to say helps them improve their own processes of decision making.

1.2 THE METHODOLOGY OF BEHAVIOURAL ECONOMICS

Before I outline the structure of this book and proceed to the main body of the text, it may be useful if I present a detailed explanation of how a behavioural economist such as myself tends to operate. This may help readers understand the ordering of the material in subsequent chapters. More importantly, though, it may help give them a feel of the lifestyle idea that I will be developing. The latter possibility arises because an economist's (or any other scientist's) methodology really defines his or her 'way of life' whilst working. In other words, each economist has a set of 'ways' for dealing with, and defining, the subject matter of economics, just as an individual may have a methodology for dealing with everyday life. Different economists operate in different 'ways' and if we know what these are, we may be able to anticipate with a good degree of accuracy the kinds of contributions they may choose to make. Just as one might seek to classify consumers into groups with nearly enough identical ways of trying to cope with the world in general, so one may usefully classify economists, even if their individuality means we shall sometimes be surprised by their behaviour. Whereas we may have nine American lifestyles, there seem to be seven schools of economics: neoclassical, Marxian, neo-Ricardian, neo-Austrian, institutionalist, Post Keynesian and behaviouralist. My own brand of behavioural economics overlaps in some degree with all the other schools; for example, a Marxian might see similarities between my discussions of consumer anxiety (see Chapter 4) and Marx's concept of alienation, but it would be most unwise generally to classify my work as Marxian! There would be far less danger of confusion were I classified as an institutionalist or Post Keynesian (the latter particularly), rather than as a behavioural theorist. What follows should be recognised as very much a personal view of a behavioural approach to economics; it is not guaranteed to overlap 100 per cent with other self-confessed behaviouralists' views (see Katona, 1980; Cyert and Simon, 1983).

1.2.1 The Subject Matter of Economics

A behavioural economist does not confine her attention only to resource allocation decisions that involve market transactions. Rather, like the maverick neoclassical economist Gary Becker (1976), she is interested in resource allocation in general, including choices such as those concerning marriage and social interaction. Many will doubtless object that the latter kinds of choice are really the province of the social psychologist. The dividing line is far from clear. As far as society is concerned, decisions about personal relationships are certainly not without 'economic' implications of the conventional kind; in fact, Duck's (1983) recent survey of the social psychology of close relationships opens with a catalogue of the economic consequences of ill-managed relationships. Decisions about marriage, divorce and acts of infidelity will have major impacts on the consumption lifestyles that the individuals involved wil be able to adopt; so market choices may not appropriately be separated in all cases from choices of personal relationships. But we should also note that, within the confines of 'non-market transactions', people are pursuing goals that can be, and often are, pursued by others who use the market to a much greater extent. Market transactions presuppose choices between using the market to produce particular outcomes, and either 'doing it oneself' or 'doing it via social exchange'.

1.2.2 The Purpose of Theoretical Analysis

Like any other economist, a behavioural theorist would claim to be theorising not for theory's sake but in order to assist in the design of policies that seek to avoid wasting opportunities for achieving desired outcomes. However, an economist such as myself holds a controversial view concerning the form such assistance might take. The prevailing wisdom—which may have much to be said in its favour if the world is not full of surprises—seems to be that policy makers should be provided with simple-to-manipulate deterministic models that so far have not been demonstrated to be false. This viewpoint, following Friedman (1953), also considers that there is no need to complicate models by introducing assumptions that seem closer to reality, unless this enhances their predictive capabilities. The behavioural theorist, by contrast, emphasises that the future is not in all respects going to be the same as the past and thus warns that deterministic models may suddenly cease to predict with their usual reliability, much to the embarrassment of their users. Such a theorist therefore does not pretend to be able to say what *will* happen. Instead, she sees her role as being to open the mind of the policy maker to pertinent possibilities—varieties of things that seemingly *could* happen—and to assist in attempts to evaluate how seriously these might be taken. It is absolutely vital that the second aspect of the role is not neglected; for if it is, the economic advisor is liable simply to produce confusion in her paymaster's mind when she presents open-ended models or multiple perspectives on a single problem. Once presented with lists of possibilities that seem difficult to dismiss, the policy maker may then choose in ways that leave her in a position to grasp opportunities or deal with difficulties that would otherwise have come as complete surprises. However, despite the best efforts of behaviouralist economic advisors to decide upon the bounds of possibility, there may still be occasions on which the unexpected does happen and past decisions are regretted.

For the policy maker with limited resources at her disposal, a problem will be posed by advice that suggests a broad range of rival outcomes should be taken seriously. Insuring against highly undesirable outcomes, like ensuring one's capacity to make the best of highly desirable outcomes, is a costly business: there is the possibility of spreading resources needlessly thinly if one hedges one's bets. Hence, despite the advice that she has received, the policy maker may well gamble in the hope that the actual outcome lies within a narrower range.

1.2.3 The Building Blocks of Behavioural Analysis

In searching for possible ways in which decision makers might seriously be imagined to act, the behavioural theorist follows lines of enquiry that conventional theorists, seeing their roles differently, studiously avoid. To begin with, the upside-down model-building philosophy of mainstream economics is inverted. The orthodox approach has been incisively characterised by Coddington (1975, p. 151) as follows:

Instead of asking how reason can be applied to the knowledge that men can or do have of their economic circumstances, [neoclassical economic theory] asks how reason can be applied to circumstances that are perfectly known. The problems of what can be known and how it can come to be known—problems of ignorance, uncertainty, risk, deception, delusion, perception, conjecture, adaptation and learning—are then tackled as a complication or refinement of the theory....

The existing mainstream of economic theory has developed in a manner which has accommodated these knowledge deficiency problems as refinements to the theory of economic action rather than rudiments of it.

Behavioural theory gets straight to the heart of the matter by treating such problems as analytical rudiments.

Inevitably, this involves calling at an early stage upon contributions from other disciplines. For example, suppose I am considering how changes in the state of information may affect consumer behaviour. The conventional economics literature, particularly that associated with the 'rational expectations hypothesis', assumes that all relevant information is taken account by decision makers. However, it does not discuss how people decide which information is relevant, when different pieces of information conflict. Since the information may concern possibilities that would represent great departures from the present situation as well as ones that imply 'no change', I cannot in practice judge how people might reasonably be expected to react unless I understand how they form their beliefs and why they dismiss some notions as unbelievable. To offer advice, I must either develop my own analysis completely from scratch—a daunting task to say the least, and possibly one involving a great waste of my time—or I must investigate the literature of psychology, possibly also of sociology, including any pertinent studies of what people so far have been able to believe (though I must keep in mind the possible dangers of extrapolating such findings into new contexts).

This willingness to examine the work of other behavioural sciences is one reason why the term 'behavioural economics' is not an inappropriate one for characterising the work of theorists such as myself: the analysis that emerges is in large part shaped by findings concerning the inability of people to behave in practice in particular ways, and evidence concerning the ways in which they are often observed to behave instead, given these limitations.

Perhaps most significant are results from experimental psychology concerning the ability of decision makers to handle information. The overwhelming message is that the capacity for human minds to formulate and solve the problems that may surface in everyday life is far short of what would be required for objectively rational choice. In most situations, people have trouble keeping in mind more than about seven things at any time (see Miller, 1956) or dealing with more than about ten pieces of information in a second (see Marschak, 1968, p. 12, and Simon, 1979). In short, the consumer suffers from what Simon (1955) calls 'bounded rationality' and is forced to simplify her processes of decision making, the more so the less time she has at her disposal.

1.2.4 The Satisficing Principle

Of all the behaviouralists' departures from orthodoxy, none seems to exasperate mainstream theorists quite so much as the replacement of maximising/optimising ideas with the notion that decision makers merely seek prospects that 'will do'—that are judged 'satisfactory' in terms of targets set by the choosers themselves. The basis for this departure is not well understood: behavioural theorists are often accused (I speak from experience!) of failing to see that their analysis is just constrained maximisation of the orthodox kind, with an added constraint—the finite computational capacities of the decision maker. Hence it is suggested that if, for example, decision makers use 'rules of thumb' to deal with their own bounded rationality, these rules are chosen as the optimal decision-making procedure, not because they are merely judged capable of generating satisfactory outcomes (see Baumol and Quandt, 1964). Such an attempt to rationalise subversive ideas into conformity with conventional modes of thought is entirely to be expected. But it is ill informed.

The basis for the idea that choice is a satisficing activity—by which people seek to meet self-defined aspirations that may fall far short of what might, in principle, be possible—lies in the logical impossibility of a decision maker being able to identify an optimal choice even if she happens to make one. In forming her expectations and deciding what to do, a decision maker first faces the problem that the lists of what she might do, and of what might happen as a result of, or despite her choice, are not given but have to be constructed. In other words, she must first identify her constraints before she can engage in constrained maximisation. In principle, absolutely anything might happen, so these lists cannot be complete; surprise is always a possibility. Gathering ideas together—for example, building up an agenda of possible options and evaluating their properties—is not without its costs: for instance, if one is trying to widen one's agenda, one may be unable to evaluate the properties of already recognised options so carefully. Hence the chooser must decide how, and how far, to engage in a search for ideas that could improve the quality of her decision. Logically, the marginal return to marginal search cannot be known in advance; search may improve one's choice, but it need not do so. Search choices thus involve exactly the same problems as the uncertain choices to which they relate. A problem of infinite regress thus stands out as a fatal barrier to attempts to avoid satisficing behaviour. As Elster (1984, p. 135) observes, in an excellent discussion of the attempts of Simon (1955, 1976) and Winter (1964) to justify the satisficing concept, 'at some point this infinite regress must be cut short by intuition, unsupported by formal reasoning, and why not then make the cut-off point as close to the action itself as possible?'

Having selected particular aspirational cut-off points in order to circumvent the infinite regress problem, a decision maker may, in the event, find herself disappointed with the outcome. If so, it is unclear what she should do; just as it is unclear whether success should be taken to imply that she could regularly be setting higher targets. The basic presumption of behavioural theorists (see Simon, 1959) is that a run of failures will normally provoke search and/or experimentation with new approaches to choice and, if unsatisfactory results persist despite such measures, sights will be lowered. A run of successes may convince the chooser that she could be raising her targets and meeting them with little extra difficulty, or be taking bigger short-cuts in this area of choice, thereby leaving herself with more time for other decisions. By experimentation, decision makers *might* stumble upon patterns of outcomes that seemed at once sustainable and impossible to improve upon. This last possibility has been taken by some theorists (most notably Day, 1967) to imply scope for satisficing behaviour to generate results akin to those presumed in orthodox maximising models; hence it might seem perfectly satisfactory to theorise as if bounded rationality and infinite regress problems did not pose barriers to constrained maximisation. In some situations, this could be a safe way for the theorist to proceed as well as an analytically convenient one; indeed it is a path that behaviouralists have not been unknown to take themselves on occasion (for example, see Kay, 1979). However, environmental turbulence could pose a major barrier to the attainment of such positions by decision makers and even in a static system they will not necessarily be stumbled upon given a 'long enough' period of trial and error. Hence, a behaviouralist would usually suggest that it could be more productive for the economist to seek out and examine techniques for choice which choosers may employ very much on a 'trial' basis with a good deal of 'error' along the way.

1.2.5 Structure and Causality

Following work by Simon (1962, 1969), behavioural theorists are increasingly adding an explicitly structuralist perspective to their work; the present book, heavily influenced by Neil Kay's (1982, 1984) path-breaking behavioural/structuralist analysis of industrial organisation, is in keeping with this development. Structuralists focus on the ways in which events in a system are shaped by linkages between system components. They suggest that two kinds of linkage may be worthy of investigation. Only one of these is discussed in neoclassical economics, despite the latter's professed concern with the interdependence of system elements (or, more bluntly, its obsession with general equilibrium), and this one only surfaces in out-of-equilibrium contexts. Suppose the economic system has been in a state of general equilibrium, with supply and demand balancing in all markets, but that there is a disturbance in respect of one product. This may cause a change in its price, the responses to which rebound upon prices and quantities in other markets, *through time*. Markets may then be said to have *diachronic* relationships with each other when the system is out of equilibrium. Another example of such relationships would be the multiplier phenomenon in conventional expositions of macroeconomic theory. However, according to the neoclassical way of thinking, a general equilibrium system may be seen as a simple aggregate once it is in equilibrium. The individual consumers are therefore seen as if they act independently of each other and, similarly, equilibrium conditions prevailing in individual product markets can be analysed one at a time. In equilibrium nothing is adjusting, so time effectively vanishes from the story, taking with it diachronic interdependency.

Behavioural theorists point out that spill-over linkages between elements in a system may not be manifest merely through time, but also at a point in time. Thus decision makers may tend to construct particular bundles of activities as means to certain ends very much with a view to the *synchronic* linkages between them. To look at favoured commodity groupings as if they are simple aggregates of components may be misleading if one wishes to understand why they have been put together. In fact, decision makers may be taking careful account of the *indecomposability* of the groupings they are selecting: they may well realise that if a particular component has to be given up, a disproportionate impact may be produced on the usefulness of the others. Likewise, they may be carefully considering the ease with which new, improved components may be slotted into an existing grouping—in other words, the question of compatibility. From this standpoint, choice involves much more than the selection of one bundle of commodities or product attributes at the expense of another: it concerns the selection of one *design of system* at the expense of another. Commitments to one set of synchronic linkages at a particular point in time may rebound upon the evolution of the system through time.

The distinction between a simple aggregate and an incompletely decomposable system may be new to many readers, so the following example is offered by way of clarification. A single-engined aeroplane cruising at a steady altitude might be said to be in some kind of equilibrium. It might also be characterised as a mass of components—engine, wings, cabin, tailplane, tailfin, undercarriage, and so on. Added together, they equal an aeroplane, just as two dollars plus three dollars is five dollars. Now suppose the engine fails: we are out of equilibrium, but to know whether or not we still have a viable aeroplane, we need to know how the other components function in relation to the engine. Wings will not provide so much lift if the forward motion normally produced by the engine is absent, so the 'aeroplane' loses height. Can it be controlled as it glides downwards? The answer here may depend on whether or not the hydraulics are driven by the engine. If they are, and if there is no manual back-up, disaster looms ahead. The moral then becomes: if one survives the impending crash, travel next time in a twin-engined aircraft, or at least one with a non-engine-dependent control system. To understand the subsequent choice of aircraft, onlookers need a knowledge of linkages between components: a knowledge of aircraft design.

This example can also be used to show how some components from a system may be easier to sacrifice than others. The failure of an aircraft's rudder *may* not prevent it from being steered safely to its destination, since the engines and other movable surfaces can be used as rather less convenient substitutes—so long as the pilot knows how to use them to this end, and so long as the rudder's failure is not a symptom of a complete breakdown of the plane's hydraulics. A structuralist perspective on an aircraft leads one to expect system designers to favour dual hydraulic circuits, as well as multiple engines, but not usually to wish to incorporate twin rudders. The view that an aircraft is a simple aggregate is short on content when a need arises to explain why particular designs tend to be favoured.

As far as the present book is concerned, the structuralist perspective means that I will be emphasising complementarities far more than orthodox economists do, and I will be de-emphasising substitution. Readers might find it helpful always to keep in mind the idea that homes and ways of life may be contrived by consumers not as simple aggregates but as systems wherein some potential linkages are experimented with and others are excluded. It might also be noticed that I seek to highlight linkages amongst component sections of this book, via frequent forward- and backward-looking pointers (for example: see section ...); the book may be broken up into chapters and sections to ease comprehension, but quite often the message will be enhanced if it is not read in a simple linear manner.

1.2.6 Strange Loops and Tangled Hierarchies

Anyone who has encountered computer scientist Douglas Hofstadter's extraordinary (1979) book *Gödel, Escher, Bach: An Eternal Golden Braid* has something of a head-start when it comes to understanding the differences between behavioural and neoclassical approaches to economics. Like Hofstadter, behavioural theorists are prone to be intrigued by the concept of the multilevel system in which attempts to find an analytical base or independent building blocks run into difficulties unless one imposes some 'bottom' from outside or divides up an integral system in an essentially arbitrary manner. Hofstadter's famous trio of figures all explored questions relating to 'strange loops' and 'tangled hierarchies': Gödel used mathematical reasoning to explore mathematical reasoning itself; Escher produced many fascinating works of art involving multilevel loops (waterfalls successively descending yet seemingly ending up providing the initial source of the flow, thereby defying both gravity and optical perspective; hands drawing hands; and so on); while Bach experimented with musical structures in which resolution could be achieved only by repeating a thematic pattern in a higher key, ever rising in pitch and eventually passing though the original key at a higher octave, still with no end in sight. This book may be seen frequently to run into parallel phenomena in relation to consumer behaviour.

One obvious example is the infinite regress problem that neoclassical critics of satisficing notions tend to ignore: to deal with uncertainty in choice, uncertain choices must be made between schemes to search for more information, and so on. The way out for the chooser involves imposing an *arbitrary* cut-off: assume particular targets are attainable, search until it seems sufficiently likely that they may be met, and then stop and act. (Note here that satisficing is going on in a dual sense—see section 8.5—and that the initial assumptions concerning what is attainable may themselves be predictions from theories built on yet other assumptions—see section 6.2.) Another example encountered in these opening pages concerns the discussion of the proposed methodology for exploring ways of life, which noted that a methodology is a scientist's way of life in her work environment; this point will be meaningless to readers unless they can break into the circle via some *prior view* of either a 'way of life' or a 'methodology'. This strange loop is just part of a more general problem: all language is metaphor, and the concept of metaphor can only be defined in relativistic terms.

To see economic events as part of history and the march of history as involving a 'strange loop' may help clarify further the perspective from which this book is written. Here, recent work by Bausor (1982, 1984), Hamouda (1983) and Shackle (1984) is especially instructive. Bausor depicts the economic process as a loop in which four elements are chained together. One can break into this chain by noting that recent choices of *strategies* may affect the allocation of resources and generate *outcomes*. Outcomes may change the information available in the system, thereby possibly causing some decision makers to change their *perceptions*, their understandings of the nature of things. Changes in perceptions may cause decision makers in turn to change their *expectations*—the things they anticipate may happen. As a result of changing their expectations, decision makers may then change their *strategies* for dealing with life. And so life goes on.

Now, of course, history is actually extending itself forward in time, so we might prefer to follow Hamouda and Shackle and consider Bausor's loop as an endless helix that starts in the past and which will coil forward, in an unforeknowable way, into the future. But whether we see the process as a loop or a helix, the strategies/outcomes/perceptions/expectations chain of interactions certainly highlights the problem of where one should decide to draw the boundaries of economics. Whatever we do, we have to start the analysis somewhere. Neoclassical economics essentially starts by taking expectations as given. It examines the choices implied by the application of a particular kind of reasoning to these expectations, and then stops. If the choices result in compatible trades, and if experience with the traded commodities does not then falsify expectations and does not provoke innovations, then we might well expect the future to be the same as the past: enter equilibrium, exit history. By normally proceeding 'as if' these 'ifs' do indeed eventuate, neoclassical economists neatly extricate themselves from the loop/helix and from the study of expectation formation; expectations are given at the outset and they stay as they were. The behavioural theorist *might* choose likewise to begin with the convenient assumption of a given set of expectations (compare the ordering of chapters in this book with the one chosen in *The Economic Imagination*) and then examine the kinds of reasoning that choosers might seriously be imagined to apply to the problem of choice. However, such an economist would then recognise the scope for individuals to make incompatible choices of strategy and to experience surprises. Therefore she is unwilling to proceed as if equilibrium is normally achieved when choices are made. The problem is then to explain how, through historical time, the system lurches forward from one set of outcomes to another. It no longer seems adequate to continue to ignore the question of how expectation-forming processes work, for these play a decisive role in determining the path of movement.

1.2.7 Attitudes Towards the Testing of Theories

As I have already noted, behavioural theorists seek out empirical material on behaviour in economic systems at the start of their investigations, rather than begin with abstractions that offer analytical convenience but bring with them considerable grounds for disbelieving the possibilities generated from them as 'as if' representations of reality. Putting things crudely, we could say that behavioural theorists try to 'make their assumptions as realistic as possible'. However, just because they begin work in this way, one should not jump to the conclusion that they insist on the 'Austrian' a prioristic approach, rejecting the idea of a need for empirical investigations of the theories they produce. Members of the Austrian school, such as Mises (1966), have argued that the way to assess the validity of economic theories is to seek out their roots in human action, checking for logical consistency along the way. Indeed, as Hutchison (1938 Ch. V; 1977 p. 159) has pointed out, the a priorist tradition held that economists enjoyed a great advantage over natural scientists when they came to assess theories, for they, as economic actors themselves, could uncover their fundamental propositions by introspection. The behaviouralist, by contrast, recognises that these roots involve 'matters of psychology, upon which even psychologists have differences of opinion' (Littlechild, 1983, p. 43). As Popper (1976, p. 57) has pointed out, 'there is no such thing as an unprejudiced observation'; observations are inevitably theory laden, whether they relate to fundamental propositions that might serve as a basis for model building, or to tests of hypotheses from models thus developed.

Whilst welcoming empirical investigations of their theoretical propositions, behavioural theorists find themselves in a tricky position when it comes to deciding what to make of such work. The ultimate aim of engaging in it is to assist the economist in assessing which possibilities she should take seriously in relation to questions of policy advice. However, empirical studies can only relate to particular past contexts, so at best they can only be

Introduction: Lifestyles and Economics

suggestive concerning what could happen in the future period in respect of which decisions need to be taken. All of the proposals for empirical work outlined later in this book could, if followed up, only produce results suggesting that, in the past and in a particular proportion of cases, subjects were observed to behave in ways consistent with or at odds with particular propositions. In future contexts, different results could be generated. Possibilities that eventuated in no cases in a past sample might in latter periods seem to be happening relatively often, and vice versa for once seemingly common outcomes. The past cannot tell us how seriously to take suggestions about how the future could look.

We seem here to have another 'strange loop': the point of conducting empirical investigations is to assist us in assessing how seriously to take possibilities, yet we have no obvious way of deciding how seriously to take empirical findings. If so, why bother to test our propositions? (note the parallel here with the quotation from Elster in section 1.2.4). As with other such loops, the way out of the tangle is provided by a *prior view* in terms of which the theorist chooses to try to see things; what we make of empirical work is very much an outcome of our personal judgemental processes. Any advice we give is going to be highly subjective, whatever our degree of diligence in conducting empirical work. It is quite possible that even a behavioural theorist, for want of any obviously better procedure, is going often to end up extrapolating past findings, albeit cautiously, into the future (see sections 5.5, 6.1–6.4 and 8.6). Behavioural theorists, like any others, can only judge after the event the adequacy of their own intuitions in respect of empirical work; the proof of the pudding has to be in the eating and sometimes the recipe may produce a severe upset for the person who tries it.

The kinds of empirical material a behavioural economist is inclined to take seriously are much more diverse than those that appeal to neoclassical economists. Amongst orthodox theorists there is a preference for econometric work employing published statistics; they display a general hostility towards case study work, in which the economist actually asks questions of decision makers. Whenever case study work is produced that seems to run counter to the core ideas of orthodox theory, the defence seems to involve the allegation that the work is biased, due to the nature of the questions asked and the attitudes of the respondents to the investigator, and that sample sizes are too small. (Two classic instances of such defences are Machlup, 1946, and Robinson, 1939, p. 539, respectively. Forty years after it first appeared, Machlup's paper is still used with tedious regularity as a club with which to fight back against intrusive behavioural ideas.) The orthodox view plays down the extent to which published data are themselves products of information-gathering processes involving human decision makers and the asking of questions (Morgenstern, 1963), while drawing little attention to the possibility that published econometric work may be misleading as a result of the non-revelation of 'poor' results from slightly different data series or functional forms, or more devious instances of 'data mining' (Feige, 1975). Sometimes, the claims of neoclassical theorists to the effect that their ideas have support from hundreds of econometric studies border on the downright fraudulent—see Cyert and Simon (1983) for an exposé that deserves to be more widely known.

If all observations, being theory laden, are open to bias then it may not be unwise to seek out diverse sources of them in the hope that possible inconsistencies, anomalies and biases will be revealed. And here, when I say diverse, I really mean diverse, not simply formal case study/market research work to supplement econometric analysis of published data. I am quite prepared to consider the possible implications of my own and other people's casual observations of behaviour and see if these can be argued to be inconsistent with my own and other people's ideas. Such observations may not be obtained under 'controlled conditions' or from systematic search, but they may at least make one stop and question the basis of some things that some economists believe. What writers say in novels and consumer magazines may likewise provide useful material that can be subject to scrutiny for possible inconsistency with particular theoretical notions about the bases of choice: for example, since uncovering the psychological material employed here in Chapter 4, I have been repeatedly struck by the way in which the nature of human action has been portrayed in a similar way in novels (J.B.Priestley's works in particular have provided a whole series of examples). Of course, my reading *is* selective and I *am* trying to see whether I can make a particular interpretation fit, but I would also be selective if I gathered data for econometric estimations and then tried to see how well hypotheses fitted in statistical terms. At least novelists or consumer journalists would not know they were writing material that economists might examine in attempts to appraise theories; unlike the providers of statistical data for official publications, or the respondents in case studies, they would not be expected to be liable to bend what they said in order to dupe or pander to economic researchers.

In the pages that follow, I outline hypotheses that seem worthy of serious investigation and I describe pertinent research methods, but I provide no new systematic investigation myself. I keenly look forward to seeing my suggestions taken up in future by those with a greater comparative advantage than myself in empirical work—either by academics who have more experience than I in such lines of enquiry and whose minds are not overflowing with theoretical ideas, or by final year honours students and postgraduates who are required to produce empirically-based economics or marketing dissertations.

However, the fact that I have not built this work around an original empirical study should not lead readers to jump to the conclusion that my analysis lacks empirical content. Reference is made to many previous but relevant investigations by authors in a variety of disciplines. The analysis is also replete with factual examples from everyday life. (As one who makes pretty deviant choices in respect of matters such as food, appearance, what car to drive, and so on, I have found it hard to avoid being on the receiving end of the kinds of reactions that people come up with in the face of consumers who challenge the 'conventional wisdom'.) Particularly conspicuous will be my tendency to highlight in parentheses pertinent phrases that crop up so often in everyday life that they have become clichés—for example, 'stuck in a rut' or 'settling down'. These more anecdotal pieces of information about how the world sometimes seems to work cannot of themselves tell us how frequently particular propositions could be found to have been disconfirmed. But they may in some minds serve to suggest that, in some cases at least, the possibilities that I outline warrant serious consideration in advance of more systematic empirical work that may be able to demonstrate past tendencies in respect of disconfirmation frequencies. They usually serve in this role by raising doubts about the generality of orthodox conclusions whilst being consistent with the alternative analysis that I propose.

The role of such diverse sources of evidence should not be confused with my use of what one might call the 'hypothetical story'. To help clarify in readers' minds how a particular group of propositions work, I often employ scenarios that refer to familiar situations in everyday life. Sometimes particular scenarios were chosen very much in the light of personal experience or things that other people have said. Other scenarios are entirely imaginary, as are many details of the experience-inspired ones. Although as a rule I treat with scepticism any proposition that I cannot discuss in terms of a seemingly plausible scenario, it must be understood that I am not asking readers to take such scenarios as general statements about precisely how the world has worked on some occasions in the past; they are merely devices designed to aid the comprehension of theoretical propositions and problems. Of course, this is not to say that they may not provide the inspiration for future carefully conducted case studies of how people think and choose.

A diverse collection of activities and consumer goods figure in this book in relation to various kinds of evidence and illustrative scenarios, including family planning, holidays, cameras, television programmes, hi-fi systems, career paths, cars, houses, furniture and food. However, most commonly discussed are choices that relate to motoring (particularly in Chapter 10). The wide-ranging coverage may help to underline the potentially broad significance of my arguments, whilst concentration on a particular area of choice may help reduce my liability to the charge that I am selecting examples in an unsystematic manner in order to bolster up what I have to say. Motoring was chosen for most frequent discussion for a number of reasons:

(1) Cars have been a particularly popular subject in previous studies of the relationship between brand sales and product attributes.

(2) Motoring expenditure is one of the largest components of the budget of the typical household and involves choices that consumer affairs organisations find particularly prone to result in buyer dissatisfaction. (The importance assigned to motoring might also be seen as evidenced by the extent of media headline coverage given to announcements of changes in the price of petrol.)

(3) It is easy to talk about people choosing cars as multidimensional products without it being necessary to mention characteristics that are likely to be meaningless to the general reader. This was very much on my mind when I needed a focus for a discussion of the relationship between product lifecycles and the decision making procedures employed by consumers. The car market might seem rather slow-moving in technological terms compared with, say, the markets for home computers or electronic keyboards, yet it was perfectly adequate for my purposes; I did not have to write whilst feeling personally distant from the product, as would have been the case with home computers, and neither was I running the risk of bewildering the vast majority of readers by discussing verdicts in multiple keyboard tests from 'home recording and electronic music' magazines which refer to mysterious characteristics such as 'musical instrument digital interface (MIDI) compatibility'. If economists themselves are also consumers who are in reality not fully informed about which characteristics are available and the purposes they serve, an economist writing about consumer behaviour has to be very careful indeed in choosing examples that will be generally accessible.

1.3 OUTLINE OF THE REST OF THE BOOK

In deciding how to structure this book, I felt it necessary to do two things: to make the ideas accessible to readers coming to them with the preconceptions of conventional economics, and to ensure that the analysis followed the helical conception of the unfolding of economic processes in historical time that I outlined earlier. Thus in Chapter 2 I attempt to construct first a bridge between orthodox ideas and the analysis I subsequently develop. The chapter shows that some economists have modified the traditional static theory in a way which enables it to accommodate new products as well as price changes. This modification portrays households as if they rather resemble firms, and as if they make choices with a view to the characteristics that can be obtained by engaging in particular transactions. The latter idea is greatly emphasised in empirical work in marketing which economists rarely mention. The bridging chapter also discusses this work and argues that marketeers who are surprised by poor statistical results are often blind to alternative processes whereby consumers could often be evaluating the different characteristics mixes available to them.

Chapter 3 takes on seriously the idea that it may be useful to explore similarities between households and firms. However, it argues that to get very far we could do better to use the recent behavioural literature on firms and corporate *strategy* as our reference point, instead of continuing to focus on neoclassical production theory. To do full justice to this material, especially that concerning the implications of 'internalisation theory' for the study of consumer behaviour, an entire book would be required. However, even the limited treatment provided in Chapter 3 should suffice to convey an unsettling message to readers who are used to the determinacy of neoclassical economics. The chapter highlights the ambiguities that abound in respect of strategic decision making and carries the implication that it is all too easy for consumers to end up 'jumping out of the frying pan and into the fire' in attempting to manage their exposure to hazardous situations. For the behavioural economist, this ambiguity is not a source of despair but a signal to consider new questions, such as 'what will consumers make of the sequels to their choices?' and 'to the extent that they feel new strategies or tactics are required, how might they *judge* what to do?' In Chapter 4, I begin investigating these issues and break with conventional practices by incorporating psychological material on consumer motivation. The kind of psychology employed – personal construct theory – happens to mesh very well with my focus on turbulence and strategic aspects of choice, since it is built around the theme that people may usefully be seen as if they are essentially concerned with trying to predict and control their lives.

Chapters 5 and 6 use this psychological foundation to move further around the helix, examining processes whereby consumers gather information about possibilities, interpret it and, in some cases, change their minds and form new expectations about what they could be doing with their lives as well as about which goods might in various ways help towards the attainment of their goals. Chapter 5 is particularly concerned with the forms that expectations may take, while Chapter 6 devotes a good deal of attention to possible determinants of resistance to change and to techniques for investigating and anticipating such phenomena.

By the end of Chapter 6, we will have completed one full loop of the helix, arriving back at the stage of consumers having expectations on which choices of the kinds discussed in Chapters 2 and 3 might depend. It is then time to re-examine, in the light of the analysis of expectation formation, *how* people may make their choices in the face of complexity and ignorance about the future. Chapters 7 and 8 deal, respectively, with these two issues. What emerges in them is at times very different from the ideas discussed in Chapter 2. In particular, I call into question the general principle of substitution—the notion that *every*thing has its price—that is so central to the research programme of neoclassical economics. Chapter 9 is an attempt to show how theorists have reacted to previous moves away from the substitution idea and seeks to demonstrate that the issue warrants far more careful attention than it usually receives. The reason for devoting a chapter to this task is that the implications of the ideas in Chapters 7 and 8 turn out in Chapter 10 to be far from trivial. It seems natural to devote this last chapter to an examination of what a conventional theorist would see as the 'bottom line' of consumer theory, namely how it relates to processes of price and non-price competition.

2 Characteristics, Household Production, and Choice

2.1 INTRODUCTION

One of the claims I shall be making later in this book is that revolutions in ways of thinking always represent incomplete breaks with past modes of thought. Part of the inspiration behind this contention comes from the writings of the late Arthur Koestler on the subject of creativity. Koestler (1975, p. 120) argued that: 'The creative act is not an act of creation in the sense of the Old Testament. It does not create something out of nothing; it uncovers, selects, re-shuffles, combines, synthesises already existing facts, faculties, skills'. I will be using this idea as I attempt to analyse how consumers come to change their patterns of behaviour through time; but it is an idea that is also relevant right now, in relation to my own actions as an economist trying, with revolutionary intent, to construct a fresh view of consumer behaviour.

I have warned that I am going to employ the unorthodox behavioural methodology to make headway in the area of consumer choice. However, I will begin by discussing some of the ideas from a branch of *neoclassical* consumer theory that deserves to be more widely known, and with whose main thrust I feel a strong accord. These ideas form the basis of what is known as 'household production theory' or the 'new' approach to consumer behaviour. As they first attracted attention around twenty years ago, the word 'new' is now something of a misnomer, but even after twenty years they still only rate at most a single chapter in most texts (for example, Chapter 10 of the state-of-the-art graduate text by Deaton and Muellbauer, 1980). Household production theory was itself an adaptation of the 'old' approach to consumer behaviour, namely Hicksian indifference analysis. What I shall be doing in this book might be seen as an attempt to take this incompletely novel research programme and purge it of the restrictive elements that remained in it from the old mode of analysis, meanwhile putting their place elements from behavioural theory.

The aim of this chapter is to introduce the main ideas of the 'new' approach to consumer behaviour and to show how they relate to other lines of research in consumer theory. Section 2.2 is concerned with the 'old' Hicksian analysis. Household production theory is outlined and reviewed critically in sections 2.3 and 2.4, respectively. Section 2.5 shows how it ties up with work on quality indices that involves using the 'hedonic technique'. The penultimate section (2.6) explores the overlap between economists' writings on the 'new' approach to consumer behaviour, and some of the theoretical and empirical work that is to be found in the marketing literature. Section 2.7 concludes the chapter by highlighting the limited extent to which this 'new' analysis has opened up economists' minds and changed their practices as researchers.

2.2 THE HICKSIAN LEGACY

After many a day of battling to open the minds of neoclassically-blinkered students and colleagues, I end up concluding that, much as I admire many of his contributions (especially those in the area of monetary theory), Nobel Laureate Sir John Hicks has much to answer for in respect of the current crisis in economics. If the Hicksian foundations of orthodox degree programmes in economics were removed, most of the conventional wisdom would come crashing down. The macroeconomics of intermediate-level textbooks is very much an outgrowth of Hicks' (1937) attempt to depict what he saw as the essence of Keynes' (1936) *General Theory of Employment, Interest and Money*. That attempt grew into the juggernaut of IS-LM analysis. Likewise, the microeconomics introduced in intermediate-grade texts has its roots in the ordinalist analysis of consumer choice that Hicks pioneered with Sir Roy Allen and then integrated into a general equilibrium framework in his (1939) book *Value and Capital*. The Hicks-Allen theory of consumer choice displaced Marshall's (1920) cardinal utility theory and led consumer theorists to become fascinated with the implications of the idea that changes in relative prices produce both 'income effects' and 'substitution effects'. The indifference curve/budget line juggernaut thus built up momentum.

Once they are moving, especially downhill, juggernauts are notoriously hard to stop—even when the person who built the prototype cries out, belatedly, that a terrible mistake has been made and that a major safety defect exists. Hicks has twice (1976, 1980) repudiated IS-LM analysis as a vehicle for serious analysis of macroeconomic issues. But despite this, and despite the best attempts of many contributors to the *Journal of Post Keynesian Economics* to highlight the limitations of IS-LM and present an alternative view (see also the books by Davidson, 1972, Minsky, 1975, Dow and Earl, 1982, and Chick, 1983), IS-LM still dominates the teaching of macroeconomics and influences the construction of macroeconometric models. Hicks (1976, pp. 137–8) has also admitted that his approach to consumer theory, though formally more tractable than Marshall's analysis, can hardly be claimed to be a more realistic approximation to the actual processes of consumer choice (see also Loasby, 1976, pp. 22–3). Marshall depicted consumers implicitly as looking at possible choices in terms of the value for money they seemed to offer: the Marshallian consumer asked herself whether she valued marginal amounts of retained generalised purchasing power above the extra value she could obtain from buying more of the commodity upon which she was focusing or, if she was looking at an indivisible product, from buying a more expensive substitute. Such a consumer would push her shopping trolley round a modern-day supermarket and fill it as she went, in the light of sequential appraisals of what she discovered to be on offer.

Hicks, in contrast to Marshall, asked his readers to conceive of consumers as if they were comparing rival feasible sets of commodities, with no restrictions being placed on the number of mental trade-offs they might be imagined to undertake. His analysis was set in terms of an n-dimensional goods space and assumed continuous divisibility of goods. The Hicksian consumer would examine the relative prices of the thousands of goods on supermarkets' (note the plural!) shelves, work out the best feasible bundle, and *then* go fill her shopping basket. Despite the greater common-sense appeal of Marshall's idea in a world where consumers are short of time and information-handling capacities, and where the market environment is in a constant state of change, it is Hicks' theory that students are asked to master by lecturers who simultaneously preach positivism and fail to note the theory's limited empirical content.

The Hicksian analysis of consumer choice has achieved its place as one of the key building blocks of modern orthodoxy, despite the fact that it is a failure in terms of its designer's own goals. Hicks (1939, p. 5) noted that his interest in consumer theory 'began with the endeavour to supply a needed theoretical foundation for statistical demand studies' and claimed that it had 'a definite relevance to that field'. To be sure, applied economists working in this area need 'theoretical foundations' as guides to the statistical relationships they might seek to uncover, and as pointers to the kinds of situations in which the relationships they have discovered might break down. However, Hicks' indifference analysis is not much help in this respect: it yields no testable hypothesis beyond that relating to the sign of the substitution effect. This may in large part explain why orthodox empirical work on demand has generally been concerned with estimation rather than with hypothesis testing (see the remarks of Brown and Deaton, 1972, pp. 1150–2).

Perhaps the most impressive statistical demand study of the post-war period is that by Houthakker and Taylor (1970); it is noteworthy that its authors were perfectly able to get by without recourse to a foundation of indifference analysis. Houthakker and Taylor tried to predict the composition and magnitude of consumers' expenditure in the United States for over eighty commodity classes. They decided to try a very simple explanatory focus with the following intuitively plausible dimensions: (1) income changes, (2) the sizes of pre-existing inventories of durable consumer goods, and (3) the volumes of goods previously consumed in each category (which they thought might serve as a proxy for habitual attachment to each category of expenditure). Their major findings (1970, pp. 304–5) were that 'consumption in the United States is characterised more by habit formation than inventory adjustment', and that 'prices [relative to income] play a fairly modest role in explaining United States consumption'. The latter finding seems to run counter to the Hicksian idea that relative price changes should be the focus of an analysis of consumer choice, for it suggests that substitution effects are not strong between commodity classes. There is no point of contact between Hicksian analysis and the findings of Houthakker and Taylor on habit formation, for their conceptualisation of habits refers to time-series data, whereas Hicks' theory is ahistorical.

Hicks also needed to construct 'theoretical foundations' at the level of the consumer in order to get very far with his attempts to demonstrate that an economic system might be able to feel its way towards a sustainable position of general equilibrium. If demand curves were not downward sloping, serious questions would be raised about the stability and uniqueness of hypothetical equilibrium configurations; so he needed a theory of choice which would predict that, as the relative price of a commodity is increased, people will buy less of it. He did not put it quite as bluntly as this, but instead claimed that his primary concern was to develop 'a technique for studying the interrelations of markets' (1939, p. 20); and, in respect of his work on choice, he suggested that:

We want to deduce from [the principle of the diminishing marginal rate of substitution] laws of market conduct—that is, laws which deal with the reaction of the consumer to changes in market conditions (1939, p. 23)

and later (p. 27) that:

we seek information about the conditions governing quantities bought at given prices in order that we may use them to discover how the quantities bought will be changed when prices change.

On the principle of Occam's razor, Hicks (1939, p. 18) sought to meet this end with the minimum of axioms. But since his theory admitted the possibility of Giffen goods (1939, p. 35) he was unable ultimately to achieve a purely axiomatic choice-theoretic foundation for his later analysis. Rather, like so many theorists before and since, he had to derive the downward slope of his market demand functions 'from the theory plus intuitive notions about consumer behaviour which have been excluded from the axiomatic base and have not been fully articulated' (Lipsey and Rosenbluth, 1971, p. 132).

It will be evident from the quotations from Hicks (1939) that his original contribution treats changes in market conditions as synonymous with changes in prices. This attitude remains in modern texts despite the fact that the competitive environment is populated by oligopolistic firms that often prefer not to use price changes as market weapons and recognise instead the importance of product changes and selling strategy (see Koutsoyiannis, 1982, pp. 2–4). Hicks' theory has nothing to say on the processes whereby new products gain market shares or on some occasion fail to take off. Nor can it offer any explanation of why some goods are seen by consumers as closer mutual substitutes than others. These are practically significant holes which the 'new' theory of consumer behaviour has looked like it might be able to help to fill.

2.3 LANCASTER'S APPROACH

Hicks had constructed his theory in terms of the goods space, with a dimensional axis for each of the goods between which choices might be made. He had depicted each commodity in an holistic manner, as something from which consumers might derive satisfaction directly. However, it struck a number of economists in the post-war period (beginning with Houthakker (1952) and Gorman, in his unpublished (1956) paper) that it might be more useful to begin to theorise with the recognition that consumers often discriminate between goods on the basis of the characteristics they contain—these elements determining the 'value for money' offered by the goods under appraisal. This would imply the construction of theories in terms of the characteristics space, not the goods space. In fact, as Loasby (1978, p. 3) has pointed out, the idea that consumers are interested in the different qualities of goods as well as their prices is to be found in the work of Marshall (1920, pp. 86–91); but it has become firmly attached in most economists' minds with the accessible yet suitably rigorous work of Kelvin Lancaster (1966a, b, 1971).

Lancaster combined the characteristics idea with another theme (posited almost simultaneously by Becker (1965) and Muth (1966)): one should see households as being rather akin to firms in neoclassical production theory. Firms purchase inputs and use them to produce other goods, from whose sale it is hoped profits will be realised. The neoclassical entrepreneur has to choose between different mixes of goods that might be used as inputs to produce particular outputs—that is, between different production technologies—and between different combinations of output. Prospective profits are maximised when expected net revenues can be increased by changes neither of technology nor of the mix of output. Households, likewise, face production technologies that limit the outputs of characteristics they can produce using goods inputs, including the scarce time inputs of the household members. Typically, household production technologies yield joint products—that is, more than one characteristic output—to which the household members may attach a value. For example, suppose I start out with a laundry basket full of dirty clothes. I can produce the valued characteristics of cleanliness and odourlessness, and the negatively valued characteristic of temporary dampness, by putting myself, my washing machine and my washing powder to work on the contents of the basket. From this standpoint, changes in relative prices of consumer goods (for example, different brands of washing machine, or the number of leisure hours I must give up to earn enough to buy a washing machine) have implications for households rather similar to the effects that changes in relative prices of different kinds of inputs and outputs have for firms. Likewise, the introduction of new consumption commodities, differentiated by the different characteristics combinations they can be used to produce, has an obvious parallel with the introduction of new, more cost-effective techniques of production for use in firms.

With such a starting point, Lancaster is able to offer an interpretation of differences in the degrees of substitutability between goods. His analysis rests upon the idea that the overall consumption technology faced by choosers is decomposable into a number of smaller technologies wherein subsets of characteristics can be produced only by particular subsets of commodities. For example, one might expect gardening and oral hygiene technologies to exhibit minimal overlap: a spade is no use as a toothpick and no one would dream of using toothpaste as a weed-killing agent. For all practical purposes, perfect decomposability is not required, merely that, if there are some 'universal' characteristics, any subsets of otherwise technologically separate goods should each be able to yield only a small proportion of the total output of these characteristics (see Lancaster, 1971, pp. 132–9). Some evidence that consumers do indeed see goods as intrinsically grouped according to the characteristics with which they are associated is to be found in the work of Pickering *et al.* (1973) and of Doyle and Fenwick (1975) (who reworked the data employed by Pickering's team, using multidimensional scaling rather than discriminant analysis). But it should be noted that this empirical work is not inherently antithetical to the notion that some fairly universal characteristics figure in the technology of consumption, and one can easily see, for example, that most commodities contribute in a positive or negative way to a person's self- and social-esteem, her ability to find time for other activities, or the degree of stress and anxiety she sees in her life (see sections 3.2 and 4.4).

Ratchford (1975, p. 66) has suggested that an operational definition of the concept of an industry follows readily from the idea that goods can be sorted into categories on the basis of the characteristics they can help to produce. He argues that Lancaster's analysis means that the economist no longer has to define products as belonging to particular industries on the basis of high versus low cross-elasticities of demand, without being able to explain why such elasticity patterns should be observed. Goods will be close substitutes to the extent that they yield the same characteristics, and complements if they need to be used together to produce a particular characteristic. Changes in the mix of goods consumed in one technology grouping will not affect the yields of characteristics associated with other technology groupings, and may therefore be considered in isolation.

In considering choices between rival brands within a particular technological subset, Lancaster focuses his attention on the output of characteristics that a person may obtain by spending a previously assigned sum of money on a single brand or on a combination of brands with differing characteristics. An example, illustrated with the aid of Figure 2.1, may help the reader to achieve the appropriate focus (see Douglas, 1983, pp. 105–21, for an excellent textbook treatment using a variety of other examples).

Consider a person who is choosing between rival brands of toothpaste, upon which she expects to spend a particular sum in order to obtain teeth that are relatively white and free of decay. Initially she can choose between two brands. If she spends all of the money on 'Snowdent', she can reach point F on the technology ray OF. If she spends all of the money on 'Toughdent',

32   Lifestyle Economics

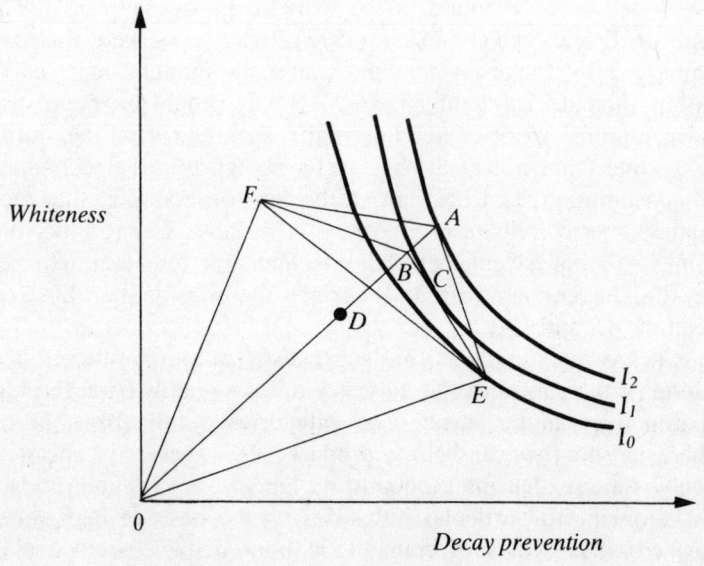

Figure 2.1: Toothpaste choices in characteristics space

she can reach the point *E* on the technology ray *OE*. Alternatively, she can buy a combination of both brands during her planning period and attain a point somewhere along *FE* (precisely which point depends on the combination she chooses). In fact, her preferences are such that she maximises her utility by purchasing only Toughdent, an act which enables her to reach indifference curve I_0. Now suppose a third brand called 'Dekkadent' is introduced, a brand which offers the mix of characteristics depicted by the ray *OA*. Dekkadent's ability to pick up sales depends on three things: its technological efficiency, the subjective preferences of consumers, and its price. The more technologically efficient it is, the less of it consumers will need to buy to produce a particular output of characteristics; so, given its price, its efficiency will determine how far along *OA* a consumer can get by spending a particular sum of money on it. If its efficiency and price were such that the consumer under consideration could only reach point D if she spent all of her allocation on it, she would never buy it, even if she sought to obtain the characteristics mix implied by the ray OD. She would always do better by buying a mixture of Toughdent and Snowdent that offered this mix of characteristics. At such a price it would be technologically inefficient for her to purchase Dekkadent, whatever her own preferences in respect of whiteness versus decay prevention. However, if Dekkadent sold for a rather lower price, such that spending her allocation on it would take her to point B, then it would pick up a market share. The frontier of technologically efficient choices would become $FB-BE$. Her personal preferences would cause her to choose point C on this frontier, and she would thus buy a combination of Toughdent and Dekkadent. An even lower price, which would enable her to reach point A if she bought only Dekkadent, would further change the frontier of cost-effective choices, to $FA-AE$, and in this case she would indeed only buy Dekkadent.

Evidently, Lancaster's analysis provides a neat way of explaining brand loyalty patterns and the tendencies of consumers often to have in their homes stocks of more than one brand of particular classes of seemingly closely substitutable products. (Many people may only use one kind of toothpaste, but they will have varieties of food, clothing, records, video tapes, and so on, that they will use on different occasions through time, some of them more frequently than others.) Unlike Farley (1964), Lancaster does not need to explain brand loyalty in terms of information costs; indeed, he only needs to adduce consumer misinformation to explain why goods lying inside efficiency frontiers at market prices obtain any market shares at all. The demonstration that it will in many cases be rational for consumers to choose several brands, even if they are only slightly differentiated, also raises some interesting issues in respect of welfare arguments over economies of scale versus variety of choice: Lancaster has explored these in detail in his more recent (1975, 1979) contributions.

2.4 CRITICISMS OF LANCASTER'S APPROACH

Despite the fact that it is essentially a modification of the Hicksian goods-space approach to choice, involving ordinal convex preferences (but over characteristics rather than goods) and constrained maximisation, and despite the new perspectives it has provided, the consumer theory associated with Lancaster's name has so far failed to displace Hicksian consumer theory at the core of mainstream economics. Rather, it has been subject to criticism on a number of counts.

As far as neoclassical economists are concerned, the most important case against the idea that they might develop their models in characteristics space is that it is not actually necessary to do this to explain differences in cross-elasticities of demand. As Haines (1975, pp. 77–8) and Katzner (1970, p. 156) have pointed out, the 'utility tree' view of preferences as hierarchically separable in the goods space is a simple extension of the orthodox model, which also seems to provide such an explanation (see Strotz, 1957, and Green, 1976, Chapter 10). Indeed, it is interesting to note that the utility tree literature was a major inspirational force behind Muth's (1966) production–theoretic view of the consumer, and Muth actually writes, for much of his paper, as if households combine goods to produce other goods (for example, a 'meal'), not characteristics, from which they derive utility.

Casual introspection certainly serves to indicate that quite often when budgeting one does *think* in terms of wholes (for example, 'holidays' versus 'new furniture', and then, 'a holiday in New Zealand' versus 'a holiday in South Australia') and not always explicitly in terms of the wants to which they minister; findings which show that the utility tree concept is not empirically unreasonable are detailed in Bettman's (1974) review of consumer information-processing techniques. However, to assume the existence of hierarchically separable preferences in the goods space is really to beg the question of why people separate out their resources in the way that they do. For example, it may indeed be the case that, once I have decided on a particular division of my resources between holidays and furniture, changes in the relative prices of different kinds of holidays will not impact upon my furniture choices. But on what basis do I decide to divide up my resources between holidays and furniture in the first place? I may have defined for myself at some point in the past the rates at which I am prepared to substitute holidays for furniture, and in this sense I may be said now to possess goods-space preferences;

yet my past assessment will surely have involved characteristics-orientated thinking at some stage.

It may be helpful to argue that Lancaster's theory and the utility tree analysis are most wisely seen as complementary constructs. After all, particular characteristics only become meaningful dimensions of choice because goods offer different performances in respect of them, while goods can only be defined in terms of their likenesses and differences in respect of various characteristics (see section 4.2). Lancaster himself does seem to have in mind some multistage budgeting process, since his model presumes a particular sum of money has already been allocated for producing the technologically separate subset of characteristics under consideration. Thinking back further in the process implies a need to consider how the consumer trades different characteristics subsets against each other. There one might presume that the technology rays refer to alternative budgeting combinations that will exhaust a particular allocation from a yet-higher level of choice. For example, one might have a $2000 luxuries budget with an efficient $1200/$800 holidays/furniture option represented as a ray yielding one mix of characteristics, and a rival $1000/$1000 holidays/furniture option represented as another ray yielding a different mix of characteristics. But whether or not one *needs* to consider the underlying characteristics-orientated nature of budgeting processes in this way will depend upon the phenomena one is investigating; Lancaster's approach may have a greater 'depth' than the formal goods-space utility tree literature, but it is characteristically(!) more demanding to handle. I shall return to the question of budgeting in section 3.3.

A second kind of criticism of Lancaster's model, raised in a paper by Watts and Gaston (1982), concerns its assumption that consumption technologies are linear (so that doubling expenditure on a commodity doubles the output of each of the characteristics it produces). It is this assumption that ensures that the technology rays are straight lines and the efficiency frontier is composed of straight-line segments. Yet it is not obviously a reasonable approximation to make in all markets. For example, the ability of a particular brew of alcohol to produce intoxication may not be noticeably a linear function of the number of pints consumed, even though each pint is physically the same as before. Watts and Gaston show that if one or more goods exhibit a strictly concave consumption technology, it is logically possible that the consumer may find herself unable to decide upon a unique optimal bundle of commodities, even though her preferences may be convex in characteristics space.

The origin of this result may become clearer in the light of Figure 2.2. Here, goods B and C, represented respectively by the rays OB and OC, are associated with linear technologies. Good A, however, has constant returns to characteristic Y and increasing returns to characteristic X. It thus has to be represented by the curved technology ray OA. If good B were unavailable, the efficiency frontier would be the solid line AD and the broken line DC, while if good C were unavailable the efficiency frontier would be the broken line AD and the solid line DB. When all three goods are available at the prices implied by their respective rays, the efficiency frontier is actually the solid line AD–DB–BC. Evidently, the chooser's preferences might be such that she had a convex indifference curve which was tangential with several points on the efficiency frontier, and some of these points might even carry implications of 'Giffenness' if relative prices were changed (see Watts and Gaston, 1982, pp. 286-7). In Figure 2.2, the curve I_0 is tangential to two points on the efficiency frontier, so that the consumer would be indifferent between particular combinations of A and C (at the tangency with the solid part of AD) and of B and C.

In effect, Watts and Gaston have identified as equivalent phenomenon in household production theory to the 'badly-behaved production function problem' in capital theory. Thus, just as the Cambridge controversies in the theory of capital (documented in Harcourt, 1972) showed that one cannot in general expect there to be a unique ranking of capital/labour combinations in respect of the profit/wage rate relationship, so the non-uniqueness of optimal quantities ('reswitching' of consumption bundles) and/or of optimal types of goods ('reversal' of consumption bundles) along the consumer's efficiency frontier opens up the possibility of badly behaved demand functions. As Watts and Gaston (1982, p. 282) observe:

Since reversal (and reswitching) along the efficiency locus only occurs over certain sets of relative prices, the demand curve for a particular good may consist of two or more distinct and possibly overlapping segments. The existence of such demand relationships would seriously undermine the constrained maximisation equilibrium analysis of orthodox economics.

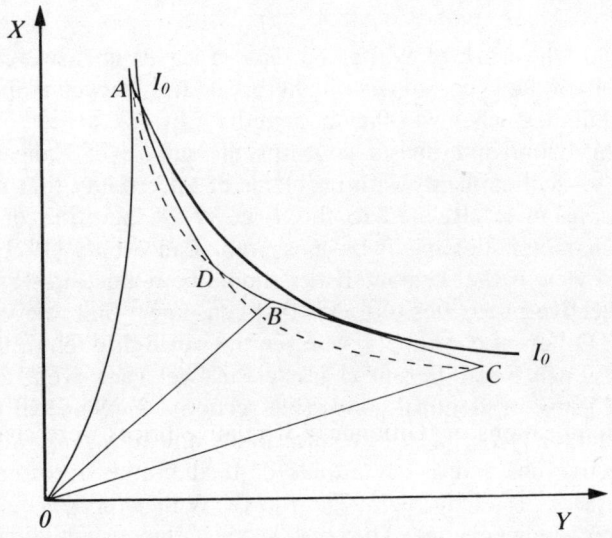

Figure 2.2: Non-unique consumption bundles

Evidently, a general equilibrium theorist can only accept Lancaster's analysis in its original form, though even then, as Lipsey and Rosenbluth (1971) have demonstrated, it makes Giffen goods look still more plausible than does orthodox Hicksian theory. However, if one is not building up an analysis around the idea of the possible existence and stability of general equilibrium configurations, then one should welcome the findings of Watts and Gaston, for they serve to alert economists to possibilities of which marketeers have long been aware. To quote from one of the pioneers of motivation research, Harry Henry (1958, p. 137):

The smooth 'demand curves' used to corrupt the young, by economists who have spiritually never set foot outside their universities and who have no acquaintance at all with the facts of economic behaviour, just do not exist in real life. The effects of price changes on the total market may be jerky in the extreme: up to a certain point they may be negligible, and then beyond that point a very small price change may exert a very great influence on sales.

However, the work of Watts and Gaston leaves unanswered the question of how consumers might break ties between optimal goods bundles, whenever they occurred.

A third line of criticism concerns the failure of Lancaster's model to deal explicitly with problems of uncertainty that might beset consumers. Related to this issue is the question of how some characteristics might be measured. Lancaster's (1971, pp. 114–15) view is that characteristics should be defined in terms of the objective properties of goods that consumers find relevant to choice. Different consumers, who see the world through different blinkers, will find different characteristics relevant even if they choose between identical goods (see section 4.2). Some of these consumers may be faced with uncertainty and they may rate the prospective characteristics outputs of rival brands according to brand prices (Ratchford, 1975, p. 74). With experience, their perceptions may change. They may see new dimensions of choice and/or rate goods differently in terms of their original repertoires of dimensions. The technology of consumption may not have changed in any 'objective' sense, so one might, like Lancaster, argue that such changes of outlook are to be represented as changes in preferences. But as far as consumers are concerned, the rerating of goods in terms of their abilities to produce certain characteristics may be seen rather as a change in the technological constraints with which they have to deal. Considerations such as these call into question the 'objective' approach of Lancaster's model and the idea that it is safe to leave it to the analyst to decide where one should draw the dividing line between preferences and constraints.

In the present work, I shall depart from Lancaster in this respect and follow Pickering (1977, p. 12) in emphasising the 'psychological perceptions of products'. Consumption technologies will be analysed as if it were the consumer who draws the dividing line between changes in her preferences and constraints, and who has her own, personal criteria of evaluation, which she could verbalise to a researcher. In practical applications of my analysis, this may raise problems for interpersonal comparisons, but to seek to understand how consumers themselves judge products may be a far less misleading methodology for market anticipation purposes than one which forces consumers to express their preferences against laboratory-derived evaluations of the characteristics outputs produced by rival brands. It also means that the researcher is not driven to impose further blinkers simply because, with many goods, 'the characteristics they yield are either nebulous to begin with or else present major problems of definition and measurement' (Taylor, 1975, p. 76). It is this inability to find published 'objective' measurements of many of the characteristics produced by goods (for example, what are 'self-esteem', 'whiteness' and 'decay prevention' and how do we quantify them?) that has driven many economists to continue to carry out applied demand work purely in the goods space.

Fourthly, there is the question, raised and answered by Rosen (1974), concerning the mechanics of handling indivisibilities in the context of Lancaster's theory. Lancaster depicts consumers as considering the output rates of various characteristics they might produce per dollar they spend on each rival brand. They mentally juggle around rival bundles containing differing quantities of various commodities until they find the one with what seems to them to be the most desirable prospective mix of characteristics. This vision has an obvious appeal with divisible goods—food, toothpaste, alcoholic beverages, and so on—that fill one's weekly shopping basket in the supermarket, but it looks less satisfactory if we are considering infrequently purchased consumer durables, such as houses, cars, furniture and electrical appliances. Rosen's solution to the indivisibility problem involves plotting goods as points in characteristics space, with one characteristic dimension being their price. It is not then necessary to specify characteristics-per-dollar technology rays. To ensure continuity on characteristics scales, one can assume, not unrealistically, that a proliferation of slightly differentiated brands is available. The consumer's task is then twofold: first, to define, for the technological subgroup under consideration, an efficiency frontier for the combinations of characteristics that are available at each possible level of expenditure; second, to decide how much to spend—how much she can afford—within the subgroup under consideration. It is not rational for her to buy a more expensive brand if her marginal valuation of the extra characteristics it may yield exceeds the marginal utility she expects she will forgo by not having the money to spend on another class of commodity, which would produce a different set of desired characteristics. If one recognises, as Hicks (1976) so belatedly did, that the consumer may not usually have in mind a fully specified picture of what the forgone commodities and associated characteristics might be, it might seem appropriate to regard the consumer in neo-Marshallian terms, as if she equated the marginal utility of additional characteristics with the marginal utility of the money that would have to be spent to obtain them (but see section 10.3 for a rather different view of what consumers are doing as they decide how much they 'can afford' to spend).

For my own part, I would raise two further points about Lancaster's theory. First, the idea that one might usefully look at household behaviour in the light of literature on the theory of the firm appeals to me so much that it is disappointing to see that household production theory has hitherto only explored the analogy in terms of the neoclassical theory of the firm. As I will try to show in Chapter 3, further significant insights are to be obtained by looking at household choices from the standpoint of recent contributions to the behavioural theory of the firm. Second, it should be noted that it may be a misleading approximation to theorise as if consumers can always perform or even bother to try to perform the kinds of multidimensional trade-offs that the 'new' theory of consumer behaviour, every bit as much as the 'old' one, assumes they carry out in their minds. For example, when I purchase toothpaste, suppose I employ the following simple procedure: 'choose the cheapest brand (per ml) with fluoride, out of those that I know to have a suitably fresh taste'. This procedure leads me to purchase only one brand, but I would hardly dare to suggest my choice should be represented as a corner solution on one of Lancaster's diagrams: I display outright intolerance in respect of non-fluoride brands and would not dream of spending more to get a better taste if I expect I can meet my target by buying the cheapest brand; nor have I the time to spare to agonise over the amounts of fluoride per ml or the likely accuracy of claims made by toothpaste manufacturers about the relative abilities of their brands to produce whiteness. Busy, boundedly rational consumers may frequently be driven to employ choice procedures with very different implications from those that Lancaster presumes they employ, even though they are thinking in terms of product characteristics (see section 3.2 and Chapters 7, 9 and 10).

2.5 THE 'HEDONIC PRICING' LITERATURE

Household production theory, particularly Rosen's extension of it to encompass indivisible commodities, has widely been taken as having provided 'theoretical foundations' for an empirical technique pioneered by Court (1939) around the time that Hicks' *Value and Capital* appeared. This is the 'hedonic' technique, which involves the use of multiple regression methods to determine functional relationships between the market prices and the non-price characteristics of rival products. The form of the regression is shown in equation (1).

$$P_i = a_0 + a_1 Q_{1i} + a_2 Q_{2i} + \ldots + a_k Q_{ki} + e_i \qquad (1)$$
$$i = 1, \ldots, N$$

Where:

P_i is the price of the ith model (often stated in logarithmic terms);
N is the number of products in the (cross-sectional) sample;
$a_o, a_1, a_2, \ldots, a_k$ are the regression-derived weights;
$Q_1, Q_2, \ldots, Q_k$ are the levels of characteristics $1, 2, \ldots, k$ produced by the ith model, and if characteristics have a strictly dichotomous nature (for example, 'saloon' versus 'hatchback') they will be represented by dummy variables (for example, 0 if a saloon, 1 if a hatchback) in the regression;
e_i is an error term.

Once the regression coefficients have been estimated, one can calculate an expected price for each product, given a knowledge of the particular characteristics mixes. This price is given by equation (2), in which the 'hats' over coefficients serve to denote estimated values.

$$\hat{P}_i = \sum_{j=0}^{k} \hat{a}_j Q_{ji} \qquad (2)$$

These prices may then be expressed against actual prices in ratio form; the ratios will usually differ between products.

The hedonic technique has been applied in over fifty studies, which together encompass cars (by far the most popular), tractors, washing machines, housing, computers, pick-up trucks, refrigerators and audio cassette decks. These studies have used the technique for a variety of purposes, which do not always involve the same interpretations being imposed on the a_i weightings. It is possible simply to regard these weightings as reduced-form coefficients that reflect both supply- and demand-side factors. However, one may also try to interpret them *either* as reflecting consumer evaluations of the relative importance of characteristics, with consumer sovereignty acting so as to force market prices to correspond to these evaluations—hence the 'foundation-providing' role for Lancaster's analysis—*or* as indicators of the marginal cost to the typical firm of adding a particular characteristic to its products, in situations where oligopolistic firms are pricing according to cost-plus methods.

Clearly, if it is legitimate to see the weightings from the standpoint of Lancaster's theory, as some kind of measure of the values that consumers place upon particular characteristics, then one possible use of the hedonic technique is in the construction of price and standard-of-living indices that take account of quality improvements in consumer goods. This is the application associated particularly with the work of Griliches (1961) (see also Griliches (ed.), 1971), and it usually involves combining cross-sections for several years and using year dummy variables to capture price changes net of the effects of changes in characteristics between years. However, Muellbauer (1974) has questioned the legitimacy of interpreting hedonic relationships within the household production framework, and I will now note the essence of his case.

If all households had identical indifference curves and incomes, and if markets were strongly competitive, then one might expect many different combinations of goods to evolve which would yield identical combinations of characteristics, although different varieties of goods would then only be produced as a result of 'variations between firms in the costs of producing goods with a given set of specifications' (Deaton and Muellbauer, 1980, p. 265). Everyone would face the same shadow prices for characteristics and would have the same marginal rates of substitution. However, as a result of differences in income levels and/or tastes, consumers may not in reality have identical marginal rates of substitution if they each perform attribute trade-offs and find optimal product/attribute combinations for themselves. (It is interesting to note that Muellbauer at no point considers the possibility that consumers may not all weigh up the pros and cons of rival choices in the manner assumed in neoclassical household production theory.) Therefore Muellbauer (1974, p. 980) argues that a serious aggregation problem exists: strictly speaking, a hedonic analysis of changes in standards of living should look at market segments for consumers with similar marginal rates of substitution. But he then points out (p. 981) that it may not even be possible to identify marginal rates of substitution using the hedonic technique. This is because demand-side interpretations of hedonic regressions must assume indifference loci are linear (indifference curves in characteristics space would thus be downward-sloping straight lines), since the regression weights do not vary according to the relative amounts of characteristics. Such indifference loci will always involve corner solutions in Lancaster's model: there is thus no guarantee that hedonically estimated shadow prices for characteristics will reflect consumers' willingnesses to make marginal trade-offs and, even if market populations can be segmented into groups of nearly enough identical consumers, the hedonic approach fails as a means for making consumer welfare comparisons across time.

Cost-side interpretations of hedonic equations have been used in the work of Fisher *et al.* (1962), which attempted to assess the cost of providing the American automobile consumer with specification improvements (higher power, automatic transmission, power brakes and so on) during the 1950s. They found that the costs of model changes since 1949 were running at $5 billion a year, totalling about a quarter of the purchase price per car by the late 1950s. The possibility that consumers did not realise what these improvements were costing seems, however, to be qualified by the fact that they could have purchased in the late 1950s, at significantly lower prices, hedonically similar cars to those they on average purchased ten years before. All they needed to do was to buy base models that lacked the modern refinements. The enormous resource cost implied in the moves 'up market' that the affluent American consumers were making in this period must surely make one pause and think seriously about Galbraith's (1958) arguments about the balance of 'private affluence' and 'public squalor' in the United States. A Galbraithian would wish to enquire whether the up-market shifts made by consumers reflected their undistorted preferences for automotive refinement over a pleasant environment, or whether these shifts in behaviour might be better seen as acts of conspicuous consumption engendered by the marketing campaigns of car manufacturers—whose incentive to enter the market for environmental improvements instead is minimal given its different skill requirements and its scope for failure in the face of poorly defined property rights and consequent high transactions costs.

Most obviously of interest in relation to the present work (in particular, to Chapter 10) are applications of the hedonic technique to the task of explaining the determination of relative market shares of differentiated products. Where actual and hedonically estimated market prices deviate, one would expect that, other things equal, there would be some impact on market share. This is because a model with a positive residual in a regression of prices on characteristics is inefficient in the sense that, compared with an average model at the same price level, it yields a lower output of (measured) characteristics. If an 'inefficient' model is able to achieve a surprisingly high market share, then one might seek to explain the observation in terms of product characteristics that have been omitted from the regression due to measurement problems. Alternatively, one could appeal to consumer misinformation, inertia, or market 'imperfections' such as advertising. The last possibility is one that has particularly attracted the attention of Professor Cowling and his colleagues. In a hedonic study of the market for tractors, Cowling and Rayner (1970) proposed a model of brand share determination which was applied by Cowling and Cubbin (1971) to data on the UK car market in the late 1950s and early 1960s. The latter study concluded (1971, p. 343) with the observation that 'The quality adjusted prices have been found to be significant determinants of market share, along with advertising expenditures. This result provides further evidence in favour of the hedonic quality adjustment procedure'. With later data cross-sections, it would be natural to notice the growing market shares of imported products and hence to try to study import penetration with the aid of the hedonic technique. This is precisely what Leech and Cubbin (1978) attempted to do in respect of market shares achieved by cars sold in the UK. They tried to quantify the roles played by: value for money in terms of product specification, fuel consumption and insurance costs (both hedonically scaled against product specifications), advertising expenditures, size of dealer network, length of guarantee, delivery time, and reliability as measured by the average number of days a model spent being repaired. Amongst other things, their analysis of the data inputs for the year 1975 suggested that reliability had a significant role to play in determining the market share a model achieved, but that the number of 'extras' included in the price (an area in which domestic cars fared poorly against Japanese ones in particular) and delivery times did not.

The Leech and Cubbin paper appeared at a time when official thinking (as typified by the work of Stout (1977) at the National Economic Development Office) was calling attention to 'non-price factors' in UK trade performance, so its results may not have been lacking in significance in matters of policy formation. But the limitations of such a cross-sectional study must be carefully recognised if misleading inferences are not to be drawn from it. Take, for example, the finding in respect of delivery. This seems to contradict the conclusion of a survey-based study of the market in 1973-4 (CPRS, 1975, which Leech and Cubbin, 1978, p. 295, briefly mention in a footnote), that poor delivery was a very important reason for not buying British cars. However, since the hedonic study refers to a year of excess capacity, it may be unsafe to assume that the delivery coefficient would not be significant in years characterised by a consumer boom and/or major disruptions of domestic supplies due to industrial action, which resulted in a failure of UK firms to meet consumers' delivery *targets*. (Here, as when I remarked about my intolerant procedure for buying toothpaste, I am foreshadowing the non-compensatory decision-making procedures discussed in Chapter 7.) A coefficient may appear insignificant because rival brands in a sample year all meet adequacy criteria in respect of delivery times, but that is not to say it would not be significant if some of the brands were to fail to do so in the eyes of a significant number of would-be buyers in a year when conditions were different. Policies formed by UK motor manufacturers in the belief that 'It seems that in statistical terms delivery doesn't matter much' could produce surprisingly bad results, whereas import control strategies that were based upon quotas might be remarkably effective if they caused waiting lists for imported cars to become unacceptably long (see sections 10.4 and 10.7).

This short review of part of a burgeoning literature is, I hope, sufficient to suggest that the hedonic technique should be used with great caution. Although it *may* tell us something about the impact of customer preferences in a particular year, the results one obtains may simply indicate something about the pecuniary costs of incorporating certain characteristics in a particular product. Furthermore, even if it is appropriate to see hedonic findings at least partly from a demand-side perspective, they should not be taken as validating Lancaster's idea that consumers make up their minds by trading off anticipated characteristics outputs against each other in compensatory manner. Hedonic regressions are concerned with what is happening at the level of the market, but markets are populated by individuals who decide what to buy according to personally evolved evaluative criteria. Aggregative results may thus be consistent not merely with firms having been constrained in their pricing policies by consumers with fairly similar values who weigh up prospective characteristic yields as in the Lancaster model; they may also be consistent with pricing reactions by firms to market pressures that actually result from a disparate mix of individual decision-making procedures, some of which involve considerable simplification, some of which do not involve attribute trade-offs, and only a few of which closely approximate to what is proposed in orthodox approaches to household production theory.

2.6 COMPENSATORY MODELS IN THE MARKETING LITERATURE

In theoretical and empirical work with multiattribute 'conjoint' choice models in marketing and other behavioural sciences, one can discern an obvious parallel to the line of thought embodied in the economists' works I have so far considered. (And, as with parallel lines, these contributions tend not to overlap.) If anything, marketing scholars have been even more prolific than economists in this area: in their 1973 survey, Wilkie and Pessemeir reviewed forty-two articles; many more have since been published (see Akaah and Korgoankar, 1983, for many of these references). These papers contain many subtle variations on the same basic idea: that consumers, or decision makers more generally, can be thought of as if they compute expected values for rival schemes of action in a way which allows poor scores in some dimensions possibly to be compensated for by good scores on others. In this section I will describe in detail the most popular model, that associated with the work of Fishbein, briefly contrast it with some related models that involve different estimation techniques, and finally comment on the empirical findings that this research effort has yielded.

Fishbein's original (1963) expectancy value model focused on the overall attitudes of a decision maker towards particular objects of choice. In its more recent and popular format (in Fishbein and Ajzen, 1975) it focuses on attitudes towards alternative activities (such as rival purchasing actions that a consumer might undertake) and takes the form of a simple linear regression equation:

$$B \approx BI = \left(\sum_{i=1}^{n} b_i e_i\right) W_1 + \left(\sum_{j=1}^{N} NB_j MC_j\right) W_2$$

in which:

B = overt behaviour, which is approximately equal to BI, the degree of correspondence depending on contingencies that occur between expressing intentions and taking a decision to act;

BI = behavioural intentions, expressed as the person's subjective percentage likelihood that she will undertake the activity;

W_1 and W_2 are weights derived by the regression process;

b_i = the person's own assessment of the likelihood that performing the activity will produce consequence i;

e_i = the person's own evaluation of the goodness/badness of outcome i;

n = the number of salient beliefs the person holds about performing the activity; Fishbein follows Miller's (1956) rule that people can only keep in mind 7 ± 2 things at a time, and thus expects n usually to be only between five and nine;

N = the number of other people whose opinions matter to the decision maker in the context in question;

NB_j = the person's assessment of whether referent j thinks she should undertake the activity;

MC_j = the person's motivation to comply with the opinion of referent j.

Fishbein's model essentially suggests that a decision maker's attitude towards an activity may be seen as depending upon the relative influence she assigns to her own assessment of its pros and cons, and her overall willingness to comply with the collectivity of opinions which she believes her reference group has about the desirability of her undertaking the activity. Depending upon the assessments she makes, counter-desired expectations about particular consequences may be offset by desired ones, while the imagined disapproval of some of her reference group may be offset by the imagined approval of other members of the group. It is even possible that she may choose to do something because she allows the approval accorded to the activity by her reference group to swamp her own critical assessment of its desirability. In separating out the social influences on choice, Fishbein has created a somewhat more complex model than those produced by many of his fellow theorists; often marketeers' models resemble, at the level of the individual, the regression equations that economists estimate in 'hedonic' exercises at the level of the market.

The fact that the estimation of the Fishbein model involves the decision-making subject in judging attribute levels, and in revealing her own valuations of them, places it in what Akaah and Korgoankar (1983) have called the 'compositional/self-explicated' category of models. A less-complicated model which also comes into the self-explicated category is that found in Hoepfl and Huber (1970): the decision maker assesses attribute scorings and relative importance, and these measures are then combined in a weighted manner to predict her overall preference for alternative options with similar characteristics.

Rather more convenient to estimate are the class of models that make use of a 'conjoint, *de*compositional methodology'. This methodology is the marketing equivalent of the hedonic technique and it turns on its head the 'build-up' approach of the self-explicated models. Subjects are asked neither to assess phenomena in terms of their characteristics nor to specify what values they attach to each characteristic. Rather, they are supplied with details of the phenomena and are asked simply to rate each of them overall on a scale. The work of Huber *et al.* (1969) illustrates this method neatly. They gave 'objective' seven characteristic descriptions of twelve hypothetical hospital wards to senior hospital staff and asked them to give their total rating of each one on a 0-100 scale. They then tried this data in a variety of multiple regression models (linear, addilog, multiplicative) without trying to find optimal regressions by dropping the less-significant variables. When they compared the regressions they had obtained using these models for each individual's data set, they formed the conclusion that although individuals had consistent ways of evaluating multiattribute phenomena that were part of their everyday experience, there was only moderate consistency among subjects in their evaluations.

One can also discern a 'hybrid' methodology in some attempts to estimate compensatory models (for example, see Green *et al.*, 1981). Such studies attempt to improve predictions by combining self-explicated and regression-derived attribute valuations within a single equation.

The fact that there has been a proliferation both of the estimation methodologies and of the forms of models estimated should mean that the reader will not be surprised to hear that the researchers have so far failed to find a model which performs consistently well and demonstrates a clear lead in predictive ability. For example, consider the Fishbein model; Tuck (1976) is highly enthusiastic, whereas studies such as those by Ryan and Bonfield (1975) and Warsaw (1980) are critical of it. The critical studies suggest that the model typically suffers from high multicollinearity between independent variables and often produces weak and inconsistent predictions. However, such findings have not prevented Fishbein's theory, or variations upon its basic theme, from acquiring and maintaining the dominant place amongst models of consumer product evaluation processes in leading marketing texts (see section 9.4).

Studies of compensatory models increasingly compare a variety of forms and estimation methodologies. One of the more recent ones to attempt this is that by Akaah and Korgoankar (1983), and it is something of a disaster in predictive terms. It involves a study of attitudes to rival 'health maintenance organisation schemes' (a new variety of health insurance in the US, whereby no significant charges are made for outpatient visits). Akaah and Korgoankar (1983, p. 195) lament the fact that:

the percentage of correct first-choice predictions, even among the best models, is only 25 per cent compared with 16.7 per cent that would be expected from random selection. Four of the nine models performed worse than chance. The relatively low percentages probably stem from the noisy nature of the data.

Like so many researchers before, they conclude (p. 196) that there is a need for further testing, with different samples of respondents, different products and variety of data collection methods.

But when one examines the reason Akaah and Korgoankar adduce for their 'noisy data', an alternative conclusion stands out as a possibility. They point out (1983, p. 193) that their respondents were asked to evaluate the rival plans in a way that involved thirty-three complex trade-offs, and suggest that this resulted in the respondents being lax in their evaluations, owing to fatigue. Their remarks echo the comments of Green *et al*. (1981, p. 33) that 'the relatively large data requirements that are needed to estimate individual utilities are becoming increasingly burdensome on respondents', and of Hoepfl and Huber (1970, p. 409) who note that 'an analysis of variance suggested that increasing the number of factors included in the descriptions caused the subjects to be less able to make consistent evaluations even in the small range included in the study'. The alternative conclusion to be inferred is that boundedly rational decision makers, if left to their own devices, may not in fact perform attribute trade-offs in situations where this is cognitively highly taxing. So what could be needed are not yet more attempts to estimate varieties of compensatory models, but new models that do not centre on the idea that people always average out or add together characteristic ratings for individual schemes when they are trying to reach decisions.

2.7 CONCLUSION

In his prescient paper of 1952, Houthakker argued that to build models in which consumers were thought of as having preferences for combinations of characteristics would represent 'a fundamental change in the approach to consumption theory, since attention [would be] paid to the reasons why consumers want certain goods', and it might 'prove interesting for studies of the demand for newly invented goods' (1952, p. 163). But there is a sense in which the change that has occurred—limited as it is in terms of the number of economists who have turned away from a focus on goods-space preferences—is not really all that fundamental. As Haines (1975, p. 78) has argued, and as should be evident from this chapter, empirical work has largely continued to involve estimation, rather than the testing of new hypotheses, with the results thereby obtained being judged in terms of their statistical 'fits'. Much of this empirical work is decidedly unscientific in the sense that it does not involve analysts in seeking and assessing fundamentally different ways of explaining observed phenomena; usually one finds only variants on a compensatory theme being compared statistically.

The practical results of focusing on such models to the exclusion of other possibilities may be far from trivial if the focus is heavily in need of qualification and this is not spelt out to policy makers who use academic findings as a guide to action. The welfare of consumers on the receiving end of policies formed as a result of this focus could suffer unnecessarily. Mindful of the policy significance of adherence to a possibly mistaken view of decision processes, I shall spend the rest of this work attempting to open readers' minds to the implications of taking the basic ideas that households are production systems and that choices are often seen in terms of rival bundles of characteristics and of then facing up to the problems of uncertainty, complexity and the non-static nature of preferences in a world of change. This will involve me in taking the analysis one layer deeper than even Houthakker was proposing, for I will be attempting to shed new light on the reasons why consumers want particular characteristics in the things they choose. Marketing researchers are, of course, used to trying to penetrate this layer of decision processes, but they may none the less profit from my distinctive analysis.

3 The Enterprising Consumer

3.1 INTRODUCTION

If one intends to discuss the nature of consumer behaviour in terms of analogies with the behaviour of firms, it is vital that one uses an appropriate analysis of corporate behaviour as one's reference point. In the previous chapter I examined previous attempts to examine households as if they were production systems; all these attempts sought to view consumers from the standpoint of the neoclassical theory of the firm. The neoclassical theory is concerned almost exclusively with optimal choices of production technology and product mix/scale of outputs, in particular with how these choices will change, in both the short and long run, *following* the addition of 'new pages to the book of blueprints' and changes in relative prices of inputs and/or outputs. Substitution possibilities are at all times the centre of attention. With such a theory of the firm as its inspiration, it is hardly surprising that the orthodox approach to household production theory takes the form it does, focusing on marginal changes in feasible and optimally preferred mixes of characteristics outputs that may follow changes in the list of technological possibilities and changes in relative prices.

As a way of seeing firms—let alone consumers—in a turbulent world, the neoclassical approach has major limitations. It does not take much thought to realise that there is more to running a firm than the reactive activity of making marginal substitutions amongst factor inputs and product outputs as relative prices change; yet this is about all that the decision maker in the neoclassical firms seems to do. Neoclassical economists typically do not concern themselves with problems of internal organisation and management in firms; with methods of discovering, creating and grasping opportunities for growth; or with managers' strategic actions aimed at dealing with the possibility that they may be *mugged* by sudden, discontinuous ('kaleidic') shifts in market demands for their products, in supplies of their inputs and in government regulations, by striking workers or by rivals' technological breakthroughs; and so on. (See Kay, 1982, 1984, for penetrating discussions of these omissions.) The neoclassical firm is not usually represented as something whose long-term ability to survive and grow depends crucially upon the entrepreneurial and judgemental skills of its leaders. Yet a firm directed by people who can neither anticipate nor control events—both in the marketplace and within the corporate organisation—with at least as much success as its rivals is going, sooner or later, to be driven out of business. To seek to justify ignoring such matters by saying that the market will eventually be populated only with skilled survivors seems a highly unconstructive stance to adopt if adjustment processes are long and painful and if the nature of the necessary skills is always changing.

The absence of any discussion of such issues in the neoclassical theory of the firm would not be significant in attempts to use the theory in relation to consumer behaviour if precisely the same issues did not arise in this context. However, it does not take much thought to realise that, in a turbulent world, there is much more to being a consumer than the reactive activity of making marginal substitutions in a household production system as opportunities change. If one is to be a consumer whose life involves non-abortive attempts to take on new activities and achieve enhanced social standing, one needs to possess considerable entrepreneurial, managerial and judgemental flair. Without it, one's life will get into a distressing mess or at best stagnate, as the following examples may serve to suggest (see also section 1.1). The fact that second-hand markets are highly imperfect means that products which fail to come up to expectations can only be exchanged to the accompaniment of a proportionately significant capital loss. A failure of one's supplies of finance to come up to expectations may result in a forced need to dispose of parts of one's wealth on highly unfavourable terms. A career choice based on a mistaken expectation can send one off towards a 'dead end' from which one may be unable to return, owing to having become 'too old' by the time one discovers the error. A choice of job or leisure activity may turn out to be a nightmare beyond one's control if one is unexpectedly unable to manage the events it entails. (Just think of executive stress and its accompanying ulcers, or the hazards of affairs of the heart and pursuits such as sailing, skiing, hang-gliding, bush-walking, and attending football matches, to name but a few.) Like firms, consumers risk being 'mugged', not merely in the conventional sense of the word, but also by unfaithful spouses, by used car salespersons, by government policies, by firms that introduce products which render previously purchased goods obsolete, out of fashion and/or less valuable in second-hand markets, and so on. If consumers are to be able to make anything at all out of their lives in a world of turbulence and surprises, they must, like firms, have at least some degree of control over the events they encounter, and to achieve this they must possess some degree of predictive competence.

In Chapter 4, I will be discussing the anticipation and control of events in relation to consumer motivation—what consumers are trying to produce with their choices—and later chapters will examine processes of expectation formation. In the present chapter, my intention is to show how a recognition of the 'entrepreneurial' facet of the business of being a consumer takes the focus of theoretical analysis away from relative prices and marginal substitutions. This will involve me in making considerable use of recent developments in behavioural approaches to the theory of the firm. The analysis is divided up into four main sections. Sections 3.2 and 3.3 are concerned with the various levels of abstraction and degrees of problem-solving activity in terms of which consumers try to cope with the complexity of their lives. These discussions involve a substantial departure from the philosophy of neoclassical consumer theory in both its Hicksian and 'new', production-theoretic guises; for orthodox analysis, in respect of consumers as well as firms, normally treats all choices as if they are essentially the same. (The 'utility tree' literature mentioned in section 2.4 is an important exception within the neoclassical paradigm that deserves to be more widely mentioned in intermediate microeconomics courses.) Section 3.4 examines how we would expect choices characteristically to be affected by perceptions of increased environmental turbulence. In the last section (3.5), there is a discussion of the question of household organisation and disintegration, something that warrants attention given changing male/female role expectations and the frequency with which marriages nowadays end in divorce.

3.2 DELIBERATIVE AND ROUTINE DECISIONS

If a decision maker has easy access to information and is not prone to suffer from information overloading, and if her decision-making environment is relatively placid, then it would be natural to predict that she would think carefully about possible opportunity costs each time she needed to take a decision. On recognising a problem, she would seek information about potential solutions, evaluate them in detail and choose the seemingly best available option. Such a decision process seems less plausible if the decision maker faces information problems, or if the environment is turbulent. First consider a situation where the environment is relatively stable but information is costly to obtain and process. Here, a decision maker who has evolved or has been given suitable simple selection rules as means of dealing with particular problems can rapidly 'decide' what to do without going through the process of seeking out and evaluating alternatives. Such decision rules we may term 'routines' or 'recipes for success'. Often they will simply involve repeating previous actions: for example, 'there is only one tin of baked beans in the cupboard, so I must get two tins of Heinz at K-Mart on Friday night'. (This is a five-element routine, for it involves consideration of neither (1) substitutes for baked beans, nor (2) alternative volumes of beans, nor (3) alternative brands, nor (4) alternative shopping venues, nor (5) alternative shopping times.) Sometimes a particular routine will be unworkable, so subsidiary ones may be brought contingently into play, as automatically as one changes down a gear when a slow-moving car thwarts one's progress when driving up a steep hill. (As an aside we might usefully note that driving routines can be economised upon at some cost by buying a vehicle with automatic transmission and thereby delegating the 'decision' to the car itself.)

In using any set of contingent routines, the decision maker is experimenting, for their success is not guaranteed. But if they usually enable her to keep things under control and there are no reasons to doubt they could continue to do so, the decision maker may feel confident in keeping in the set a rule of inertia: 'if it works, don't mess with it' (see Hoch, 1984, and, noting that a rule for keeping rules is an example of a 'strange loop', see sections 1.2 and 6.2). Thereby the hopeful consumer frees her mind for the task of deciding what to make of unfamiliar situations, albeit at the cost of not discovering the kinds of results that can be obtained by using routines which do not yet have proven track records. To make successful decisions, the chooser does not need to know how her recipes for success work; she merely needs to be in possession of a set that *does* work. In this respect, the image of a '*recipe* for success' is a useful one to bear in mind; strictly speaking, cooking is chemistry of a somewhat complex kind, but a person armed with a recipe book of instructions on how to prepare meals for particular occasions may be able to impress her party or dinner guests despite having no knowledge at all of chemistry.

A turbulent environment would at first sight appear to be a place where such procedure-based forms of behaviour are not going to be viable. Certainly, there are many cases where decision makers can be seen to have got into difficulties because they tried to apply to newly turbulent environments routines that had worked very well in more placid times (see Earl, 1984). However, in many unfamiliar situations, a detailed evaluation of options may be precluded by complexity and ignorance. Hence, when trying to cope under pressure with surprises, the decision maker may be forced for want of any better ideas to seek out familiar patterns under the surface of her problem—patterns to which she has attached particular routines for making selections. What looks like agonised or coolly calculating deliberation may therefore actually end up reducing to a form of routine behaviour. Experimental investigations of ways in which people play chess— a game that is only fascinating as a result of bounded rationality allowing surprises within a well-defined rule structure—suggest such a view warrants serious consideration. This work (Chase and Simon, 1973a, b) suggests that 'good' chess players win more frequently not because they can think further ahead and over vastly more options than can novice players; rather, they have larger repertoires of 'successful' patterns to look out for and are often no more able to specify precisely what a particular move is expected to achieve in respect of the state of play some moves into the future. This is *not* to say that the expert players always reach snap decisions without looking at a variety of possibilities, but it could be taken to imply that they ultimately choose in a manner that might usefully be described as *programmed* or *reducible to a system of principles.* This is the essence of the thinking underlying the analysis of deliberation put forward in Chapters 6–8 of the present book.

The distinction between routine behaviour and deliberative choice (programmed or otherwise) has often been drawn in behavioural literature on corporate and bureaucratic decision making (see Cyert and March, 1963, Steinbruner, 1974, March and Olsen, 1976, and Nelson and Winter, 1982). Yet it is surprisingly infrequently encountered in non-neoclassical discussions of consumer behaviour. Up until about 1980, even marketing texts on consumer behaviour followed the economist's approach of depicting consumers 'as if' they always reached decisions only after careful thought about possible options. This seems surprising, given that the marketing literature on industrial buyer behaviour carefully distinguished between 'new task', 'straight rebuy' and 'modified rebuy' decisions and made much of limited search undertaken by firms (the paper by Cunningham and White, 1974, includes empirical material on the absence of careful search that neoclassical theorists might find rather disturbing). Things changed following the publication of a provocative paper by Olshavsky and Granbois (1979). They argued (1979, pp. 98–9) that:

For many purchases a decision process never occurs, not even on the first purchase.... Purchases can occur out of necessity; they can be derived from culturally mandated lifestyles or from interlocked purchases; they can reflect preferences acquired in early childhood; they can result from simple conformity to group norms or from imitation of others; purchases can be made exclusively on recommendations from personal or non-personal sources; they can be made on the basis of surrogates of various types; or they can even occur on a random or superficial basis....
...even when purchase behaviour is preceded by a choice process it is likely to be very limited. It typically involves the evaluation of few alternatives, little external search, few evaluative criteria, and simple evaluation models. There is very little evidence that consumers engage in the very extended type of search and evaluation a product testing organisation like Consumers' Union performs routinely.

So now marketing texts normally include at least one apologetic chapter that, despite the small volume of literature on simplifying choice behaviour, tries to correct the impression given in earlier editions.

Unfortunately, there are signs that marketeers have incompletely understood the nature of such behaviour. Typically they distinguish between 'high-involvement' and 'low-involvement' choices, arguing that if a choice matters a lot to a consumer she will go to a great deal of trouble in making her selection. However, a consumer may be so highly involved with a particular idea that she fails even to think of alternatives. For example, there can be few more important decisions in life than those concerning getting married and having children, yet Richards (1985) found that a majority of her sample of Australian couples had not considered the possiblity of not aiming to marry and have children (though many did consider alternative times for having children). There are many passionate believers in the conventional Western family who have never seriously examined its opportunity costs and who would find suggestions about other ways of life simply unthinkable (see sections 5.2 and 6.2).

Whilst marketeers may have missed some of the message that Olshavsky and Granbois sought to convey, orthodox economists seem utterly oblivious of it; they typically read neither the *Journal of Consumer Research*, in which the article originally appeared, nor marketing texts that have tried to grapple with it. Economists use routines themselves to avoid information overload and normally end up writing, suboptimally, as if consumers *always* consider opportunity costs prior to choice. (Many seem aware that Becker, 1962, once proposed an analysis of demand based on random behaviour, but few—Hey, 1983a, is an exception—have bothered to take such an idea at all seriously).

3.3 STRATEGIC PLANNING BY HOUSEHOLDS

The idea that households engage in strategic planning in a manner somewhat akin to corporations is one that I have yet to see an economist putting forward in a text on consumer behaviour. In high-level analysis, neoclassical economists typically follow Debreu (1959) in depicting the consumer as choosing, once and for all, between rival *fully specified bundles* of commodities: time and uncertainty are taken account of in these hypothetical acts of choice by defining commodities, not merely according to their physical characteristics and place of delivery, but also with respect to their date of delivery and the 'state of the world' in which they are to be delivered. Thus 'Economic Man' orders a particular kind of child safety seat to be delivered for his car on a particular date 'if and only if a baby has appeared in the household' by that point. If that contingency has not arisen, the contract will not come into operation and other contracts will be invoked pertaining to the 'no baby' state of the world: for example, on the date in question, the person might have a claim to see a concert 'if and only if there is no new baby and if I am not indisposed due to illness'. Economic Man does not face up to life with open-ended and incompletely mapped-out plans, the details of which are only inked in as and when particular contingencies arise. Rather, Economic Man is depicted as if he is able to insure himself against every possible eventuality and, having done so, able simply to go through life ensuring that the pertinent, and exactly appropriate, contracts are implemented.

In reality, many consumers may often devote a good deal of thought to methods of organising their lives in a world of uncertainty and change, whilst making rather restricted use of insurance possibilities. (This is not to say that a good deal of their time is not spent simply carrying out routines; the use of routines gives them time to plan.) They try to plan their career paths, but do not make advance orders for goods to be delivered 'if and only if I have been promoted to position P by date Q'; rather, they make the order of their acquisition of particular goods contingent on how their careers seem in fact to be shaping up. They also choose the order of their purchases with a view to the information that might become available about their possible needs for particular commodities, about what is likely to become available and about trends in relative prices (for example, 'if I buy a compact disc player this week, it could be a mistake since prices may not yet have reached a floor level and next month's car service could be horribly expensive; but now might be the time to get the extra fan heater while summer prices are lower—*that* should still leave me with enough room on the Visa card even if the worse comes to worst on the car front'). They may sometimes commit themselves to package tour holidays with detailed itineraries, as well as to travel insurance, but often they prefer to plan for themselves a loose timetable that gives them scope for lingering at places that take their fancy and for passing swiftly through those that do not. In planning their families, they might sometimes insure against multiple births, but they do not insure against the disruption caused by any failure of their attempts to preclude children 'for the time being'; rather, they set about revising their plans to cope with the reality of surprise. In planning their retirements they may seek to accumulate funds, and guard against dying and leaving their spouses in poverty, with the aid of life assurance policies. Having retired they may commit themselves to annuity policies on their long-dreamt-of retirement homes in Florida, Cornwall, Surfers Paradise, or wherever. But they will usually only take steps actually to create their retirement lifestyles in detail (or even plan broadly what they are going to do) when (or if) they get near to retiring at the planned point in their lives. In a turbulent world, redundancy may force them into early retirement, as may ill health, and if so, they will revise their expectations and plans, making fresh choices; they will not merely see to it that different sets of prearranged contracts come into operation.

To see why consumers opt to construct, and if necessary revise, their own rather loose plans of action for shaping their lives, instead of trying to insure against the vagaries of the world in which they find themselves, we need only consider how turbulence and complexity combine to produce many situations in which it may seem to pay not to organise one's life via the use of contingent claims contracts. First, as Heiner (1983) has emphasised, the infinity of things which might happen means that it will be impossible to avoid being exposed to all manner of unpleasant possibilities, even if the costs of concluding any single insurance contract are small. One only needs to think of the behaviour of a hypochondriac to see how constraining it is to try to preclude undesired states, many of which will remain forever as mere imagined possibilities even if no precautions are taken. If Economic Man happens to be as sterile as the theories in which he is the central character, then all manner of baby-related contracts he might negotiate will turn out to be useless. On the other hand, if conception occurs at the first attempt, many such contracts aimed at later possible arrivals of children will also be redundant. It is likely to appear better to choose now with an eye to the possibility of a pregnancy if one is trying to start a family (for example, avoid buying a two-seater car that one would then have to trade in at some cost), but only to commit oneself to baby-specific goods once the baby's arrival seems guaranteed.

Second, we should note that amongst the infinity of things which could happen are possibilities which no one has yet imagined, either at all or in enough detail for them to be made the subjects of precise contracts. Thus while Economic Man might be able to order a 'hi-fi' system for delivery on a particular date, if and only if he has not lost his hearing, he is going to run into trouble if he starts insisting on entitlement to an as-yet uninvented system as part of the contract: to specify the 'state of the art' at the date of delivery would open up all manner of scope for argument about what gets delivered, and it might not even be a system compatible with his existing recordings. Working out a deal to encompass as-yet-uncreated and undreamt-of musical works would be even more problematical. If Economic Man tries to avoid keeping his life open ended, by concluding contracts in respect of what has thus far been envisaged, he may needlessly debar himself from great opportunities to take advantage of pleasant surprises or to cope with events that come 'like bombshells, out of the blue'.

Third, insurance markets are prone to failure due to (a) the phenomenon of 'moral hazard' (having insured themselves, some people are less than usually careful about trying to prevent the situation against which they have insured); and (b) the failure of low-risk groups to insure, which means that prohibitive premiums have to be quoted to the groups most at risk (see Akerlof, 1970). Finally, insurance and guarantee arrangements may founder in situations where it is difficult to establish what has happened (see Williamson, 1975, p. 24); for example, consumers may never be quite sure whether faulty workmanship is the cause of a breakdown, while firms may decline to offer guarantees if they find it difficult to police whether or not consumers act within the letter of such agreements. Either side could have powerful incentives to indulge in guileful, opportunistic behaviour at each other's expense. If sufficient trust cannot be engendered, *any* kind of transaction may be precluded.

If people have reasons for not trying to face up to the future via contingent claims contracts agreed to *right now*, then they will not be choosing amongst rival fully-specified bundles of commodities. Instead, they will choose first between rival plans of a strategic nature and will then try to implement them via a *sequence* of lower-level choices. These subsequent choices will be made in the light of how things actually seem to be shaping up, yet the options thus considered will be ranked with respect to their compatibility with the chosen plan given the commitments already made by way of implementing it. We might usefully regard the behaviour of consumers who have chosen particular plans as being programmed in a broad sense. They will only change their pathways (and often only after a good deal of heart searching—see section 6.6) if it becomes sufficiently obvious that events are not unfolding as broadly anticipated and that a better plan of action might be conceived and put into effect.

There are two senses in which we may regard households as making *strategic* choices amongst entire plans or in the process of executing their plans. The first is the meaning that Bausor (1982, 1984) attaches to the word 'strategy' in his looped, historical view of economic processes (see section 1.2, part (6)). Bausor's (1984, p. 366) idea of a strategy is that of a choice influenced by anticipations of what *could* happen, where the decision maker's preferences over rival schemes of action are not 'a simple translation of preferences over outcomes'. In other words, 'Pursuing a plan reveals nothing unambiguously about outcome preferences and attitudes towards surprise. It means only that the person judged the chosen strategy to be correct' (p. 367). A consumer's choice of a plan of action would be a strategic one in Bausor's sense if it were affected by her desire, for example, to stand prepared 'if something *un*expected happens' or to be ready 'just in case X *does* happen'. On such an occasion the consumer would not be choosing a course of action (say, Y) in the belief that a particular state of the world (say, Z) *will* materialise, in which event Y would be the best course of action to have committed herself.

The second sense in which consumers may make strategic choices is one that we can generalise, to the context of household production theory, from Neil Kay's (1982, especially pp. 52–5, 1984) structuralist analysis of the firm. Kay conceptualises business 'strategy' as something distinct from 'tactics' in the light of the thinking of the nineteenth-century military strategist Carl von Clausewitz. In a war, the generals have two kinds of decisions to worry about. One is how to set up and win *individual* battles. The other is which *combinations* of battles they should get involved with in order to win the war. The former, Clausewitz called tactics: the latter, strategy. In business behaviour, as depicted by Kay, tactical choices include pricing and output choices for a particular product that a firm makes, *given* the conditions and scale of production of the firm's other outputs—outputs that may be seen as *linked together* in particular ways with the product in question. Strategic choices, on the other hand, include questions about which choices of activity combinations to engage in, given apparent cost and revenue possibilities. A strategic question might thus be 'does it make sense for us to start producing aluminium tennis racquets, given that we already produce aluminium skis, or would it be better to start producing ski-jackets and sell them under our brand name?' But a tactical decision might be 'given the change in popularity of tennis whilst we've been getting our tennis racquets ready for production, how should we set our racquet prices?' Some readers may have noticed that the orthodox analysis of the firm is essentially concerned with tactical choices of price and output, and even treats investment decisions in tactical terms, since linkages between different production activities are rarely mentioned. However, it should also be noticed that, even once investment decisions have been made, it is by no means always appropriate to treat the pricing of an individual product as a tactical decision, since its price may have repercussions for the sales of other products in the firm's catalogue. Wherever one activity is in some way linked to another, choice becomes strategic in Kay's sense of the word (see sections 4.5 and 6.5, as well as the next section).

It should be evident that the 'strategic' and 'tactical' kinds of decisions that Kay has in mind might both be addressed 'strategically' à la Bausor, since both could involve unavoidable uncertainties. It should also be evident that analogous strategic and tactical choices arise in the context of consumer behaviour. For example, a young professional couple may strategically decide to try to postpone starting a family until they have both got their careers established. Given this choice of lifestyle for the immediate future, they may then choose tactically between alternative contraception technologies. Similarly, a young graduate trainee who has committed herself to a city centre job may see herself as faced with a strategic choice between, say, (a) using an old car to commute into town from the suburbs where rents are cheaper (especially the rent her parents may charge if she lives at home), and putting much of her income aside towards a house deposit; (b) commuting from the suburbs but using much of her first few years' income to make repayments on a new car instead of rushing to save up a house deposit; (c) sharing a flat in the city centre, thereby saving travel costs and time but paying higher rent, and trying to accumulate money for a house deposit whilst relying on public transport; (d) sharing a flat in the city and making great use of the city's entertainment facilities, at the cost of accumulating little capital, on the ground that 'you're only young once'; and so on. If she chooses (b) over (a), she may be doing so because a new car seems to offer reliability, something which she sees as essential if she is to get to work on time and make a good impression. Her particular choice of type of new car may also be linked with her other activities; for example, she may strategically set out to look for a station wagon 'so that I can camp in it when I go off windsurfing at weekends', because windsurfing is a sport with which she has previously become heavily involved. (Such an involvement would pose a barrier to preferring strategy (c) or (d).) As Cairncross (1958, p. 16) has observed in an early plea for the integration of production and consumption theories (his paper is cited by Becker (1965, p. 496) but by neither Lancaster nor Muth, and is proposing a much more radical programme than neoclassical household production theory has delivered) 'each fresh purchase has to be fitted, not just into an existing pattern of consumption but also into an emerging way of life'. Only at the brand level—which new station wagon?—does the choice of car become a tactical one.

Kay's view of the distinction between tactical and strategic choices may be more clearly drawn in relation to the issue of system decomposability, mentioned in section 1.2. A purely tactical choice can be defined as one in which the set of rival possibilities has been preselected by the consumer to ensure that the choice of one option at the expense of its rivals has no impact on the payoff to other choices of activity, even if each member of the set of rivals is linked with other activities. For this kind of choice to be possible, the members of the set of possibilities must be linked with other activities in identical ways. Then, by taking these common binding properties for granted, the consumer is able to decompose her choice problem. For example, the consumer may choose strategically 'to buy next week, if possible, a new station wagon within the price range of $T – $U'. Her choice is strategic in that it relates to the activities of 'commuting into town during the week' and 'camping/windsurfing at weekends'. Her choice between the rival station wagons within her budget range and available for rapid delivery is then a tactical one, made with reference to characteristics that were not considered for their strategic significance—for example, features such as 'velour versus vinyl trim' or 'soft ride versus good handling'.

Complexity is likely to force consumers often to treat choices as tactical ones when there is, in principle, scope for looking at them in strategic terms: a series of partial choices may seem the only way of confronting an indecomposable problem. Consider the question of how much it might be worth spending within a particular commodity category. I have already mentioned the use of a 'budget range' as a device for selecting a tactical choice set in respect of a decision to purchase a car. Such a price range would have been an element in a budgeting plan chosen not merely with a view to technological spill-overs between expenditure categories in the possible combinations the consumer brings to mind (for example, living a long way from work at the mercy of an old car or public transport may be incompatible with punctuality), but also with a view to the fact that various activities may produce non-trivial amounts of some common characteristics, even if they are technologically independent (for example, the amount a person spends on clothes and the amount she spends on a car may both contribute to the image that she can establish of herself). These relationships may be hard enough in themselves to assess when the person contemplates the possible results of choosing one plan at the expense of the rivals she is considering. However, once a budget range has been used to define a tactical choice set for a particular category, further opportunity cost issues arise.

For example, if the consumer buys a station wagon at the lower end of her budget range, she will have smaller monthly repayments and could use the money she avoids committing to motoring in a huge variety of ways. In principle, she might ask herself, 'do I prefer vinyl trim and lower repayments plus more trips to concerts each month, to velour trim and higher repayments, to vinyl trim plus a better camera?' and so on. In practice it would be overwhelming to try to do this for a large array of specific possibilities. Plush upholstery may help establish one's status, as may one's camera or appearance at public concerts; but, then, what value might one place on musical aspects of live concerts as opposed to foregone automotive or photographic features? *Each characteristic in one category that costs time or money to obtain could warrant consideration against the characteristics that would have to be foregone from any of the other expenditure categories.* The potential trade-offs seem endless. If the consumer could deal with all of these trade-offs among different characteristics and among different ways of producing particular amounts of individual characteristics, and if she could take account of all the technological spill-overs she could see, she would have no need to form budgets or think in terms of a variety of levels of choice with varying degrees of abstraction. The Kay-type dichotomy between strategy and tactics would vanish.

In practice, bounded rationality will ensure that the consumer ignores many trade-offs; her high-level choices will focus on relatively basic characteristics and general classes of products, not on precise brands (though some brands occasionally may be used as reference points); low-level choices will focus on characteristics specific to the particular category of products. At either level, highly programmed choices may be made instead of deliberative ones. For example, lifestyle plans may include a strategic intention to get married that has been incorporated without consideration of the merits or otherwise of alternative household set-ups, and marriage partners may be 'chosen' not after a good deal of searching—'is *this* person the one for me?'—but by way of doing the 'done thing' following an earlier failure to think about the possible implications of a tactical action (for example, a decision about 'your place or mine?' that was not preceded by the question 'should we take precautions?').

It should not be a cause for surprise to find that, in situations of novelty and complexity, as well as those of high passion, consumers only consider some significant strategic implications of their choices *after* they have acted upon their tactical decisions (see section 6.6). For example, suppose someone decides strategically to 'purchase a decent camera' to capture the sights she sees on hiking trips. Suppose further that she has little knowledge of photography and opts for a good quality automatic camera as her tactical choice—say, a 'Canon Snappy'. She has now equipped herself with a camera that will not accept a variety of lenses and yet, if she ends up getting 'hooked' on photography, she will come to require the ability to switch lenses. Had she thought ahead and examined the activity of photography more carefully, she would perhaps have seen a strategic reason for buying a 35 mm reflex camera with 'breech-lock' fitting for its lens. Such a camera might be somewhat less simple to operate, but it would at least leave her options open. As it is, she may to her regret find it expensive to adapt to her growing area of interest.

3.4 WAYS OF LIFE IN INCREASINGLY TURBULENT SITUATIONS: THE EVOLVING CONSUMER (1)

A consumer's recognition that some areas of her life are more hazardous and prone to variability than previously she had imagined may reflect either changes in the nature of these areas (for example, higher risks of job losses due to technological change) or simply changes in her perception of how risky some parts of life actually are (for example, she may have learnt the hard way how dangerous solo bush-walking can be, or how much it can cost to run a particular kind of car). Either way, a variety of kinds of strategic shifts stand out as likely candidates for adoption. It will be seen that all involve some costs and/or risks of error; so it will not be surprising to find people choosing different strategies, or combinations of strategic responses, even if they have started out with similar combinations of interests and commitments and have reached similar conclusions about the need to change their behaviour.

3.4.1 Take out new insurance policies

In the previous section I discussed possible barriers to the use of insurance (contingent claims contracts) for coping with uncertain environments. But it would be foolish to claim that they rule out every kind of insurance; in affluent economies, where people have a lot of valuable property and income flows they stand to lose or have damaged, insurance is big business. However, if costs of insuring are significant for administrative and transactional reasons, and if she judges herself to be less at risk than other people assessed as being in her risk category, then the consumer is likely to investigate alternatives to using the insurance market to guard against undesirable eventualities, even if policies to cover them are actually available in the market. The incentive to investigate other possibilities is enhanced by the fact that, even where it can be arranged, an insurance policy may fail to offer compensation that covers fully the costs associated with the undesired outcome to which it pertains (see sections 7.4, 8.3, 8.5 and 9.5). For example, it is indeed difficult fully to restore a badly damaged car to its pre-accident condition; while holders of life assurance policies may hardly relish the prospect of themselves being dead even if their families are well provided for, and no amount of money might suffice to stop their families' grieving in the event of their deaths.

3.4.2 Move to relatively less risky environments and products

Examples of consumers pursuing a policy of 'flight' or 'playing safe' are easy to find. Reports about the dangers of high-cholesterol diets lead people to cut their consumption of eggs, meat and dairy products, and do wonders for the sales of 'Flora' margarine. The spread of AIDS leads some of the 'dirty raincoat brigade' to indulge in their sexual fantasies with the aid of pornography, not prostitutes. Expensive mistakes by motorists who have tried to run out-of-the-ordinary vehicles result in some of them switching to more mundane cars: as *Car Magazine* ('The Good, The Bad and the Ugly', May 1984 issue, p. 147) notes, the Toyota Corolla 'sells in huge numbers because it offers no surprises'. However, the consumer is at best likely to find herself obtaining only relative security and giving up one risk for another. A striking illustration of this concerns the fortunes of a Canadian family who migrated to the Falkland Islands in the late 1970s. They have yet to observe quite how safe their haven is in the event of the nuclear war they foresee between the superpowers, but they have already found out what it is like to be mugged by invading Argentinians. Less dramatically, we can note that the bitter experience of disappointments as a result of 'leaving it to chance' in respect of finding accommodation on a touring holiday, or tickets 'at the door' of a concert, may lead a consumer unknowingly to make advance bookings of unattractive accommodation in relatively uninspiring locations, or for concerts that in the event she will be unable to attend. Mises (1966, p. 113) is by no means exaggerating wildly when he claims that 'Every action is speculative. There is in the course of human events no stability and no safety'. Moreover, the costs of trying to insulate oneself from life's risks through one's choice of activities may be considerable: like a firm which confines itself to its established market niche and so fails to grow very far, the consumer who seeks to avoid risks wherever she can is unlikely to accumulate great wealth or a wide range of personal experience. These factors will militate in favour of continuing to act in an enterprising manner—which by no means needs always to involve behaving recklessly, on impulse—when life seems to have become more problematical.

3.4.3 Devote more resources to trying to control environments newly perceived as hazardous

The idea that people spend a good deal of their lives trying to preclude counter-desired events without fleeing from risky arenas is a major theme in the next chapter. New perceptions of risks may make them concentrate even more on keeping things under control. For example, reports about a high incidence of thefts of audio systems from cars may lead people to install burglar alarms, even if they continue to park in high-risk locations such as inner-city streets and long-stay car parks. More bizarrely, we can note how firms that produce male contraceptives may suddenly have a new market consisting of gay males fearful of catching AIDS and yet reluctant to abstain from their risky practices.

3.4.4 Seek more flexibility

This strategic response to increased perceptions of environmental turbulence is one to which Albert Hart (1940, 1942, 1945, 1947) devoted great attention in work on business and macroeconomic policy that deserves to be much better known. Hart argued that, in situations of perceived uncertainty, even a wise decision maker is unlikely to find herself using the production technology that is the least-cost way of dealing with the situation in which she has found herself. Looking forward, she might rationally prefer an (*ex post*) 'inefficient', but flexible, way of producing what she could wish to make, and might not choose something which is perfectly adapted to what seems the 'most likely' situation or the outcome equivalent to a weighted average of probable outcomes, and yet which is not easy to adapt to other, less likely, but seemingly possible states. In criticising Keynes for his tendency to speak in terms of 'certainty equivalent' expectations, Hart (1947, p. 422–3) summed up as follows:

Generally speaking, the business policy appropriate for a complex of uncertain anticipations is different in kind from that appropriate for any set of certain expectations.... *Flexibility* (of which liquidity is an aspect) is worth incurring costs for, because it avoids wastage of information accruing between the date of planning and the date for which plans are made.... Economists will be able to give better council if they form the habit of analysing contingencies and designing policies to hedge against uncertainties.

Hart's philosophy has been reinvented in business strategy literature on 'scenario planning' (for example, Jefferson, 1983) and is one I use in my own writings (see section 1.2, part (2), and Earl and Kay, 1985). I would expect to find many consumers unknowingly living by it as they choose adaptable plans and production technologies to insure themselves against the vagaries of a world of turbulence.

Such consumption strategies are not without their costs. For example, a person who believes she could have to move house in the not-too-distant future would be likely to judge it unwise to commit herself to new furnishings specific to her present home. However, *modular* furnishings that are easily adapted to a variety of alternative housing conditions may not be available at the desired quality level or may be more expensive because, by their very nature, they will involve more edges than do integral systems. None the less, such decomposability costs may be seen by some consumers as well worth incurring. (This example is inspired by my own experience with a non-modular 'corner-unit' settee which was perfectly adapted to the shape of my first home but which could only be sited in one corner, and not the ideal one, of the lounge in my second: in retrospect, a three piece suite looks like it would have been a better idea.) Secondly, we may note that modular hi-fi systems give their owners flexibility in the event of technical progress—if I have a separate amplifier and AM/FM tuner, I need only replace the tuner when AM stereo is introduced.

However, separate casings, extra wiring connections, and so on are going to mean higher prices; a 'receiver' is usually cheaper than a comparable pair of tuner and amplifier 'separates'. Even bigger savings can be made by choosing a 'hard-wired' integrated music centre, yet anyone who wishes to keep abreast of technical developments in sound reproduction will usually prefer to pay extra for a decomposable system.

Hart's remark that liquidity is an aspect of flexibility is significant not merely because the extreme flexibility-seeking strategy is totally to avoid commitment and hold on to one's purchasing power. If consumer durables could be traded in at little cost for replacements that were perfectly adapted to new requirements, then adaptability would not be a sought-after characteristic: easy marketability could seemingly substitute for physical adaptability. Unfortunately, many consumer durables are exceedingly illiquid, for reasons that are not hard to see. Indeed, the less adaptable something is in physical terms, the harder it is going to be to sell it in a hurry at a price anywhere near its new price, even if it is in excellent physical shape and has not been rendered less attractive by technical progress.

Consider furniture as an example once again, not forgetting that its colour may play a major role in determining its compatibility with existing systems. Its bulk prevents sellers from conveniently moving it from buyer to buyer until an acceptable offer is obtained. Its lack of standardisation makes its quality difficult to specify if one is trying to get would-be buyers to come to inspect it: for example, 'a velour corner-unit' might be exactly what a person is looking for but, then again, it might be in too bad a condition or the wrong shape, size or colour. Whether they are intermediaries or users, buyers of second-hand furniture require a good deal of know-how if they are to avoid paying inappropriate prices, and sellers, likewise, need to be well informed if they are to get a good deal (especially with antiques). Informational economies are clearly difficult to obtain if one is not a frequent participant in the market and products vary greatly. Taken together, these factors ensure that furniture, like most other consumers durables, is an illiquid asset (see Streissler, 1973, and Casson, 1982, Chapter 9). Most trade in second-hand furniture will therefore *not* involve people switching furniture that was 'perfectly suited' to their former home, for similar grade furniture that is 'perfectly adapted' to their new home. Rather, it will be in furniture that is trickling down from affluent homes to poorer ones as affluent consumers renew their somewhat tattered furnishings or correct past mistaken choices of expensively inflexible items that do not suit their new houses.

3.4.5 Introduce bigger safety margins

This policy is a variant on (3) and (4) and is one that all drivers are trained to employ: the more hazardous the driving environment seems, the bigger the gap there should be between oneself and the car in front, so that one has 'room for manoeuvre' in the event of trouble. When consumers recognise they are moving into surprise-prone environments, we should expect them to choose budgeting plans that leave them with more spare time and money (or larger unused credit card balances) available for dealing with difficulties, anticipated or otherwise. They may also be expected to purchase greater quantities of inputs for tricky household production processes than they would actually need if everything worked out perfectly. (For example, the past experience of difficulty in cutting kitchen tiles may lead one to purchase an extra box of bathroom tiles, just in case one breaks some when decorating the bathroom—one is exchanging the risk that they may be unnecessary, for the risk of being unable to finish the job as planned without another trip to the hardware store.)

The 'safety margin' idea is another one that deserves to be associated in economists' minds with the work of Hart, who, in discussing it, introduced the 'principle of linkage of risks' (Hart, 1948, pp. 198–202). Our lives are often organised in ways that ensure a chain of misfortunes will be set in motion if we allow ourselves to fall victim to a single unpleasant surprise. To demonstrate the role of a cash reserve as a buffer against such spillovers, Hart used the example of a motorist on a long business trip who has taken only just enough money to pay for petrol and meals. If the traveller is stopped for speeding and cannot pay an on-the-spot fine, her trip turns into a disaster: she suffers a night in jail, the humiliation of having to call friends to ask them to send money, and perhaps fails to conclude the business deal as a result of failing to arrive on time. Similar unfortunate escalations could have arisen as a result of her car breaking down. In a turbulent world, the person who tries to run her life in a very taut manner is going to have to be very careful not to put a foot wrong or allow herself to be 'mugged' by events. This is going to make for a very stressful existence and one which could easily get into a mess. By contrast, the consumer who chooses to build a good deal of slack into her way of life can take a 'laid back' attitude to events, for an individual misfortune will not have wider ramifications (see section 6.5).

3.4.6 Seek greater diversity in one's commitments and avoid making the viability of one dependent on the simultaneous success of another

With this strategy, the linkages theme is maintained – though with more of a synchronic than a diachronic emphasis—but we turn for inspiration back to Kay's (1982, 1984) work on business policy, for once again his analysis is open to generalisation to the realm of consumer behaviour. Kay argues that, in a placid environment, a firm will choose additions to its product portfolio very much with a view to their complementary relationships with its existing activities. He identifies three main kinds of overlaps: (i) common requirements in respect of research and development, (ii) common production know-how requirements and facilities, and (iii) a common market. The firm's existing commitments mean it has a head start in respect of common know-how if not also in the form of spare capacity (released by learning processes) and, by taking on related products, it can spread the costs of design, manufacture and marketing over a larger volume of output (see section 4.5). The new product may aid sales of existing ones, and vice versa, because of a shared brand name; for example, some of the image of an 'up-market' model rubs off on to less luxurious models, whilst buyers who entered the market by purchasing something from the lower-priced part of the firm's catalogue may carry on buying the same brand as they move up-market. Hence by pursuing scope for linkages and exploiting complementarities amongst activities, the firm achieves *synergy:* the returns from undertaking the activities together are greater than the aggregate of returns that would be enjoyed if the products were designed, produced and sold entirely separately. However, Kay suggests that the firm will recognise that, as its environment becomes more turbulent, there are risks in concentrating on a few markets and technologies and exploiting synergy wherever possible. By increasing the number of markets in which it operates and the number of technologies in which it has expertise, the firm can try to insure itself against an individual failure being a disaster for the corporation as a whole. By choosing activities that can stand on their own or which, if linked to other activities, are not dependent for their viability on the success of any single other line of activity, the firm may be forgoing short-run profits that might be generated from more synergy-rich activity combinations. But so long as its activities generate enough profits for it to be able to survive against firms that are surviving for the moment on the basis of highly synergistic activity combinations that give them lower costs, its long-run position may be more secure.

Although many lay consumers have not heard of the word 'synergy', they are normally very well aware of the risks of 'putting all your eggs in one basket' in hazardous environments and of the costs of spreading themselves thinly across a variety of activities. Consider how their choices of vacation strategies parallel corporate portfolio choices. A British family might normally take a holiday in Spain in a single fortnight and stay at a hotel they know well. But if taking their holidays in Britain 'for a change', they may choose to have two separate weeks to insure themselves against the vagaries of British weather, even though this will mean two lots of packing and travelling. They may also hedge against unfortunate choices of holiday resorts and accommodation that they have not previously experienced by booking up for one week in one location and one in another, even though this will involve them in the cost of familiarising themselves with two places. Choices of skiing holidays might likewise differ from choices of holidays in familiar Spanish resorts, where the weather seems near-enough guaranteed to be fine. For example, the strategy of choosing adjacent weeks in separate resorts in the same country may enable the consumer to avoid a huge misfortune due to a single commitment to a resort where the weather turns out to be awful most of the time, the runs uninspiring and the accommodation below par. Weather risks may be reduced still further by including more widely separated resorts in the plan, but more time will then be lost in transferring between them.

But perhaps the most obviously synergistic activity a person can enter into is that of an intimate relationship with someone else with whom she/he has much in common. By setting up a joint household, they reduce the costs of duplication in household equipment, of working out at whose place they will be spending time, and of reduced specialisation in performing household functions. By doing things together that they might hitherto have done within a larger circle of friends, they cut down the cost of cultivating and coordinating a number of continuing relationships that they exploit only to a limited degree. So long as the relationship lasts, they may also reduce their vulnerability to the risk of being individually unable to generate income (see Pollak, 1985). However, if a close relationship of this sort turns out to be a stormy one and culminates in a break-up—or if they find it impossible to reconcile their separate career ambitions— each of them will find themselves facing substantial start-up costs as they construct independent households once again. Such a split will be particularly painful if, in making the most of the relationship, they have lost touch with their former supportive acquaintances. To the extent that people anticipate difficulties in maintaining close personal relationships, we might thus expect them to avoid constructing 'couple-centred' ways of life, and either to forgo altogether the economies of a joint household or to try to obtain them via, for example, 'apartment-sharing' arrangements with others from whom they remain relatively detached.

3.4.7 Consider previously-avoided 'institutional/ transactional' methods for attempting to produce particular kinds of outputs

This suggestion, opaque as it no doubt will initially seem, is inspired by literature on corporate behaviour that has recently grown up out of seminal contributions by Coase (1937) and, much later, Williamson (1975). This new body of ideas—known as internalisation theory—seeks to understand how perceptions of environmental turbulence bear upon the relationship between physical linkages between activities and the extent they are undertaken *within* firms or via transactions *between* firms. The ideas seem amenable to application in the context of consumer behaviour theory (or, more significantly, they can be seen to make the division between theories of the firm and theories of the household all the more artificial), but so far only Casson (1982, p. 193) has noted this, and then only in passing.

In the corporate context the basic theme—which I have myself explored at greater length in Earl (1984, Chapter 2)—is simple: the choice between trying to get things done in the market-place or within a corporate organisation depends on the strategist's perception of the different risks and costs (particularly transaction costs) associated with the rival institutional arrangements; neither mode is perfect, but the likely problems of using either vary with the state of the environment. Diachronic linkages between stages of production and distribution processes do not intrinsically involve the vertical integration of activities within the boundaries of a single firm, for subcontracting arrangements can in principle be used to handle every stage from retailing back to the extraction of raw materials. Similarly, synchronic linkages of risks and possible returns do not intrinsically require the horizontal integration of activities within a single corporate boundary. Synergy can in principle be traded amongst firms and investors can hedge their bets by buying shares in a variety of undiversified companies instead of a tranche of shares in a single diversified conglomerate corporation.

In earlier parts of this section, a number of my examples implicitly involved consumers in taking internalisation decisions that were affected by the extent of perceived environmental turbulence. Consumers insure themselves against disasters not always via market-based insurance contracts and guarantees, but often by careful (though by no means costless) choices of activity mixes that limit their commitments and vulnerability. One obvious example was the choice between a couple-centred joint household, an apartment-sharing arrangement, and life as an independent single person living alone; this choice essentially concerned the question of how precisely, and where, household boundaries might be drawn. Readers may have noted that I did not tie the couple-centred joint household case to the formal institution of marriage. But marriage is not an intrinsic feature of such a system and marriage/'living together' choices may themselves not be unaffected by the turbulence of the environment. For example, the costs of dissolving a *de jure* relationship may deter a couple from entering into it if they were not confident of being able to keep their relationship viable (see Becker, 1974, p. 22, for some evidence on the relationship between the incidence of marriage and the ease of divorce). On the other hand, however, fears about doing badly in the event of the break-up of a *de facto* relationship could make marriage an attractive institutional arrangement to insist upon if one were taking the risk of setting up a joint household; the willingness of the other party to agree to this could display much about his/her confidence in the relationship's durability and about the genuineness of his/her commitment. Internalisation theory raises some question marks about the wisdom of the idea that love and marriage 'go together like a horse and carriage'; true love is likely to be blind to strategic reasons for getting married or avoiding doing so, and hence likely to be indifferent between *de facto* and *de jure* arrangements. (These issues receive no attention in Pollak's 1985 survey.)

Let us now move to two other kinds of internalisation questions that households may recognise. First we can note that, in stable environments, the costs of arranging and maintaining rental agreements for flows of services from durable goods may make consumers feel inclined to buy them outright. However, in turbulent situations, rental arrangements may have advantages. If video recorders seem likely to undergo rapid technological improvements, then to buy right now would seem to carry risks of capital loss. These risks are difficult to insure against in any other way than by renting (the forward market for used VCRs being conspicuous by its absence). Similarly, if a person is not sure that she will be staying for long in a particular area, she can try to avoid legal bills and reselling costs (including possible costs of a bridging loan to avoid having hurriedly to take a knock-down price if, at the time of moving, the market happens to be thinly populated with buyers) by renting accommodation instead of buying it—though at the cost of missing out on possible capital gains and security of tenure.

Secondly, we can note that if bitter experience leads a person no longer to trust garages, she can try to maintain her car herself instead of subcontracting the work out to garages. If she does so, she may need to incur great expense in terms of forgone leisure or income-earning time and by way of obtaining know-how and appropriate tooling that will get used only occasionally. (She *might* be able to rent the tools, of course, but not necessarily just when she desperately needs them; or she might be able to rent out her own tools, at the risk of finding it difficult to get them back at the right moment. With lower-value tools, the costs of arranging rental agreements are easily likely to swamp their purchase prices after only a few hirings.) By internalising the maintenance of her car, she at least knows what *has* been done, but there is always the possibility that, despite the investments she makes in this activity, her own lack of expertise will result in her finding herself stranded at the roadside. 'Do it yourself' and 'subcontracting' strategies each involve set-up costs (which, it must not be forgotten, include costs of obtaining competitive quotations) and risks of unpleasantly surprising outcomes, and decision makers may assess these differently. So we should not be surprised to find a great variety of internalisation strategies being used even in situations where people have similar income-earning opportunities and are trying to produce similar end results. The risk-related and transactional aspects of the economics of 'do it yourself' warrant far more attention than they have hitherto received from consumer theorists.

3.5 HOUSEHOLDS AS ORGANISATIONS

Once one has devoted attention to issues that may bear upon the formation of multiperson households and on the internalisation by such households of activities that might be arranged via the market, some questions come to mind that economists normally do not bother to consider: how are households organised and what stops them from disintegrating when the going gets tough, given that their members are unlikely to have identical goals? In seeking to provide some answers, a potentially useful starting point is to characterise households as organisational *coalitions*. It is then possible to generalise some of the ideas of Cyert and March (1963), who depicted firms as coalitions of people with partly complementary and partly antagonistic interests. Members of such coalitions put up with the disadvantages of participation in the hope of meeting aspirations that otherwise they would be unable to meet. They exit from the coalition when the disadvantages of membership become intolerable and/or the payoffs insufficiently great.

In a turbulent environment, the disadvantages and payoffs to coalition membership would tend to be in a state of flux. But this does not necessarily mean that a coalition immediately becomes fragile if turbulence increases. Room for manoeuvre may be provided by the fact that, in order to economise on the costs of putting the coalition together, relationships between the coalition members will have been only partially specified. (Coase, 1937, would argue that a 'firm' which involved fully specified relationships between participants, covering all possible contingencies, would not be a firm at all in an organisational sense: nothing would have been internalised, and there would be no need for managerial decision making as pre-specified contingencies arose.) The vagueness of the relationships between coalition participants permits them to engage in discretionary behaviour to economise on the disadvantages of their membership and improve their payoffs. Because coalition members are unsure of the conditions in which their fellow participants would exit from the arrangement, they will hold back from 'pushing their luck' so long as things seem at least adequate from their own standpoints. The result of this combination of moderation and the failure of all the parties to 'lay all their cards on the table' is the existence of a buffer of 'organisational slack'; in good times, some or all of the coalition members may be enjoying returns to membership in excess of their minimum acceptable targets. When the going gets tougher for some members of the coalition, other members may be prepared to contribute more to, or moderate their claims on, the coalition's various productive activities in order to keep the arrangement together. Even if the other members are not prepared to contribute enough to make good all of the shortfall suffered by those who are finding life more difficult, the relationship may still survive owing to the threatened attainments having hitherto been sufficiently in excess of minimum acceptable levels. Thus a measure of 'give and take' may enable the coalition to weather difficult periods.

Tensions in a household coalition may arise not merely as a result of shocks (for example, job losses, price rises, breakdowns) that make a given collection of aspirations more difficult to meet. They may also come about because of sudden shifts in aspirational targets and in perceptions of attainment possibilities outside the present relationship. Here we should take serious note of the social context in which household members live their lives: external reference standards will be used in the formation and reformation of aspirations; people will not simply adjust their criteria of adequacy into line with their own repeated attainments.

For example, consider the position of a wife whose rosy expectations of married life have been shattered: she now expects that, if she keeps her present relationship intact, she will be a victim of domestic violence on occasions when her husband finds his life is going badly and 'takes it out on her' in attempting to keep intact his own expectations (see the discussion of hostility in section 4.4). She may know about the fates of women like her with, say, small children, limited educational achievements and without established careers whose marriages have broken up. Their experiences may make the prospect of life outside the institution of marriage look even worse than life inside it. If many of the women she knows also confess to being tied to violent husbands, her chances of improving things via a change of partner may appear so slim as to not make search seem worth while. Thus, despite periodic batterings, she may not take steps to terminate the relationship. Meanwhile, in material terms at least, there may be little to grumble about; her husband may normally be quite easy to bargain with in respect of household equipment and items of conspicuous consumption that will match the standards set by people in whose league she believes her household to be. However, suppose that, by one means or another (see section 5.2), she comes across feminist ideas. These could lead her to undertake a revolutionary reconstruction of her aspirations, the upshot of which is that she now ranks the avoidance of *any* domestic violence above the attainment of material security. Unless she can get her husband to change 'his ways', this household coalition is no longer going to be viable. Major changes in social service provisions, female employment prospects or in divorce laws with respect to maintenance payments might also produce household fragmentation by raising the opportunity costs for women of continuing to participate in unsatisfactory relationships.

In households, as in firms, a good deal of scope for tensions and possible disagreement is eliminated by the specialisation of individuals with respect to particular roles, including income-earning versus internalisation activities. If roles are agreed upon in broad terms, along with pertinent allocations of broadly specified complementary resources, the designated individuals can then attend to the details of their tasks without persistent negotiation; special routines can be developed and more can be achieved, though on some occasions coordination problems may arise. Specialisation helps generate organisational slack, since the non-specialist is poorly placed when it comes to judge how easy it is to perform a particular task; husbands and wives playing traditional household roles may have very little idea what their spouses actually do during working hours. But, of course, role specialisation makes household members vulnerable in the event of the household's disintegration. In turbulent times, feminist arguments against male/female role stereotyping, and in favour of the sharing of tasks, can be augmented with a strategic dimension; for by acquiring a broad range of domestic management skills and their own capacities to generate income, members of households can insure against finding themselves all at sea in the event of separation, a partner's disability, or bereavement.

Such a sharing of household roles would not merely reduce the vulnerability of individual household members. It would also help to remove the hierarchical characteristics that many households share with corporate and bureaucratic organisations. In the household context, and leaving aside the question of child/parent authority relationships, Galbraith (1975, Chapter 4) has argued that many women are reduced to the status of 'crypto-servants' who specialise in consumption administration under the authority of their husbands. For example:

The wife of the somewhat senior automobile executive need not be intellectually alert or entertaining, although she is required to be conventionally decorative on occasions of public ceremony. But she must cook and serve her husband's meals when he is at home; direct household procurement and maintenance; provide family transport; and, if required, act as charwoman, janitor and gardener. Competence here is not remarked; it is assumed (Galbraith, 1975, p. 48).

In such a household, the wife may exert a superficial control over the purse strings, yet the major decisions, the strategic moves, are made by the man who provides the money (Galbraith, 1975, p. 52). His wife is a doormat to be moved from place to place as his career demands and who is expected to undertake the duties of homemaker without questioning her role or status.

As with the 'economics of do it yourself', the economics of the household as an organisation appear as a field ripe for further research—indeed, internalisation and organisational issues tend to go hand in hand. Attention might usefully be devoted to the comparative strategy advantages of extended families, communes, Kibbutzim, and so on, as well as to marriage, living-together, flat-sharing and living-alone arrangements, and to the various organisational problems and possibilities associated with each (see Pollak, 1985, for a review of previous contributions). Clearly, more attention also needs to be given to processes of bargaining (see Earl, 1983c, pp. 184—8, for some of my earlier suggestions) and joint decision-making processes generally. Marketeers have for some time been exploring such issues (for example, see Curry and Menasco, 1979), but economists have largely continued to treat household and individual choices as interchangeable. During the chapters that follow, readers should bear in mind that decision-making procedures may include criteria concerning the likely acceptability of an option to other household members, as well as criteria concerning characteristics in which the individual in question has a personal interest. Choices may be made by an individual on her own account, by an individual acting alone but on behalf of a multiperson household, or they may concern the acceptance or rejection of particular proposals made by a fellow participant in a joint decision.

3.6 CONCLUSION

In this chapter I have tried to show that there are gains to be had from extending the basic neoclassical picture of the household as a production system by introducing themes from recent behavioural contributions to the theory of the firm. Many of these themes were ones that I employed in my earlier (1984) work on the origins of corporate mistakes. In this earlier work, I argued that, although much of the new literature on corporate strategies has been presented as describing how companies in general *do* operate, it might often be better seen as analysing strategies that decision makers *should* consider employing in particular situations. Very much the same remarks could be offered about attempts to construct an analysis of strategies of consumer behaviour. Although I have tried always to use examples from everyday experience to illustrate the theoretical analysis, I recognise that much of what I have argued may involve more subtle thinking than many consumers will undertake prior to making significant choice in turbulent environments. If companies get into trouble by, for example, tackling potentially strategic choices as if they are simple tactical ones, then we should not be surprised to find households getting into similar kinds of difficulties. By considering the arguments in this chapter and the ones that follow, consumers may find themselves[1] able to improve the quality of their decision making.

Although the discussion has largely focused on reasonable strategies and routines for coping with anticipated turbulence, the arguments may easily be turned round to shed light on modes of behaviour in environments that are perceived as placid, either by nature or as a result of the consumer having implemented seemingly successful control measures. In such situations, consumers would be expected to *settle down*, in the sense of adapting precisely to conditions and committing themselves to inflexible, immobile, 'lumpy' activities from which it is difficult to switch without loss. They will combine these activities to form highly integrated, synergy-exploiting ways of life. Having done so, they will then largely be involved with simple routine choices. When turbulence appears unexpectedly in their lives, it will be particularly disruptive, not merely because of the integrated nature of their lifestyles and inflexibility of their commitments, but also because of the shortness of their menus of proven 'recipes for success' for coping with surprise-prone environments.

4 The Inquisitive Consumer

4.1 INTRODUCTION

Having first departed from orthodox analysis by highlighting the strategic dimension of consumer behaviour, I am now going to take an even more deviant step and consider from an explicitly *psychological* standpoint what consumers are trying to produce as they make their strategic and tactical decisions. The kind of psychology I will be employing is known as personal construct theory. It is an approach that is increasingly being used by clinical psychologists as a means for understanding why distressed patients are finding that life is getting on top of them, and for showing them how they might improve their situations. Personal construct theory is by no means the only kind of psychology that the economist might think of employing—for example, in trying to understand the problems of affluent consumers, Scitovsky made extensive use of behaviourist and physiological psychology in his (1976) work *The Joyless Economy*—but it will be seen to be a particularly natural one to employ, given our strategic perspective on consumer choice. Furthermore, its comprehensiveness enables it to offer us the prospect of being able to understand expectation formation and resistance to change (the subjects of Chapter 6) as well as motivation, and it also comes complete with a well-developed set of research techniques that can be used to map evolving consumer perceptions and preferences.

The chapter is divided up as follows. Section 4.2 introduces the main ideas of personal construct psychology, while section 4.3 shows in some detail how they relate to consumer choices. Section 4.4 presents an analysis of the significance of 'emotional' factors in decision making, and shows how they can be conceptualised in usefully precise terms. Before the conclusion (section 4.6), section 4.5 examines, in the light of the previous sections, why consumers may prefer some areas of activity to others.

However, before we move on to the main body of the chapter, it is probably appropriate for me to explain why, unlike most other economists, I feel it is necessary to examine the psychological underpinnings of consumer satisfaction.

Economics has conventionally managed to distance itself from psychology by taking as 'given' the perceptions and preferences that underlie the choices people make. This assumptive procedure leaves the economist seemingly free of any obligation to explain what consumers are trying to achieve as they choose. And when it is 'common-sense knowledge' that everyone should be entitled to 'life, liberty and the pursuit of happiness', few economists ever stop to ask themselves whether it could be misleading to subsume all matters of motivation under the simple heading of 'utility maximisation'. Having thus taken psychological material as 'given', the economist is only interested in admitting changes in these 'givens'—and then only occasionally so—in so far as they can be presented as objective payoffs from economic activities chosen with reference to the initial preferences, perceptions and endowments. The neoclassical consumer invests in gathering information about prices and product characteristics, and her behaviour then changes as a result of what she has discovered; or she invests in gathering information about how to use particular household production technologies, and her subsequent choices of marginal expenditures on rival production technologies are directly affected by the 'set-up costs' she has incurred in respect of some technologies but not others. In both cases the consumer's perceived constraints have changed, but her underlying preferences are treated as if they are fixed, (see Stigler and Becker, 1977).

It appears to me that, in depicting the pursuit of happiness as the budget-constrained scaling of contour lines on indifference maps, the teachers of successive generations of economists have ended up losing sight of what consumers actually feel and are trying to do with their lives. Endless talk of 'utility maximisation' seems to have led economists to focus on choices amongst 'the good things in life', on how the best possible bundle of 'good' goods or characteristics might get selected. The only 'bad' thing usually discussed is the drudgery of work. The message is that more goods and less work are the key to happiness. But now, in this age of 'sado-monetarism', we see that, for many of the millions of people out of work, employment has become a desperately desired commodity, even though, in 'real' terms, modern-day dole and redundancy payments vastly exceed those of the inter-war slump. Meanwhile, even if they enjoy good health and family relationships, those who possess and can participate in the fruits of affluence are frequently no more obviously happy than those enjoying far lower living standards. The rich and the poor alike seem to have their problems; yet within the ranks of either group one can usually find *some* people who would claim to be 'perfectly happy'. Unless we can understand the psychological foundations of such phenomena, the scope for erroneous policy recommendations would appear to be considerable.

4.2 THE CONSUMER AS A SCIENTIST

Happiness, joy, pleasure, utility—call it what you will—is a concept that makes no sense taken in isolation from some kind of reference point. Usually, when we have failed to achieve happiness in a particular situation, we would profess to feeling 'disappointed', so a potentially useful reference point for understanding happiness seems to be whatever it is that differentiates it from disappointment. Here, as so often, the *Concise Oxford Dictionary* is instructive: it defines the verb 'to disappoint' as to 'fail to fulfil desire or expectation of; to frustrate', and it defines the noun 'disappointment' as an 'event that disappoints, resulting in distress'. The implication seems to be that whether or not something disappoints or makes one happy does not depend intrinsically upon its objective properties, but upon what is *expected* of it and how it subsequently seems to match up to one's expectations. We are 'happy' when events conform with our anticipations of them and 'overjoyed' when we discover that, even in our 'wildest dreams', we have underestimated their astonishing, 'marvellous' properties.

This view of the nature of happiness is nonsensical in the world of perfect information so often assumed in neoclassical economics; for in such a world, there are no disappointments and no surprises, whether good or bad. In the real world of uncertainty and environmental turbulence, the view makes complete sense. Being a consumer whose range of activities continues to grow and whose life is not seemingly filled with disappointments is, as we saw in Chapter 3, a business that requires considerable competence in the area of expectation formation. In Chapter 3, I characterised this competence as a kind of 'entrepreneurial' flair, but it is perhaps better construed as a kind of *scientific* skill: like scientists of an academic sort, enterprising people, in firms or households, are trying to *predict and control* events.

It was around precisely this latter vision of the nature of human endeavour that an American psychologist, the late George A. Kelly (1955), some thirty or so years ago constructed the comprehensive theory of personality out of which has developed a school of thought known as personal construct psychology (hereafter, PCP). (The crucial first three chapters of Kelly's massive two-volume work are conveniently available as Kelly (1963), while helpful guides to Kelly's ideas and subsequent work on PCP are found in Bannister and Mair (1968), Bannister and Fransella (1971) and Adams-Webber (1979).) The 'personal construct' term originated in Kelly's concern to emphasise that the impressions people form of 'things' are images that they construct for themselves—there is no such thing as an 'objective' universe. Kelly's own view of the universe was that it is such a complex, integrated structure, in which everything ultimately affects everything else, that people can only make sense of it by imagining that it can be separated into distinct events. These events he saw as being imagined theoretically as mental 'templets' which are then tested, with the aid of other mental templets, for their goodness of fit. A person who can construct a variety of rival theories will try to discover which of them has the least bad fit. Quite often, even the best available fit will not be very good and, failing any other bright ideas, a person may end up having to twist some of her constructions to stop others falling to pieces.

Personality is something that PCP suggests one should see as the outward manifestation of a person's beliefs; for the fundamental postulate of Kelly's theory is that 'a person's processes are psychologically channellised by the ways in which she anticipates events' (1955, p. 46). How a person will feel about a particular environment, and how she will try to behave in it, will depend on how she construes the environment—in other words, on how she 'sees things'. People have different personalities, and often find it hard to get on with each other, because they see the world differently: Kelly's (1955, p. 55) individuality corollary holds that 'persons differ from each other in their construction of events', while his (p. 95) sociality corollary tells us that 'to the extent that one person construes the construction processes of another, she may play a role in a social process involving the other person'. The latter corollary carries with it the implication that unless marketing staff can see how potential customers construe products in the market-place, they may very easily end up selling them very little. However, the emphasis that Kelly gives to the possibility that people may fail to construe events in similar ways does not mean he rejects the idea that people may in some degree share common perspectives: the commonality corollary of his theory states that 'to the extent that one person employs a construction of experience which is similar to that of another, her processes are psychologically similar to those of the other person' (1955, p. 90). Thus although two economists, say, may differ over appropriate ways of seeing particular economic problems (or even over what constitutes an 'economic' problem) they may see certain consumption activities in very similar ways, or vice versa.

Kelly's work points to four main reasons for people forming different theories about how to predict and control events, and about which events are worth attempting to predict and control. First, people *organise* their ideas in systematically different ways. This contention of PCP will be discussed in detail in Chapter 6, but for the present all one need note is that a willingness to accept some ideas may be incompatible with a willingness to accept other ideas and hence it may be necessary to rank some constructs above others in order to avoid a state of total confusion when incompatible notions are being entertained.

The second reason for people seeing things differently follows from Kelly's (1955, p. 50) construction corollary, which states that 'a person anticipates events by construing their replications'. The events that people attempt mentally to separate from the integral and ever-changing universe can only be seen in terms of their likenesses and differences *relative* to other previously construed events. People may thus end up construing things differently because they have different reference points—different judgemental standards—at their disposal. For example, British motorists would usually see a 2.0 litre Ford Cortina as 'powerful', rather than 'economical', relative to its 1.3 litre counterpart (which was not sold in Australia), whereas most Australians, by contrast, see a 2.0 litre Cortina as 'economical', not 'powerful', relative to its 4.1 litre counterpart (which was not sold in Britain). American motorists would be unlikely to use *any* version of a Cortina as a reference point when imagining what it might be like to own a particular car.

Third, one should note that Kelly suggests that people have only limited repertoires of perceptual axes in terms of which they seek to compare and contrast events: his dichotomy corollary states that 'each person's construction system is composed of a finite number of dichotomous constructs' (1955, p. 59). These theory-forming repertoires will differ between people, resulting in some people being blind to things that others see. For example, most consumers do not seem to compare the cosmetics products they buy in terms of the construct 'involving animal exploitation *versus* produced without cruelty to animals'—despite the fact that this is a dimension in terms of which differences can be discerned. (Here it should perhaps be noted that although Kelly often gives 'dichotomous' its strict binary connotation, for example, 'cruel *versus* kind', it is by no means essential to do this and often it will be more appropriate to think of people using bipolar construct *scales*.)

Finally, we should see that, even if people use similar points of reference and similar construct axes when trying to anticipate events, they may still form different expectations because they have assigned different ranges of applicability to some of their constructs. Kelly's (1955, p. 68) range corollary informs us that 'a construct is convenient for the anticipation of a finite range of events only'. However, Kelly goes on to warn his readers that such ranges are themselves personal constructs; he notes, for example (1955, p. 69; and see also pp. 108-9) that:

One person may use the construct of *respect versus contempt* to apply broadly to many kinds of interpersonal relationships. Another person may use it to apply only a very narrow range of events, perhaps only to the choice of words in a formally structured situation, such as a court proceeding.

The range corollary means that it is appropriate to see a person's ways of looking at the world as being partially separable into broadly different groupings of constructs used for anticipating different kinds of events, though with some constructs having a very common usage and figuring in many groupings.

Differences in the ways in which people see the world—including differences in the ways in which they see themselves in the world—will mean that 'similar' events will impinge differently upon their perceived abilities to predict and control their lives. Hence 'happiness' is not necessarily related to one's material position: rather, as an old adage would have it, 'happiness is a frame of mind'. To ram home this point, before moving on to see how a Kellian view of the consumer relates to choice, I will briefly note some of the findings in studies of the psychological consequences of unemployment recently conducted by Professor Peter Warr and his colleagues.

People with greatly differing personalities may all be surprised to find themselves made redundant by their employers. Now, thrust into a new environment, they will be in for yet more disappointments and will find themselves losing control of their lives if they fail to develop seemingly valid hypotheses about the events in which they consequently get involved. Unemployment is not intrinsically the end of one's world, but it seems that many workers find it difficult to construe it as anything other than this. People commonly find life on the dole very distressing because they find it impossible to anticipate what is going to happen to them in future months (see Payne *et al.*, 1983); they can neither construct theories that seem to match unfolding events that they do not presume to be able to control, nor can they see ways of determining themselves what will happen. In important respects, being unemployed is like nothing many workers have hitherto experienced. Unemployment is usually seen to offer a few new freedoms—such as when to get up—but these are swamped by a perceived loss of scope for control that the unemployed associate with lost access to material resources (see Warr, 1983, p. 306). Some people see themselves as so totally lacking the ability to predict and control events that they cease trying altogether and come to display the symptoms of clinical depression—scientific activity of any kind has as its rationale the existence of seemingly *soluble* puzzles.

However, not all unemployment involves terrible disappointments. In a study of 1000 unemployed males (Jackson and Warr,

1983) it was found that some 8 per cent actually felt better off as a result of losing their jobs: redundancy had thrust them into an environment safe from the stresses of their paid jobs. A rather larger, though still small, minority of involuntarily unemployed workers seemed to cope well with the situation, even though they did not experience an improvement in their psychological wellbeing. These tended to be people who see the event as providing an opportunity for getting involved in other kinds of work, to which they felt more strongly committed. Such people maintained high levels of activity, despite their reduced access to material resources, by participating in, for example, political, religious and community groups; and they saw these activities as offering scope for the creation and exploitation of new opportunities (see Fryer and Payne, 1983). Evidently, if large-scale unemployment is here to stay, policy makers would do well to examine the possibility of devoting resources to helping the unhappy majority construe their situations along lines presently used by those for whom the experience is not an unmitigated disaster.

4.3 PREDICTION, CONTROL, AND CHOICE

The idea that we should see people 'as if' they were scientists was far from being an unprecedented suggestion even in 1955 and, since then, other scholars in diverse disciplines have unknowingly come to a similar conclusion to Kelly about the nature of human action (for examples, see Earl, 1983c, pp. 9–10; 121–3). However, my experience is that many people do not find it immediately obvious how it might be used to understand consumer behaviour, and it seems that, apart from myself, only Gutman (1982) has attempted to employ PCP in this context. (Gutman's paper complements what will be said in this section, but that is about as far as it goes.) The key to such an application of PCP is the choice corollary of Kelly's theory: 'A person chooses that alternative in a dichotomised construct through which she anticipates the greater possibility for the extension and definition of her system' (1955, p. 64). Scope for choice arises when rival things are construed differently in respect of any of the dichotomous axes/bipolar scales in terms of which a person sees them, and, depending on how things are construed and on how the person arranges her thoughts, rival choices will differ in their implications for the person's view of the world. A person's 'system'—her world-view—may be said to have been extended ('elaborated' is a synonymous Kellian term) if the range over which it may practically be applied has increased. The definition of a person's system may be said to have been increased if, instead of being able to construe certain things only in fairly general terms, a person now finds she can form seemingly well-fitting theories about their finer points. The concept of 'definition' may be more easily appreciated in the light of the word's use in an optical context ('sharpness of focus'), or if readers think of it as pertaining to increased connoisseurship in certain areas. In a world of turbulence, where predictive successes are hard to achieve or maintain, the best that some people may be able to obtain is the bare preservation of their views of the world, or a limitation in the extent to which their understandings of things become less well focused or reduced in their ranges of compass.

In seeking to extend, define or maintain her constructs, a person has to contend with the opportunity cost problem. Like any academic scientist, a consumer can only obtain limited resources to test her conjectures. Some notions that she entertains as possibilities can be tested only with great difficulty and only if she forgoes opportunities to test many other ideas or sustain many other expectations. In some cases, the refutation of one of her conjectures would be seen by a person as disastrous for her subsequent ability to predict and control events; in the 'laboratory of life' there are many conceivable *crucial* experiments that have the potential seemingly to change *irreversibly* a person's opportunities one way or another. These considerations ensure that there will be many occasions on which a person is driven to adopt the methodology of 'armchair theorising' about what was, what might be or what might have been: she makes tentative choices between rival constructions of events without subjecting some of them to a direct test. On other occasions, however, a person will be willing and able to embrace a methodology that involves trying to test the fit of some of her constructs at first hand.

With these thoughts in mind we can now turn our attention once more to the concept of the household as a production system. If we see decision makers as scientists then, like Gutman (1982), we must recognise that things are not sought 'for their own sakes' but as direct or indirect *means* towards the ends of prediction and control. Things that seem in some respects antithetical to these ends will be avoided unless they are consistent with them in other more significant respects and no seemingly superior options are available. Very many of the choices and strategies discussed in the previous chapter should on reflection fit neatly into the category of possible (though not always foolproof) means towards making life more predictable and ensuring control. Indeed, when first seen from the standpoint of PCP, a modern-day consumer may seem almost obsessively concerned with the production of control, rather than with the testing of hitherto untried theories about the scheme of things.

The image a consumer presents to the rest of the world is usually carefully contrived—even if contrived to look uncontrived—as a means of obtaining access to certain activities, eliciting certain responses from others, and *establishing herself* in her own eyes and in those of the rest of the world. The consumer has her hair shampooed and styled and may lacquer it to keep it in place (think how many hair-care products are advertised with reference to the contribution they can make towards 'manageable' hair). She (and, increasingly, he) uses cosmetics to guarantee a particular visual and fragrant impression, while smiling with carefully cleaned and often straightened and capped teeth. Her clothes help tell the world how she sees herself, as do her house and its decor, the food she eats, her car, where she goes for entertainment, holidays and shopping, and the clubs of which she is a member. Some of her assets enable her to keep her self-image intact by keeping it safe from invasion by the world at large: she sits in her car, cossetted from the rigours of public transport, perhaps her house has high hedges around it and net curtains at the windows, certainly she is concerned to keep quite a few of her activities private.

Although a very large part of the consumer's budget may seem to be spent on devices for controlling her life and ensuring that events match up to expectations, the consumer is none the less engaging in considerable experimentation. Each time she employs a 'control device' she is testing her construction of what it can achieve, and often she experiments with new measures that she imagines will have a more powerful effect—for example, a new hairstyle and outfit of clothes may make a stunning impact on those with whom she mixes, if they had not thought of her 'like that' before; yet the new image might be a dismal failure because it is in the event branded as 'not really her'. Affluence opens up considerably the chances for inquisitive activities. If a holiday location becomes boringly predictable, the modern-day consumer can fly away to see what another part of the world is like. Convenience foods and a plethora of labour-saving household appliances release time for sporting and creative activities that enable the person to prove herself—adding to the scope for self-testing that a job may permit.

A considerable part of the consumer's leisure time may be spent in front of a television. Here, she can test herself in respect of her memory (as she watches quiz shows) or her ability to anticipate events (whether in 'soap operas' or in the outside world as depicted in news programmes), and she may find a feeling of security as she recognises how safely distanced she is from the 'horrific' events she finds she cannot anticipate or which, if she experienced them, would cause considerable damage to her predictive system. Other mass media, in this age of information, serve similar functions; nowadays, a good deal of empirical work can be done from one's armchair!

While the successful pursuit of privacy may help the consumer to obtain control over parts of her life, she will often seek friends as means towards prediction and control (see Duck, 1983, and Earl, 1983b, c, pp. 171–5). However, if friends do not come up to expectations in this respect, a person will discard them, unless such an act would reflect upon the person in such a way as to cause even more damage to her predictive system than do the 'friends' who repeatedly challenge her view of things, place her in incomprehensible situations, or damage her image in the eyes of the world at large. The consumer who has friends may spend her leisure time with them, not merely in sporting activities, but giving and attending parties of various sorts: dinner parties, barbecues, and possibly even parties where experimentation concerns not merely food and conversation, but also 'sex, drugs and rock'n'roll'.

4.4 EMOTIONS AND RATIONALITY

The kind of rationality embodied in my Kellian view of the consumer is a much more modest construct than the global rationality of orthodox economics. Nothing I have so far proposed should be seen as amounting to a claim that consumers necessarily have well-defined preference systems which accord with the neoclassical axioms of transitivity, continuity, non-satiation and so on. All I have suggested is that, when consumers choose, they have *reasons* for what they do, and that these reasons may usefully be seen as being ultimately subordinate to a desire to predict and control events. But to someone not brought up as a neoclassical economist, even this may seem to be claiming rather too much: my picture of consumers so far seems to treat them in all circumstances as dispassionate, coolly calculating beings; it portrays them as lacking emotions. The lay reader might well wonder what I would make of a situation in which, for example, a consumer looks back on a decision and reflects that 'I suppose I got carried away with myself; I can't really see how else I could have come to buy it'. Most of us, at one time or another, have surely been in such a situation. We acted, but with the benefit of hindsight all we can see is that we lost control or behaved impulsively; we cannot see reasons for our actions.

Such disturbing situations may begin to make sense once we see how Kelly adds an emotional perspective to his work. In a chapter significantly entitled 'Dimensions of transition', Kelly (1955, Chapter 10) provides a systematic set of conceptualisations of emotions such as anxiety, hostility and guilt, which he relates to patterns of human action. This part of his work has been ignored by the great majority of psychologists, who reveal their ignorance by commonly criticising personal construct theory 'on the grounds that it is too mentalistic' (Mackay, 1975, p. 128).

Aggression is seen by Kelly (1955, p. 508) as 'the active elaboration of one's perceptual field'. A person is being aggressive when she sets about testing just how far her existing notions can be stretched or when she is attempting to see what sense she can make of a hitherto unexplored situation. However, aggressive behaviour may be held back by *anxiety*, which Kelly (1955, p. 495) sees as 'the recognition that the events with which one is confronted lie mostly outside the range of convenience of one's construct system'. Given a choice, a person will avoid events that she does not expect to be able to understand, just as a student will try to avoid courses that she expects to fail. But in a complex and turbulent world, there may be so many uncertainties that the consumer who is not prepared in some degree to 'take life as it comes' will end up paralysed as a result of spending all her time puzzling (worrying!) how she might arrange her affairs to ensure a predictable future.

In some situations, *all* perceived options may give a decision maker cause for anxiety. This may be the essence of many major career/lifestyle choices: a person may be unsure of her ability to cope with a job she has just been offered (see Andrews, 1949, p. 224), unsure of the options that she could be closing off from herself if she takes it, and unsure of her prospects (perhaps including her future ability to cope with disappointment in respect of her tentatively held expectations of promotion) if she stays where she is. Buying a used car is an activity similarly fraught with anxiety unless one 'knows' the vehicles one is considering. With both examples, one possible decision is to maintain one's present course (that is, to stay with one's present job or means of mobility), despite the potential for lost control this might seem to entail. With the benefit of hindsight, this may appear to be the wisest path to take, since it leaves one's options open. At the time, however, the consumer may find it too complex to have to continue to think about a wide range of possibilities (see section 5.5): a change of activity will at least, she hopes, put her on a more narrowly defined track. Moreover, some of her present options may have decision deadlines attached to them, after which they will cease to exist as possibilities. In such situations, the consumer will feel that she is being 'driven' by events, rather than feeling that she is in charge of them. Her action is an aggressive, though panic-stricken, 'plunge' and she then tries her best to cope with the events that follow. But it must be noted that her decision does have a reason behind it—a desire to preserve as far as possible her chances of developing a system for anticipating events—even though it may be exceedingly unclear in prospect *which* scheme of action is the appropriate choice in the circumstances (for further discussion see section 8.6).

Another class of 'emotional' decisions consists of actions that involve *hostility*, defined by Kelly (1955, p. 510) as 'the continued effort to extort validational evidence in favour of a type of social prediction which has already proved itself a failure'. To admit a mistaken construction of events may seem very damaging to a person's image, for it may cast her in a new role relative to those whose rival constructions seem better able to match up to events. The result may be that, unless she can construct a way of changing direction that enables her to 'save face', the person will end up continuing down her previously adopted pathway, while desperately trying to force events into conformity with her ill-fitting prediction. Such behaviour is not only common in the context of consumer choice (see Thaler, 1980, pp. 47–50); following Elster (1983), one can see it as ubiquitous: in academic science (see Feyerabend, 1975), in industrial and political bargaining (where a loss of face in the present can affect for years to come the kind of bargaining stance that one can credibly present —see Shackle, 1949, Chapter VI, and Earl, 1983c, pp. 184—8), and in corporate decisions concerning the (non-)abandonment of 'unsuccessful' investments (Earl, 1984, Chapter 5). However, widespread and disastrous as these 'Procrustean' choices often are, their cognitive underpinnings are more appropriately discussed later, in section 6.6.

A third class of 'emotional' choices relates even more directly to a decision maker's perception of an impending change in her status, either in her own eyes or in those of people whose opinions matter to her. Kelly (1955, p. 510) sees *threat* as the identification of 'a major shift coming up in [one's] core role structure', and *guilt* as 'the awareness of dislodgement of the self from one's core role structure' (1955, p. 502). Very many of the things that other people do or one does oneself may be construed as challenges to one's basic self-image. A person can usually tolerate some of these challenges but sometimes a challenge may be large enough, either by itself or when seen as an addition to other disquieting images, to take her beyond some self-constructed threshold of tolerance. Action is then necessary to keep the person's self-image intact.

Depending on the nature of an intolerable challenge to a person's self-image, the action she takes may be anything from the dramatic to the mundane. As an example of the former, one might imagine the consumer who feels driven to purchase a new car, simply because of the challenge to her self-image that she sees entailed in the fact that one of her friends or neighbours has just acquired a new vehicle (see the work on conspicuous consumption by Hirsch, 1977, and Mason, 1981); like firms, consumers are engaged in a competitive struggle with each other. Much more trivial (unless one is on the selling side of it) is the case of the consumer who is about to add a cake-mix to the collection of convenience foods in her supermarket trolley and who suddenly puts the packet back on the shelf, having been overwhelmed by a feeling of guilt. This latter example is inspired by the findings of some classic work on motivation reported by Henry (1958, pp. 126–30; p. 194). Motivation research indicated that a large part of the potential market for cake-mixes felt that, if they used them, they would 'not be taking the proper trouble' or that they would be 'being lazy'. But the research also indicated that many consumers did not have an outright resistance to these kinds of convenience foods; rather, they avoided those which seemed to be *too* convenient, and were quite receptive to the idea of using cake-mixes that involved adding an egg. As Henry saw it, the reason why this seemingly perverse change of product characteristics worked as a marketing ploy was that:

When a housewife adds a fresh egg to a cake-mix, she gets a feeling of *participation* in the cake making operation to a much greater degree than if she merely beats up an egg-included mixture. Her half-felt and often unconscious feelings of guilt, of laziness, of not taking the proper trouble, of not doing the job the way it ought to be done, all diminish in intensity. Additionally she can rationalise her revised attitude in terms of the goodness and desirability of fresh egg (Henry, 1958, p. 128, emphasis in original).... One might say, in fact, that the adding of the egg lowers the threshold of resistance (p. 130).

The cake-mix example points to the possibility that, if 'happiness is just a frame of mind', there may be considerable scope for firms to affect consumer behaviour via marketing policies aimed at moulding the emotions of potential buyers. Firms might profitably not only try to demonstrate that their products provide no cause for anxiety or guilt; they might also seek to engender feelings of guilt or anxiety in consumers who are considering purchasing the products of rivals. Economists and marketing scholars have so far not troubled to conduct much research into the use of such policies: among the few noteworthy studies are

Goldstein (1959), Ray and Wilkie (1970), Wheatley (1971), Kay (1972), Taylor (1974) and Dash et al. (1976). However, it does not take a great deal of examination of the advertisements that bombard us daily to see that modern corporations could already be making great use of them. As far as consumer welfare is concerned, the implications of such policies are ambiguous: the propaganda of rival firms *might* cancel out, though at the cost to society of whatever alternative outputs might have been produced with the resources fruitlessly devoted to the selling campaigns; naturally existing negative emotions *might* be removed, but new sources of distress *might* be generated. Economists of opposing political persuasions need to conduct detailed empirical research before jumping to conclusions one way or another.

In fact, the policy importance of emotion-oriented images seems to go beyond the realm of persuasive advertising. One can easily see how theories of wage bargaining that centre on relativity concepts (Baxter, 1980, and Wood, 1978) might lend themselves easily to integration with ideas from PCP concerning threatening and face-saving behaviour, and I have elsewhere pointed to the role of guilt, in relation to social 'norms' concerning acceptable work efforts, in determining productivity levels in firms (Earl, 1983c, pp. 182–4). But, going beyond this, one can see opportunities for incorporating an 'emotional' perspective in analyses of tax avoidance and evasion. The following passage from Maital's non-Kellian contribution to economic psychology makes perfect sense from the standpoint of PCP:

Hiking fines is essentially costless, while more frequent audits can be expensive. An economic approach to tax evasion, therefore, suggests stiffer penalties. A psychological approach, though, suggests finding ways to alter the perception of the tax system as inequitable, or to restore the feeling that evasion is morally reprehensible (Maital, 1982, p. 249).

A person may dodge possible tax payments without feeling guilty if she sees herself otherwise as a victim of the system's unfairness, and if she believes that people 'like herself' in other respects are also attempting to escape paying their taxes. However, to judge from Lewis' (1982) survey of *The Psychology of Taxation*, no one has hitherto examined the role of guilt, as seen from the standpoint of PCP, in this context. (This is not to say that the role of guilt has been ignored altogether; see Schwartz and Orleans, 1967, and Grasmick and Scott, 1982, for some significant empirical findings.)

4.5 CONFIDENCE, COMPETENCE, AND CHOICE: THE EVOLVING CONSUMER (2)

A consumer is constrained in her aggressive tendencies by her awareness that certain kinds of elaborative behaviour could result in her predictive system being damaged rather than in the augmentation of its range of convenience. The consequences of certain choices could put the consumer in situations where she is forced to form theories about events which she is poorly equipped to analyse. But environmental change may be such that her predictive system could be threatened even if she tries to avoid the prospect of failure by standing still. Her problem, then, is to try to budget her time and other resources so that she can see a way of advancing at a satisfactory rate without suffering an excessive prospect of loss of control over events (see sections 8.4 and 8.5). It is a problem of strategy, compounded by emotional concerns.

The consumer's problem is obviously not unlike the predicament facing a company: she might seek to strike out anew and *diversify* her activities, or she might try to discover the limits of her ability to come to terms with areas of the universe in which she has hitherto *specialised* her interests. Either way, as far as her perceived ability to anticipate events is concerned, she might end up worse than she started. The strategy chosen by a consumer, or by a company, will be very much dependent on perceived competence, on confidence. Differences in perceptions of competence will result in differences in choices of evolutionary pathways. In a social setting, a consumer will need to possess kinds of competence similar to those possessed by people she is trying to match, or else she will find her self-image being threatened—just as a management team who are trying to establish their company's position in a particular competitive league will require a particular overall level of ability in relation to the prediction and control of events in the market-place and within the corporate organisation.

Bound up with the strategic question of diversification versus specialisation is the question of the rate at which one should seek to advance one's position. Over the longer run, a person's access to particular activities is dependent at least in part on her ability to *control herself*. For example, if she finds she cannot cut down her expenditure on smoking and other costly vices, or if she cannot improve her concentration on her studies or how she gets on with her boss, then she may accumulate little in the way of savings and/or fail to achieve a high income. If she recognises her personal fallibility, she may deliberately impose constraints upon herself—such as a monthly savings contract—as a means of realising certain expectations (for other examples, see Elster's (1984) book, *Ulysses and the Sirens*, and Thaler and Shefrin, 1981). Otherwise, she could end up feeling, in retrospect, that she has not been able to do much with her life. And if she does not see herself as someone lacking in self-control, she will react in a hostile manner to those who assert that her lack of achievement is her own fault, not that of 'the system'.

Conventionally, economics has treated consumers as if they face well-defined short-run budget constraints. But in affluent economies—where consumers are not on the breadline, where they have access to a wide variety of sources of credit, and typically replace their durables long before they are completely worn out—demand for non-essential products depends heavily upon the *willingness* of consumers to enter into contracts and not merely upon their current incomes and net holdings of financial assets. Consumers will not spend unless they are confident that their expectations concerning the future courses of prices (including the price of borrowed money) and of their money incomes are not going to be disappointed. In a turbulent world, where relative prices are in a state of flux, it is tempting, but potentially dangerous, to take speculative chances. On the one hand, if 'optimistic' expectations are realised (for example, if house prices and money incomes shoot up as anticipated, ensuring that a nominally large mortgage is a 'millstone' for only a brief period), one's scope for prediction and control could be hugely enhanced. On the other hand, one might end up humiliated, having to contend with repossession orders, a need to make sales of one's durable assets at knock-down prices and/or retrenchments in one's current activities that topple one down to a lower level of social standing. Some consumers will see such risks as worth taking; others will register their anxiety in a preference for liquidity (see Reddaway, 1937, and Townshend, 1937).

Empirical evidence consistent with the view that budget constraints (like any others) are personal constructs, heavily dependent on confidence, has been obtained for a wide variety of contexts: for OECD countries in the wake of the 1973–4 oil crisis (Katona, 1976), for the UK in the year April 1972 to March 1973 (Pickering, 1977), for Canada (Shapiro and Angevine, 1969), for Germany in respect of car expenditures (Strumpel *et al.*, 1969), and for the US, using the Michigan Survey Research Centre Index of Consumer Sentiment (Adams, 1964, Adams and Klein, 1972, Dunkelberg, 1969, Friend and Adams, 1964, Katona, 1975, and Smith, 1975) —the last of this group of researchers also finds that as one moves up to higher income groups the importance of consumer confidence increases in its explanatory power relative to income (Smith, Chapter 7). These studies vary in their degrees of success in predicting expenditure on durables, but they share the same conclusion: a strong influence on buyer behaviour is *not* exerted by economic variables which reflect an *ability* to make purchases.

The consumer's willingness to take on new commitments may also be tempered by a consideration of the possibility that she may end up getting confused by things, not because they are inherently beyond her, but as a result of trying to do too many new things at once. Corporations are often, though by no means always, aware of such risks (see Penrose, 1959, and Earl, 1984, pp. 12–16; 67–72); this is why, for example, car companies prefer not to try to introduce altogether new models and normally change engines and body designs at different times. A consumer, likewise, will have good reason to limit the amount of novelty in her life at any one moment; for example, in giving a dinner party she will often mix untried dishes with ones she knows she can handle, while it is indeed a confident consumer who will plan to change simultaneously her job, her house, her car and the size of her family (especially if she has no experience of children). New lines of thought are so much easier to construct if one has time for reflection, free from pressure for a decision that will effect control and stave off chaos (see Kelly, 1955, pp. 128–9, and the end of section 9.2). A consumer who chooses, or is forced to take on, more than she finds it possible to handle immediately may be expected subsequently to suspend her effort to extend her perceptual system. She will only start advancing again once she has better defined and consolidated the new aspects of her life, and in the interim she will have to struggle along with a pretty superficial set of impressions of these new features.

Precisely how well defined a set of constructs a person will require before she feels it is safe to move on to new areas is something which she has to judge for herself. People will set themselves different standards for control, different requirements for order in their lives. This is a point to which I will devote a good deal of attention in Chapter 6; its significance in the present context is that such differences in standards will shape the relative rates at which people move forward in their lives. Other things equal, a 'fussy' person is going to have less time and resources to devote to elaborative activities. However, a failure to set and meet demanding standards before moving forward *may* mean that a person ends up having to confront events with which she finds it difficult to cope. For example, it is one thing to spend one's entire weekend tidying one's house rather than exploring a new bush-walking trail; it is another to leave one's house 'looking like a tip' and set off walking with a backpack that has been filled with scant regard for possible sudden changes of weather.

When a person feels free to diversify somewhat and experiment in new areas there is a question with which she must contend: which activities, out of all the possibilities newly available to her, should she try? In principle, this looks like a question which could paralyse a consumer who has not been born with a set of preferences of a neoclassical sort and who needs, instead, a set of reasons for choosing one activity set in preference to its rivals. In fact, such a question is indeed paralysing for some people—a particularly obvious instance concerns the difficulties that people may face on retiring from a busy working life, when they either realise they have *no* idea how to spend their time, or are presented with a *comprehensive* list of things which they might do. To avoid paralysis, one needs a sense of direction, something which will make some activities stand out as particularly worthy of attention.

The need for a sense of direction arises with academic scientists and with corporations, as well as with consumers. Scientists and corporate planners seem to come to focus on new activities in similar ways, and I would contend that precisely the same kinds of channels are employed by consumers. The bulk of scientific activity is concerned with solving problems using a previously developed set of tools (what Kuhn, 1970, would call a 'paradigm'). Having seemingly solved one problem, a scientist finds another that looks amenable to solution using her existing 'tool-kit'. This problem may be one that has been lying around untended for a long time, or it may pertain to phenomena which previously seemed to have been sorted out but which are now throwing up disturbing anomalies. What the scientist does not do is solve a problem in one area and then move on to investigate something that is completely *unrelated*—unrelated, that is, in terms of the subject matter or the problem-solving devices brought to bear upon whatever is studied. For example, when this book is finished, I would be unlikely to start working on international trade theory from a neoclassical standpoint, but I might well start to investigate a new area of economics—for example, development economics—from the standpoint employed herein. Alternatively, I might study in detail some relevant empirical techniques and start to do empirical work in the area of consumer behaviour. I find it inconceivable that I will abandon economics and take up, say, botany, but perhaps I might get ever-more engrossed in psychology. Clearly, what I will be doing is either going to involve an attempt to diversify while exploiting synergy that is rooted in my past investment in theoretical constructs that can seemingly be applied to new areas; or it is going to involve attempts to secure my previously attained position. In both cases I am going to have to acquire some new constructs, for example, concerning developing economies or statistical techniques respectively, but I believe my existing knowledge gives me something of a start; either way, I will not be *completely* out of my depth.

As far as corporations are concerned, Scott Moss (1981, Chapters 2 and 3) has argued that their sense of direction arises from the combined workings of 'focusing effects' and 'inducement effects'. Managerial attention is focused by the perception or anticipation of spare capacity—machines or human factors that are not producing as much as they might be. This spare capacity might be due to learning-by-doing on the part of workers, or it may exist or be anticipated for reasons associated with a bottleneck inside the firm, a failure by input suppliers, or declining competitive conditions. In the latter cases, the firm has actual or prospective declining profits to serve as an inducement to come up with a way of employing the resources it already has. It either uses the spare machines and skills on making seemingly related products (see Earl, 1984, pp. 112–15, for some examples of diversification where the relationships were not all that they seemed!); or it acquires resources on the expectation of being able to use them to remove the actual or anticipated difficulty. An obvious example of the latter is where a firm engages in vertical integration to safeguard itself against unreliable suppliers —because a failure to do so seems more dangerous than the dangers that could arise from the lack of scope for transferring *its* knowledge of production to the production of inputs, and the dangers associated with having even more resources tied up with particular final product markets.

These analyses suggest that scientists and firms are both given a sense of direction by the things they have done in the past. Through time, their activities *evolve* instead of lurching largely discontinuously between areas and/or techniques that are utterly unrelated. Quite often, they may be induced to take on activities about which they initially know very little, simply in order to guard against disappointments in areas where they have already made commitments. Otherwise, their changes of direction will be based on existing know-how in respect of which they have already incurred some set-up costs. Now let us consider how consumers fit into this pattern, using the activities of cookery and music as illustrations.

A person setting up home for the first time may be somewhat intimidated by the idea of cooking for herself, but she may feel she cannot afford not to learn how—for reasons of both self-esteem and finance. Having acquired 'some of the basics' as far as equipment and know-how are concerned, she can seek to master certain recipes. If she is successful, she reduces her dependence on costly convenience foods. But as she masters one recipe, she releases resources that can be used with others. For example, if the bread-making situation is under control, the question arises as to what might be done while the dough is rising. One possibility, of course, might be to spend the half-hour trying to bring the garden under control. But this would involve a change of costume and much scrubbing of muddy hands on returning to the kitchen. How much better it would be to spend the time trying to make a cake, or some pastry! After all, some of the ingredients are already in front of the consumer, she has her apron on, and from the recipe book it looks as if some cakes or pastries are not *that* different from a loaf to make. With practice, a basic cake will not take half an hour to prepare, so in later weeks the consumer comes to experiment with more exotic recipes. Thus she may evolve into a competent cook and, as she does, the contents of her shopping basket will change. How far she will pursue such activities will depend on how good a cook she feels she needs to become, and on how good a cook she does become. Once she has reached what is, for her, an adequate standard her attention might be focused elsewhere by other problems in her life.

To someone who has not been brought up in a musical family, nor been forced to learn to play an instrument as a child or at school, and who has not been taken to concerts while young, musical activities could seem an area of anxiety. Without strong inducements, such a person might avoid all things musical. In a social setting, however, inducements for her to devote time and money to music might naturally arise. For example, as a teenager it might be important to have some knowledge of popular music or an ability to play, say, the guitar (which is likely to be acquired in tandem with the former) in order to present a particular image to one's peers. At university, the expectation of some of one's new reference group might be that one has some knowledge of classical music, so there is a pressure to acquire some constructs, and some records, in this area. In either case, despite the lack of a strong grounding (though probably with some advice from friends and the music media), the person might take to music 'like a duck to water', rapidly picking up constructs. In the example of the university student, the person might start with well-known 'light classics' and find they are not nearly so intimidating as she had imagined. This experience might leave her feeling confident of not being completely unable to fathom out opera, less popular works by well-known and not-so-well-known composers (string quartets by Beethoven, symphonies by Michael Haydn, for example), or even something known to be mildly avant-garde. But she may still tend to listen sometimes to the music she started with, for it may remain in some senses marvellous or intriguing to her; and possibly the constructs she forms in relation to the music into which she diversifies her listening may fit the former.

One can also envisage the kind of consumer whose experimentation with music never gets very far at all. She has an excellent hi-fi system that proves to her friends how skilled she is in choosing complex electrical durables and how much money she has. However, her collection of musical 'software' is small and no one would class it as adventurous: it is 'middle of the road', 'easy listening' material, polished in execution but often insipid to the ears of experts. And when her friends are not present it all rests idle, as she spends her time dealing with problems of life that seem to her to be more pressing or open to definition and solution with the physical and perceptual resources she has at her disposal.

The closest that neoclassical economics comes to providing an analysis that parallels my emphasis on the role of competence in shaping consumer choices is in the work of Stigler and Becker (1977). In their attempt to analyse behaviour dynamics, they follow the orthodox methodology in assuming that all agents have basically the same *underlying*, and stable, preferences. However, they argue that, due to differences in the constraints they face, consumers will accumulate different kinds of skills that they can use in the production of utility. Thus people who are avid concert-goers are likely to be those who have accumulated relatively large amounts of human capital that is specific to music appreciation.

From the present standpoint, one can only give a qualified welcome to Stigler's and Becker's extension of neoclassical household production theory. For it is overly objectivist in outlook and does not consider the personality damage that incompetence may cause when it results in misconstructions of reality. It should not have escaped the reader's attention that Kelly's view of anxiety involves the *recognition* by the individual herself that she could be stepping out of her depth. A person's aspiration for the rate of elaboration of her system is a personal construct, a prediction from her theories about what she should be able to get out of life, tempered by her experience. Different people will make different predictions of what they can do, depending on the nature of their construction systems and their previous success in anticipating events. These predictions embody their confidence in the ability of their predictive structures to frame the situations which they might confront. They will not always be correct. The approach of Stigler and Becker looks rather questionable against Kelly's (1955, p. 526) comment that the patients he encountered who kept 'getting into trouble' with exotic adventures tended to have construct systems which almost anything *seemed* to fit. They confidently plunged themselves into all sorts of activities thinking they would be able to cope with them. Had they invested more in the relevant kind of 'human capital' before proceeding, and thereby successfully added to their construct repertoires, they might have realised their own limitations and held back.

To emphasise further the difference between the objectivist nature of the work of Stigler and Becker, and my own subjectivist approach, one should note the problems of euphoria and depression—problems of confidence in competence. For people with less simplistic construct systems than Kelly's 'exotic adventurers', the danger that they will misapprehend their personal capacities is greatest when they have been greatly surprised by a gross mismatch between their aspirations and their apparent attainments. If there is a large overfulfilment, existing reference points become meaningless and the response is often to adopt the attitude that 'the sky's the limit'; subsequently one may be 'brought down to earth' with a bump. If a major disappointment has been suffered, then, in the relevant area, a person may conclude she has no competence at all and may cease to function as a scientist (see my comments about unemployment at the end of section 4.2, and see the work of Beck *et al.*, 1979, on techniques of depression therapy that involve getting patients to become 'scientists' again).

4.6 CONCLUSION

The analysis of the consumer developed in this chapter is antithetical to the equilibrium notion around which orthodox consumer theory is constructed. Inquisitive activity in a turbulent world is something that will naturally be associated with changes in behaviour. From a Kellian standpoint, one would only expect consumers to seem unmoving in their choices of activities if they asked such vague questions of the world that they never knew whether they had achieved the ability to predict and control certain events; if they asked such undemanding questions that they were never disappointed and never driven to modify their constructs or try new ways of obtaining control over events; or if they had succeeded in establishing for themselves a cosy environment sheltered from the rigours of the rest of the world—an outer world which they found a *petrifying* prospect. Quite a few people, of course, do fall into this mould; indeed most of us might seem to have ceased to evolve in some areas of our lives for precisely the reasons listed. However, many people are busily trying to change their lives, carving new lifestyles, new careers, social niches, leisure activities and so on for themselves. The analysis I have proposed provides a way of explaining the behaviour of both kinds of people: we can look at people who have 'got themselves into a rut', whether they see things like this or as a comfortable existence, and we can begin to see how firms might successfully seek to change their behaviour; we can also look at evolving consumers and, mindful of possible activity relationships, we can seek to anticipate where they might move their existences in coming months and years. Furthermore, we have a way of understanding how people can have 'everything' and yet end up asking, in the words of the song, 'Is that all there is to a ...?' For if people form grand expectations about themselves and about the reputedly desirable things in life (including expectations that they will be able 'to see a lot' in such things when eventually they encounter them), then we should not be surprised to see them find that much of life is just a series of disappointments.

Had we stayed with the much simpler postulate that 'people seek to maximise their utilities', we would not have had the bother of coming to terms with PCP, but we would have remained largely mystified by such phenomena. Sceptics might none the less seek to point to a dubious paradox in my suggestions, by asking 'is not the "theory of the consumer as a scientist" itself merely an example of "pseudo-science", since there is no aspect of choice that it cannot accommodate if one constructs an appropriate rationalising tale?' Such a criticism is in fact misplaced, for PCP encompasses techniques for uncovering how people themselves see events and make judgements. I will eventually come to describe these empirical tools (see section 6.4) but, before I do, it is appropriate to examine from a theoretical standpoint precisely how people may come to see things in the ways that they do. Chapter 5 begins this task.

5 Possibilities and Potential Surprises

5.1 INTRODUCTION

A decision maker who wishes to make choices on the basis of reasoning may require information about the following:
(1) What has happened so far, either as a direct consequence of her past actions or as a result of processes whose workings she sees as conceptually separate from her own behaviour. She will be particularly interested to know whether her own anticipations were correct and whether her experiments aimed at achieving control over events seemed to have been validated.
(2) What might have happened but did not eventuate.
(3) What could happen in the future if she does not seek to control events.
(4) What she might be able to do to effect the course of events.
(5) What it could be appropriate to try to do, given 1–4.

How consumers may obtain these kinds of information is the subject of section 5.2 of this chapter. Section 5.3 examines the kinds of mental images that consumers may construct from their current stocks of ideas, as a basis for choice. Particular attention is paid to the fact that they will often come across ideas that seem to be incompatible, mutually exclusive rivals, and may consequently perceive uncertainty. The analysis in section 5.3 deals with images of uncertain events in the light of Shackle's theory of 'potential surprise', without any mention of the conventional economist's idea that people may assign 'probabilities' to events. Bearing in mind that consumers in everyday life often speak in terms of probabilities, I feel obliged to discuss the relationship between these two views of how people think about uncertain events. Section 5.4 is devoted to this task. Finally, section 5.5

examines criticisms that have been or might be raised in relation to the way I am portraying consumers as conceptualising things prior to choice.

5.2 ORIGINS OF IDEAS IN THE CONSUMER'S MIND

The ideas that a consumer may consider *en route* to making up her mind will typically come from a variety of sources, and the processes by which she gathers them together may be so complex as to defy formal modelling in any kind of deterministic manner. As far as economists are concerned, the usual response to this problem has been to try to circumvent it by assuming at the outset that 'consumers know what they want and they know how to get it'. An alternative approach would be to suggest that *chance* plays the major role in determining precisely which pieces of information a consumer encounters or is driven to seek out. I suspect that the latter would disturb most consumers—I find it quite disturbing myself to look back upon the 'chance' linkages in the chain of events that has culminated in my sitting here today in my study in a particular house in Australia writing this particular book on consumer behaviour and employed as a university lecturer. (I have detailed some of these linkages in Earl, 1983c, pp. 4–11, and elsewhere in this book.) For a long while, before I discovered and became fascinated with Shackle's writings, I anticipated that after graduating from university I would become a civil servant—things could have been so different! It is the fact that things seem as though they could so easily have been very different that makes it disturbing to consider the role of chance in our lives; it seems to run counter to the idea that we have much control over what happens to us. Faced with such a picture, many people are inclined to take refuge in astrological theories or conjectures about 'someone "up there" who is in control of our destinies'. My own view is that, although the processes by which consumers gather and process information are indeed complex, they are none the less sufficiently systematic in nature as to make them worthy of study as a means for forming bounded and not wholly misleading conjectures of what consumers may do. It would seem worth while to try to segment the population of consumers according to their relative propensities to employ the following sources of information and inspiration, and then to group them more finely according to how they use these sources—a suggestion that will come as no surprise to marketeers (see section 6.4).

5.2.1 Creative thinking in the light of personal experience

Using her existing constructs, including those relating to rules of logic and inference, the consumer may be able to create new ideas about what might happen in the future, or about what has already happened. By experimenting with wider ranges of convenience for some constructs, or with new arrangements of constructs that she would not normally tie together, the consumer may come to see new ways of looking at things—just as, in writing this book, I am exploring possibilities for widening the applicability of ideas from the theory of the firm to the study of household behaviour and am experimenting with the integration of constructs from economics and PCP. Bounds are placed upon the consumer's ability to create new ideas by the limitations of her existing ideas; to be given a new range of convenience or a new relationship with other constructs, a construct must already by part of the consumer's repertoire. (An interesting corollary of this is that a person must possess *some* constructs at birth in order to be able to make anything of the events of her early life.) This view of limits to creativity obviously underlines my earlier (section 4.5) arguments about the significance of past experience in shaping the activities people will feel confident in choosing. (For thought-provoking discussions of the nature of creative thinking, see Koestler, 1975, Shackle, 1979, and the references to 'construct loosening' in Kelly, 1955; excellent discussions of how to achieve creative and open-minded thinking are provided by Adams, 1980, and Nolan, 1981.)

Researchers studying the processes whereby people form new ideas would do well to remember that their subjects may be employing different rules of logic and inference from themselves. Like many a poorly trained scientist, the inquisitive consumer may commit all manner of methodological blunders as she exercises her creative faculties, for example the fallacy of induction, or the maturity of chances fallacy (see Ross and Levy, 1958, for evidence). Consequently she may end up taking decisions that have unpleasantly surprising sequels.

5.2.2 'Unbiased' specialist sources of information

The enormous popularity of consumer choice magazines and radio/television programmes on consumer affairs is only one manifestation of the use of this kind of source of ideas about what can and should be done. One must also note the widespread use of brokers/agents and of consultants such as investment advisors, surveyors and interior designers. Acknowledged professional experts with access to the mass media would appear potentially to enjoy great scope for determining whether or not particular products are successful, but in practice their opinions are by no means always decisive. The car market is a case in point. On the one hand, we can note the impact that Ralph Nader's (1965) book *Unsafe At Any Speed* had upon the sales of the ill-handling rear-engined Chevrolet Corvair in the United States. Similarly, the fortunes of the UK distributor of Lancia cars took a very severe knock when a feature on the BBC television programme *That's Life* highlighted the propensity of nearly-new Lancia Betas to suffer from serious structural rusting (see section 10.5). On the other hand, however, we can note the case of the Leyland P76 V8 saloon, the Australian equivalent of the Edsel in terms of its sales success. This car, which enjoyed a production run of barely a year, was Leyland Australia's belated attempt to provide a purpose-built, big, powerful car, rugged enough to stand up to local road surfaces, instead of continuing to provide variants of BL's small European models. The P76 was awarded the 1973 Car of the Year Award by the widely-read magazine *Wheels*, but the Australian motoring public avoided it like the plague and stuck to the technologically inferior and less spacious products of General Motors-Holden, Ford and Chrysler.

5.2.3 Advertisements and information from potentially biased sales personnel

The chances that these sources of information will be misleading are somewhat restricted by the incentives to firms to try to discredit any inflated claims made by their rivals. However, consumers may find it difficult to judge the 'truth' when faced with a mass of conflicting claims. They may also be distracted from the sales campaigns of relatively sincere but small firms by the sheer volume of pretentious propaganda put out by large ones. Some consumers may systematically resist making use of sales personnel as sources of information because they are not confident of their abilities to maintain control in such interchanges.

5.2.4 Information available from social communications

This information arises at three main levels. First, consumers will have particular reference groups of friends and acquaintances whose opinions they take seriously (see Shibutani, 1955). Some members of the typical consumer's reference group may possess a good deal of expertise in certain areas, while she may suspect others of being somewhat pretentious. Second, consumers will be interested to hear of the latest ideas that are circulating—what Shackle calls 'the state of the news'—regardless of whether or not members of their reference groups have reached firm conclusions as to their accuracy. Third, most consumers will look to beliefs held by the wider populace, beliefs which we may call 'the common-sense things that everyone knows' (see Garfinkel, 1967) or simply 'folk wisdom'. One reason for taking such beliefs seriously, even when they clash with those of professional pundits, is that consumers who publicly act at odds with the ideas of the majority will stand out as deviants and be called upon to justify (often in a remarkably watertight manner) their departures from 'the norm', even if the majority are acting on the 'million lemmings can't be wrong' principle and have little idea how 'the norm' was justified in the first place. Obvious examples of this phenomenon are situations in which parents react with hostility when their offspring brazenly flout conventions that decree they should marry and produce within wedlock at least two grandchildren, or where teenagers inquire sneeringly of their deviant peers 'you don't drink, don't smoke, aren't going out with anyone and don't do sport, so what *do* you do?' It takes strong principles, self-confidence and a willingness to suffer a highly restricted set of acquaintances if one is to opt to follow the lifestyle of, say, a lesbian teetotal vegetarian Marxist—all the information signals from society at large will suggest that this is a queer way to attain happiness.

Clearly, these four information sources may often contain many conflicting ideas. In the case of the Leyland P76, the folk wisdom was (and remains) that 'you'd have to be crazy to buy a P38 (...only half a car); it's just a huge boot with four wheels that is bound to fall to pieces since Leyland couldn't build a car tough enough for Australian roads', whereas if I were to try to sell you the one I drive, I'd tell you 'its engine is still super-smooth and surprisingly economical after more than 100,000 miles, while after twelve years the body is not at all rusty; everything still works and the only things that are missing are a couple of plastic interior trim inserts'. However, it will often be the case that consumers end up getting their ideas from mutually reinforcing sources. This point is central to the arguments of the Women's Movement. A woman growing up in the UK in the midst of 'conventional' beliefs about the nature of womanhood is much more likely to read *Honey* and graduate to *Woman's Weekly* than she is to read *Spare Rib*, because of her observations of what her peers read. Consequently her head will be filled with ideas about romance, marriage and how to make herself look attractive to men; the occasional article on 'career women' will provide a few clues as to the heights that women may attain in a 'man's world', but overwhelmingly the focus of both text and advertisements in orthodox women's magazines is on the woman's role as a homemaker and sex object. She may remain largely oblivious of the feminist viewpoint, carrying in her mind little more than an image of 'bra-burning women's libbers', an image that is almost wholly visual instead of being concerned with feminist beliefs.

5.3 LANDSCAPES OF THE FUTURE

Having gathered a set of ideas together, the consumer will be concerned to decide what to make of them, what constructions to place upon them. This task could prove very confusing to someone with a background in epistemology. No one can possess, let alone process, a complete list of potentially credible raw possibilities. This implies that it is not strictly meaningful to say that a particular event is perfectly possible, simply because one can see nothing to prevent it from happening. Neither does it make complete sense to assert that a particular event is absolutely impossible, since events that one has not imagined nor heard about as possibilities could combine to ensure that 'the impossible' actually happens. For the same reason it should be questionable to attach a greater rating of 'possibility' to one event than to another, simply because one can see fewer things that might prevent it from coming about. If one follows this line of argument, it is difficult to see any basis for closing one's mind about what it could be appropriate to do, what could happen or even about what has happened in the past; absolutely anything might happen but, then again, it might not. One might as well choose at random.

If one is unaware of the ideas from which such a position of scepticism follows, or if one views with scepticism the idea that one should be completely open minded and choose at random, then one can adopt a much looser view of the nature of a 'perfectly possible' event and hence of events that seem somewhat less than perfectly possible. It makes no sense for a boundedly rational decision maker to class an event as perfectly possible 'because I have every reason to believe it will happen'. However, if a person can see no obstacles to prevent a particular event from coming about, she may feel she has no reason to *dis*believe in it as a prospect. Following Shackle (1983, pp. 31–4) I would suggest that although people often speak in the terms of belief, they actually see perfect possibility as involving the total absence of perceived fatal obstacles, that is to say that perfect possibility is, in cognitive terms, synonymous with zero disbelief. By extension I would argue that the more obstacles a person can see potentially lying in the way of a particular event, and the greater their imagined sizes, the greater will be the extent of the person's disbelief in the event as a prospect and the less willing she will be to 'take it seriously'. However, it should be noticed that obstacles to possible events are themselves imagined events, in the way of which may lie yet other obstacles. Hence the more hypothetical events that a consumer can see potentially lying as obstacles in the way of obstacles she sees in the way of a particular event, the smaller will be her disbelief in the idea that this event may actually come about. It is only because a consumer possesses a finite list of ideas that she is able to come to some conclusion concerning the extent of her disbelief in any particular idea; her inability to see obstacles to obstacles beyond a certain level of abstraction extricates her from a potential problem of infinite regress (see section 6.2).

However, to speak of consumers assigning 'degrees of disbelief' to rival ideas seems altogether too formal; we are, after all, dealing with ideas which consumers may after some deliberation classify as 'hopes' or 'fears' which may seem worthy of attention or which may be dismissed as blasé. In the context of empirical research it would seem somewhat unclear as to how one might usefully get consumers to assign measures of intensity to their assessments of the extent to which they see events as potentially unblocked prospects. Shackle (1983, p. 34) has addressed this issue as follows:

Disbelief is an intellection, something which has, in itself, form rather than intensity. What psychic experience can we find, that will reflect these forms as intensities? There is one emotion which directly springs from the combination of some formal kind or source of disbelief, and an actual taking-place which belies that disbelief. This is the feeling of *surprise*. The individual may be supposed to ask himself: How much or little should I be surprised if, with no relevant change in my present knowledge, such-and-such occurred? Potential surprise seems to me a practical link between formal and emotional disbelief.

Actual surprise is something that has an upper limit, namely utter astonishment, so anticipations of feelings of surprise will be similarly bounded; beyond some point, thoughts about further seemingly unblocked barriers to an outcome that already seems to have 'the odds stacked against it' will not make it any more incredible as a prospect. At the other extreme, an event in whose way a person can presently see no obstacles will be one whose actual taking-place will be completely unsurprising to that person, unless her ideas change in the interim.

Now, suppose we ask a consumer to list all the ideas she is thinking about in relation to a particular choice, and suppose that we then ask her to state, for each idea, how surprised she would be if it actually eventuated. The answers she gives to these questions embody her conjectures in relation to the choice upon which her attention is focused. Taken together, these answers define topographical forms that can be depicted diagrammatically as a set of landscapes for each imagined option in respect of each of the construct axes in whose terms the consumer sees them. For example, consider the case of a consumer thinking about her career prospects. One dimension of her thoughts concerns her income from the near future—let us suppose from the end of 1985—as far as she can imagine into the distant future. This dimension may include both real and nominal income, but let us here just concern ourselves with her conjectures concerning nominal income, which will be heavily dependent on her feelings about possible rates of inflation. (Nominal income will be particularly relevant in relation to thoughts concerning indebtedness and rates of saving.) For each job in which she imagines herself as possibly being employed, the consumer may be able to define a set of potential surprise conjectures. These ideas concerning possible income paths, formed after due thought about what might prevent them from eventuating, are essentially three-dimensional: they concern income levels, dates and assessments of potential surprise. But they can be represented on a two-dimensional diagram with axes of time and income, and contour lines for degrees of potential surprise between zero and the upper 'astonishment' bound. Our consumer might be thinking, for example, about how much she could earn if she can build herself a career in the American university sector. Figure 5.1 shows how she might envisage this prospect. Figure 5.2 is a cross-section through Figure 5.1, depicting the consumer's expectations for such a career for the year 1995. The latter diagram treats the scale of potential surprise as if it is continuous, following Shackle's original exposition of the potential surprise curve idea (see Shackle, 1949, for his first book-length investigation of the concept); however, it is probably unrealistic to expect consumers to think normally in terms of anything more than a stepped scale with five or seven points, including both bounds.

The landscape depicted in Figure 5.1 is shaped like a widening flat-floored channel, carved into a plain. However, it is to be stressed that this is only one of many configurations that might be imagined. A consumer might be unable to see any outcomes that seem 'perfectly possible'. There may also be periods in the future which she finds it very confusing to try to anticipate, so as one moves across the landscape there might be areas that are best represented, without reference to any particular potential surprise rating, as 'rapids' that come between periods expected to be less turbulent (see Jefferson's (1983, pp. 138–9) description of how corporate planners at Shell International Petroleum characterised their company's environment in the mid 1970s). Possibilities might be thought of not as a single channel but as bifurcating after some expected crucial event, such as a political upheaval in which 'moderate' policies were replaced by those of either the extreme Left or of the extreme Right. (To gain a greater feel of these arguments, readers might do well to ask themselves whether they would dispute the expectations depicted in Figures 5.1 and 5.2 and, if so, to try to construct their own maps for this particular line of employment.)

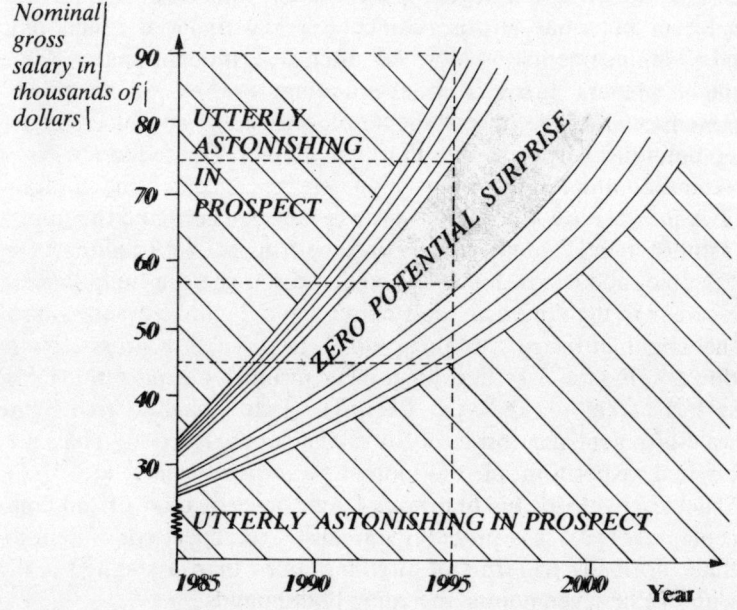

Figure 5.1: Possible earnings in the American universities sector from 1985 to the year 2000, as a would-be faculty member might see them in 1985

For our consumer to form a conjecture of how much she could earn over the period 1985–2000, she will need to ask herself not only which rates of pay could be available in particular job-slots that have come to her mind as possibilities. She will also need to ask herself how surprised she would expect to be if she were employed in each of these mutually exclusive positions, at each point in time. Her answers to these questions may depend on her expectations about whether or not she could be offered each of the jobs in each year, and on how surprised she expects she would be to find herself accepting them. Thus even if she thinks it is perfectly possible that an assistant professor in an American university could be earning $50,000 in 1995, she might expect to be pretty surprised to find herself actually in such a position in 1995, since she may expect to have achieved promotion to associate professor or beyond before then (Figures 5.1 and 5.2 might be built up on this expection), or she may expect that she would have left the academic world altogether if she had not achieved such promotion, even if presently she thinks such promotion is perfectly possible. Thus the expectational landscape of the consumer's imagined earning is not the simple product of the superimposition of her conjectures concerning possible rates of remuneration in mutually exclusive lines of employment.

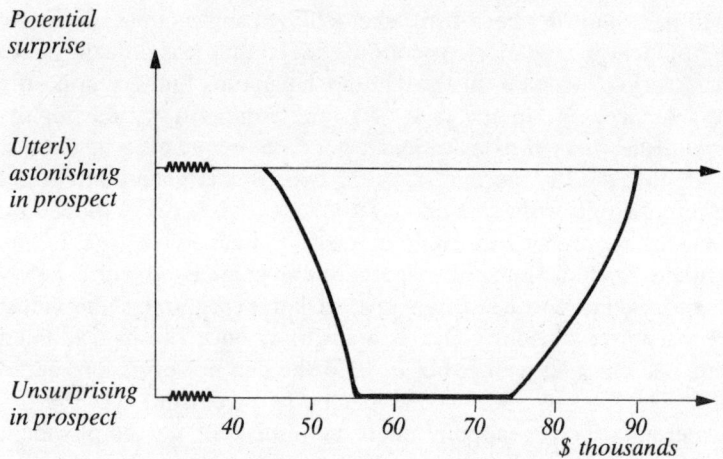

Figure 5.2: The would-be faculty member's view of her possible earnings if she is working in an American university in 1995

The kind of expectational landscape a consumer sees, at the start of 1985, for the period 1985–2000, may be very different from that which she envisaged in, say, the early 1970s. The difference may go a long way towards explaining how she feels about her current lifestyle. Consider the case of someone who, on the basis of a good first degree in the United Kingdom, obtained a postgraduate scholarship to a Canadian university in 1970. From the standpoint of 1970, she might well have assigned only a small degree of potential surprise to the idea that, by the mid/late 1980s she would have become a professor, or would at least have reached the stage where she was 'shortlisted' if she applied for professorial positions. At the same time, she might have assigned considerable potential surprise both to the idea that she would be anything other than an academic, and to the idea she would, by 1985, be employed in a polytechnic. By 1985, a whole series of surprising events could have taken place, causing her to revise her expectations. Let us consider two extreme, yet perhaps familiar, scenarios.

The first is a tale of life in the academic 'fast lane'. The consumer completes her Master's degree and follows this with a doctorate in an area which is attracting great interest. Even before submitting her thesis, she achieves some publications. By 1973, cuts in education expenditure mean that it is difficult to get a lecturing job back in the United Kingdom, but she none the less obtains one in the face of strong competition. She rapidly establishes herself as a leader in her fashionable area of interest and, in 1980, at the age of thirty-two, she is head-hunted and offered a full professorship. By 1985, she has already moved on to a more prestigious chair in an 'Ivy League' college in the United States. Her career path has encompassed quite a few surprises and she has often revised her expectations (her most recent move did not come as a surprise, once she had attained her first chair so young, but in 1970 she had not even considered the idea that, by 1985, she would be so successful), yet she has experienced no disappointments in respect of her employment opportunities.

Second, consider the following tale of life *en route* to an academic 'dead end'. The consumer completes her Master's degree, but experiences great difficulty with her doctorate, owing to an absentee supervisor and unanticipated data problems. By the time her scholarship funds have run out, she is still a long way from finishing her thesis, and she is unable to get a part-time teaching job in Canada. On returning to the United Kingdom, she is surprised by the impact of the cuts in education expenditure and unable to get a university lectureship, owing to strong competition from people with doctorates. As a 'stop-gap' measure, she applies for a job in a polytechnic and obtains it. The high teaching demands of this job make it difficult for her to find time to finish her thesis; the fact that many of her colleagues are former high-school teachers with no interest in research also means she finds it difficult to engage in fruitful discussions about the progress of her work. In the late 1970s, there appear some more vacant university lectureships in her area of interest, but she is unable to obtain one of these: she is competing against people five years younger with doctorates, or with people of her own age with proven research records. Although she has managed to turn one of her teaching courses into a fairly successful textbook, this counts for far less than scholarly articles and finished doctorates. In 1980, she is promoted to senior lecturer in her polytechnic; the money is useful, but the promotion is no great source of joy given the lack of strong internal competition, her ever-present thoughts of 'what might have been', and her memories of the rosy expectations she held a decade ago. By 1985, she sees no prospect of employment in a British university and can imagine no possible new, non-teaching career opportunities. Given repeated announcements of funding cut-backs, she feels she would be somewhat surprised even to be promoted to principal lecturer within the polytechnic sector within the next five years. She would be astonished to obtain a teaching post in an American or Australian university. Overall, she feels she has little control over her career; her domestic life is comfortable, but she is far from content with life. Job-wise, she feels she is well and truly 'stuck in a rut' (albeit a somewhat different kind of rut from that referred to in section 4.6). Her inability to finish her doctoral thesis on time seems, with the benefit of hindsight, to have been a truly tragic event, a watershed in her expectational landscape. She feels she must do something to extricate herself before it is too late, but what *can* she do?

5.4 THE POSSIBILITY OF PROBABILITY

When Shackle first wrote about expectations in terms of potential surprise and perfect or seemingly obstructed possibilities, he did so out of his dissatisfaction with the orthodox analysis of expectations in terms of probabilities. Today, despite forty years of Shackle's writings on potential surprise, economic analysis still employs the concept of probability. The lay consumer, too, is frequently to be heard speaking in probabilistic terms: for example, 'I reckon I've a one-in-four chance of getting the job', or 'I'd say we had a fifty–fifty chance of selling the house by the end of the week'.

The reason that Shackle took issue with the concept of probability as applied to decision making by individuals was that choices are essentially one-off, unique acts undertaken at particular points in the tangled and ever-extending web of events called history. Probability as discussed in the formal literature is essentially a *distributional* concept: fractional probability weights that sum to unity are thought of as reflecting the relative frequency with which particular outcomes will arise if choices are repeated. For example, take the case of family-planning choices. If tastes in respect of family-planning technology and the desire to preclude children are stable, one can use last year's statistics to anticipate the numbers of couples who may choose each method of family planning. One can also make confident projections concerning the numbers of unplanned pregnancies that will occur this year, providing one has statistics concerning the reliability rates for each of the family-planning technologies. (The opening comment about stability of tastes should, of course, not be forgotten; in a turbulent world—where a piece of news concerning, say, cancer risks associated with oral contraceptives can lead to a sudden shift in preferences—past statistics cannot tell a demographer what *will* happen in the population she is studying.) But statistical inference cannot tell us for sure which *particular* couples will be faced with unplanned pregnancies. Couples may employ published reliability statistics as guides when making up their minds about which family-planning technology to employ, but in the event they are either beset by an unplanned pregnancy or they are not, during the course of the year. Even if they employ a technique with only a 90 per cent reliability rate one hundred times during the year, they will not, for obvious biological reasons, be faced with ten unplanned pregnancies; nor can the woman become only 'one-tenth pregnant'.

To be sure there are *some* low-cost choices that an individual can repeat time and again and so end up generating a pattern of experience that is a microcosm of the aggregate experience of similar people who make similar choices. However, readers should note, in the light of my 'academic fast lane' and 'dead end' scenarios and of my family-planning example (as well as many other examples throughout this book), that some choices (for example, topics for doctoral research or methods of family planning) may be watershed events of massive significance and very expensive if not impossible to recover from if they misfire. These are, in Shackle's terms, *crucial* decisions whose sequels may lead to *kaleidic* changes in expectational landscapes, both in the mind of the chooser and in the minds of others for whom her actions have implications.

Many economists to whom I have explained Shackle's mode of thinking have reacted by saying that potential surprise curves look not unlike inverted distributions. Formally speaking, this is incorrect in anything other than pictorial terms. As Hey (1983b, p. 131) has emphasised in a recent review of the 'state of the art' in probabilistic approaches to uncertainty, the formal theory assumes that decision makers *know with certainty* the sets of options, possible states of the world and final consequences that are relevant to their choices. The only thing they do not know is precisely which state of the world will come about. (For example, consumers choosing holidays may know the precise characteristics of each available holiday, but be unsure which of a finite set of possible weather patterns will come about and impact upon the relative values of rival holidays.) The formal theory, in other words, does not admit the possibility of surprise due to unimagined outcomes. (For example, one might have been on holiday in Cyprus and be utterly astonished to find oneself in the midst of a civil war.) However, if one leaves aside this major difference, one can begin to see that it might be possible to convert potential surprise patterns into probabilistic ones. Very simply, given a set of imagined possible outcomes, one might be able to convert their potential surprise ratings into a set of fractional 'subjective probability weights' that add up to unity. In his recent and fascinating book on Shackle's theory of choice under uncertainty, Ford (1983, pp. 129–30; 146–7) has examined, in a highly technical manner, ways of performing such a conversion (or, as he calls it, 'recodification'). In the rest of this section I will consider, with the aid of some simple examples, this idea and some of the problems it entails.

First, let us think about a particularly simple potential surprise construct, where a consumer has in mind only two rival 'ultimate' events, X and Y. If she can neither imagine nor take seriously any barriers to either of them, then she would be totally unsurprised should either come about. If called upon or brought up to express her expectations in terms of probabilities that sum to unity, then the logic of the situation she envisages would compel her to say that each outcome had a 50 per cent chance of coming about. But this does not necessarily mean she will expect that, if she had the opportunity seemingly to 'trigger off' these events time and again by a given procedure, she would generate an equal division of outcomes between X and Y. All she is saying to herself is that they presently look equally unsurprising in prospect.

Now suppose the consumer suddenly conceives of a third possibility, Z, that is a rival to the original pair. Plainly, if she talks in terms of probabilities, she can no longer continue to speak of X and Y as having 50 per cent chances of coming about. If Z is an event to which she assigns only a moderate degree of potential surprise, she might now verbalise her 'subjective probability weights' as follows: 40 per cent to X, 40 per cent to Y, and 20 per cent to Z. In other words, thoughts about additional possibilities reduce the 'weight' the consumer seems to attach even to *perfectly possible* future events. This is an idea to which Shackle (1961, p. 92) is utterly opposed; to him, a small share of a total, and a share that can vary according to the length of the list of rival imagined possibilities, cannot suitably indicate the status of an outcome seen as 'perfectly possible', since perfect possibility arises from an absence of (that is, *zero*) imagined fatal obstacles.

To see why Shackle adopts this stance, it is helpful to add some more substance to our example. Suppose that the situation concerns the possible promotion of a lecturer to senior lecturer by an academic review committee. Two candidates are obvious contenders who would seem to lack nothing by way of qualifications for promotion. If our consumer (who might herself be one of the candidates) can see no reason to suppose that the committee will select neither of these candidates and no reason why the committee could favour one at the cost of excluding the other, then she will see it as perfectly possible that either could be promoted. Now imagine the consumer hears that a third candidate, not automatically due for consideration, has asked for her case to be heard. The consumer will see the idea that the extra candidate might be promoted as less than perfectly possible if this candidate appears to lack some of the usual qualifications. The third candidate's entry *only* changes the way the consumer sees the others' prospects if the new candidacy brings with it a possibility that looks like a potentially fatal barrier to the promotion of X and/or Y. For example, whilst our consumer might in normal circumstances think that 'Z is too young to be taken seriously', she may in this situation think that 'despite her youth, Z is a threat to the other candidates, for she is the protegé of the committee's most influential member'. In other words, the imagined predispositions of the influential member are now seen as a hurdle that X and Y must overcome if either is to be appointed. No longer will the consumer regard the appointment of either X or Y as perfectly possible. But if Z does not seem to bring with her a potential barrier to the success of X and/or Y—and there is no necessary reason why she will—then the standing of X and Y are not going to seem diminished when Z enters the contest.

To clarify further the Shacklean perspective, let us consider some other employment-oriented examples. Suppose I think that I am one of twenty candidates for a job, and that neither I nor my nineteen rivals lack any qualifications. (I might reason that they otherwise would not have troubled to apply.) If this is as far as my assessment of the situation goes, then I can treat myself and all my rivals as perfect possibilities; I have no reason to expect to be surprised regardless of who is, in the event, successful. But now suppose I hear from a seemingly reliable source that there are not twenty candidates, but forty. If I follow my original line of reasoning, I now have a vision of forty perfect possibilities. A probability theorist would say my subjective probability of success must fall from one in twenty to one in forty, yet in terms of possibilities I see nothing that has happened to impair my chances. However, my reasoning processes might be rather more complex: I might expect that, faced with candidates who have no unsatisfactory characteristics, the committee will start considering other discriminatory criteria, not specified in the job advertisement, or that it will apply weights in respect of performances that exceed targets in varying degrees (see Chapter 7).

In this case, the size of the field is something that *might* affect my conjectures about my prospects. For example, I might reason that, the bigger the field, the larger could be the number of additional characteristics between which the committee could find itself able to choose. More people could be applying with something to offer that I do not possess: each characteristic I lack is a barrier to my success; the more candidates there are, the more surprised I shall expect to be if I am successful. But note that I do not *have* to think like this; I might actually be exceedingly confident because I am totally unable to think of any grounds on which others might be preferred and because I can think of all manner of reasons why I might be preferred instead. If so, I will regard myself as the *only* perfectly appointable applicant and will be astonished to see anyone else being appointed, no matter how many other candidates there are. My excess of qualifications is something I see as an impenetrable set of barriers to the prospects of my rivals. (Of course, I may be failing to see that I could be turned down precisely because I am 'over qualified' and am therefore judged not likely to stay in the job for long.)

The inference I draw from these discussions is that the addition of an extra hypothetical outcome to a list of previously imagined possibilities *may* involve a decision maker in changing her assessments of some or all of the elements on such a list. This could happen if the newly considered outcome is felt to be associated with something that could get in the way of its rivals. But this need not happen. In circumstances where new thoughts about what could happen do lead decision makers to revise their expectations and assign possibility scores to newly imagined prospects whilst *downgrading* scores they had previously assigned to rivals, it may appear 'as if' they are thinking in probabilistic terms. However, people might not think of themselves as if they are carving up some *fixed* 'possibilities pie' in a new manner; some may indeed do so, but we could be unwise to presume that this is generally what happens and then, on the basis of such a presumption, to attempt to treat in distributive terms all rival thoughts about the future.

Finally, we should recognise that imagined future events are not in themselves potentially fatal barriers to each other even though they may be rivals in time to come. In prospect, rival events are just figments of our imaginations; mere thoughts cannot stop their rivals from turning into events. What *can* serve as barriers are other, *prior* events, anticipated or otherwise, which choices as well as natural processes have a power to determine.

5.5 POSSIBLE NON-PROBABILISTIC ALTERNATIVES TO POTENTIAL SURPRISE

Whatever one thinks of the philosophical conflict between Shackle and probability theorists about how one *should* face up to an uncertain future, this should not be allowed to distract us from the question of how people *do* envisage events and their possible sequels, prior to choice. By referring to commonly employed topographical terms in the previous sections, I have sought to suggest that Shackle's analysis may not be altogether misleading in descriptive terms. Ordinary consumers may lack Shackle's philosophical insight, but some of them do none the less talk about outcomes that are 'watersheds', that are 'not beyond the bounds of possibility', or that 'open up whole ranges of hitherto undreamt-of possibilities'. The 'rut' term is perhaps the most instructive, when employed by someone who is clearly disappointed with the seriously restricted set of options that seem 'open' to her. However, there are a number of alternative possibilities that might describe more accurately the ways in which some people, at least some of the time, attempt or find themselves able to face up to an uncertain and as yet undetermined future.

One possibility takes us back to the discussion of impulsive behaviour in section 4.4. People may find themselves completely unable to form constructs on some occasions; either they fear that they do not have potentially important construct axes in mind, or they find the future so foggy that they recognise that unforeseen possibilities could get in the way of events that presently seem to be unblocked prospects in terms of the construct axes they do have in mind. Here, they are recognising the limitations of their past experience and present creative capacities as guides to what the future could hold; in some degree, they might be thought of as embracing the scepticist position outlined at the start of section 5.3. A vivid example of this kind of thinking is contained in the following short passage from Marilyn French's novel *The Women's Room*. It is part of a discussion of the lifestyle choices faced by women in a male-dominated society. French (1978, p. 44) writes thus about the predicament of a woman playing the 'mating game' in the days before reliable contraception:

There was no way out of her dilemma; all the alternatives rot. Like being in a burning building, the fire beyond you, two windows in front of you, one looking down on a tiny bunch of firemen holding a canvas that looks no bigger than your thumb, the other looking down on the filthy Hudson River. When you are in situations like that, the only thing you can do is close your eyes and plunge. No amount of ratiocination can help you decide whether the fire is only a corridor deep and you could reach the staircase beyond, whether your chances are better with the water or the net.

A similar view of the nature of processes of decision making under uncertainty is to be found in the writings of Keynes. The relevant passages are actually his famous objections to probabilistic ideas, yet they would appear to indicate that he would have thought Shackle's analysis presumes choosers have a far clearer idea of what might and might not happen than is actually the case. It is noteworthy that his view is not limited to unpleasant dilemmas, such as the one facing the heroine of French's feminist novel, for Keynes (1936, pp. 161–2) asserted that:

Most, probably, of our decisions to do something positive, the full consequences of which will be drawn out over many days to come, can only be taken as a result of animal spirits—of a spontaneous urge to action rather than inaction, and not as the outcome of a weighted average of quantitative benefits multiplied by quantitative probabilities. Enterprise only pretends to itself to be mainly actuated by the statements in its own prospectus, however candid and sincere. Only a little more than an expedition to the South Pole, is it based on an exact calculation of benefits to come (emphasis added).

And, in replying to critics of his monetary theory of employment, Keynes (1937, pp. 213–4) emphasised that:

the fact that our knowledge of the future is fluctuating, vague and uncertain, renders wealth a peculiarly unsuitable subject for the methods of the classical economic theory.... The sense in which I am using the term ['uncertain'] is that in which the prospect of a European war is uncertain, or the price of copper and the rate of interest twenty years hence, or the absolescence of a new invention, or the position of private wealth-owners in the social system in 1970. About these matters there is no scientific basis on which to form any calculable probability whatever. We simply do not know.

These passages suggest that people may quite often be totally unable to look at the sets of ideas at their disposal and then feel they have a secure basis for at least partially closing their minds in a way which enables them to define expectations and reasons for their choices. They may have no basis for saying 'because' and may be unable to justify opinions about possible events even if placed under pressure to do so. In section 8.6, I shall attempt to explain how they decide what to do in such situations.

The polar opposite to extreme open-mindedness and 'empty-headedness' is that which Carter (1954) and Steinbruner (1974) have independently come to suggest. Carter's suggestion is part of his critique of Shackle's original model of choice in the face of potential surprise. In addition to arguing that it is unrealistic to expect choosers to think in terms of continuous variables (as opposed to stepped scales), Carter (1954, p. 52, emphasis in original) goes as far as to argue that, in some cases:

We may find that, in looking at a fairly close date, a man's calculations are based on a *single* typical outcome. He has made up his mind about what will, he thinks, happen; he has no side glances at alternative possibilities.

Steinbruner displays as even greater willingness to reject outright the notion that people are willing and able to keep in mind ranges of possible outcomes relating to mutually exclusive states of the world. He asserts (1974, p. 123, emphasis in original) that:

[The mind] does not match the uncertain structure of the environment in which events might take a number of alternative courses. Rather, it imposes an image and works to preserve that image. A single course of events is projected; evidence for alternative outcomes is manipulated to preserve the expectations. We might call this, then, *the assumption of a single outcome calculation*

As a general analysis of how people think about the uncertain world in which they find themselves, the 'single outcome' approach seems flawed, since it appears to deny the everyday observation that people frequently display signs of uneasiness about what is going to happen, even when they have made up their minds about what to do. However, this is not to say that people never behave in the suggested manner. On the contrary, one can, for example, note the behaviour of undergraduates doing case study work on business policy; they are all too prone to treat supplied sales projections as gospel truths, instead of realising that demand curves might be more usefully seen as conjectural bands of possible sales levels at particular possible prices. Further evidence of the tendency of people to ignore uncertainty and make single-line forecasts is provided in Jefferson's (1983) account of his experience in using 'scenario-planning' techniques in the Shell International Petroleum Company. Managers at Shell often took the view that the purpose of a planning tool is to reduce ignorance about the future. Consequently they were very hostile to the idea of using a technique which, instead of telling them what *the* result of a decision would be, confronted them with the realities of uncertainty (see Jefferson, 1983, p. 146; also see section 4.4 and note the obvious overlap between the conceptualisation of hostility in PCP and Steinbruner's mention of evidence being manipulated). Experience at Shell indicates that people often find it difficult to face more than two or three scenarios without becoming confused and apathetic. Furthermore, if one of these scenarios is in the nature of a middle course, 'base case', people tend to ignore the others and accord it an excessive degree of certainty. The avoidance of narrowminded ways of thinking would appear to be a skill that is not always easy to develop and which, if developed too far, can be a positive hindrance to the activity of trying to predict and control events.

Carter does not explain upon what basis people may feel justified in sometimes coming to focus their expectations on single typical outcomes. One simple explanation may be that they have not imagined or have not been exposed to ideas that are rivals to those upon which they base their choices. Indeed, the absence of any thoughts about rival possibilities may mean that a person moves along particular pathways in life without actively choosing at all, in the sense of evaluating opportunity costs prior to selecting a particular course of action (see section 3.2). Simple as this explanation is, we could be foolish to play down its significance, particularly in the light of my earlier comments about the tendency for people to get their ideas from mutually reinforcing sources. Sad to say, one can very easily end up living in suburbia, 'married with two kids, a dog and a cat' and holding absolutely conventional beliefs, without it ever crossing one's mind that life did not have to turn out like this and could be turned into something radically different.

Steinbruner's attempt to explain how people settle on single-pathway expectations is rather more complex and draws heavily upon experimental findings from cognitive psychology. These experiments seem to show that mental images are, by virtue of their very subjectivity, highly malleable. There is thus scope for the mind to twist ideas that might collectively suggest ranges of rival possible events into images of unique future pathways. In relation to Shackle's idea of the nature of a 'perfect possibility', for example, we can note that what constitutes a potentially fatal obstacle to a particular event is something that may be open to debate. If we *wish* to believe or disbelieve particular ideas we can, providing we 'rig' our mental lines of thought accordingly. Steinbruner (1974, pp. 114–22) details five techniques people employ to do this:

(1) the construction of images and arguments from analogy (in other words, people seek out analogies that appear to lend support to ideas to which they feel predisposed—as is done in section 6.3);
(2) inferences of transformation ('wishful thinking');
(3) inferences of impossibility (it is here that Steinbruner comes closest to Shackle's way of thinking, though at no point does he mention Shackle's work);
(4) negative images (in other words, people look around for arguments against ideas they are predisposed to reject, with their expressed preferences thus often being determined by their previously construed constraints—see Elster's (1983) book *Sour Grapes* for an excellent study of this phenomenon);
(5) attempts to obtain social corroboration (which is not the same as attempting to obtain from society ideas that would call into question the images that are being constructed).

Steinbruner's suggestion, then, is that a decision maker who wrestles with uncertainty but ultimately whittles her vision of the future into a single projection essentially *deludes* herself into believing that she has a basis for rational action. She selects one self-concocted image of the future and an implied scheme of action when, in principle, she might have dressed up any of the rejected possibilities in a suitable manner.

It should be obvious that it is by no means necessary to consign the use of the above five techniques solely to the representation of an activity that culminates in so much sense being made of a situation that all scenarios bar one are rejected. People who are less prone to delude themselves may be thought of as using these techniques as they attempt to piece together rival scenarios against which to make their choices. Indeed, it should be noted that Keynes' comments about business behaviour are entirely consistent with the idea that much decision making is based on 'deliberate self-deception' (Shackle, 1967, p. 132) in the face of an uncertain and undetermined future. I would suggest that Steinbruner's 'cognitive' analysis complements any discussion of the origins of confidence, even though I would question his claim that people *generally* are 'banking on' single expected outcomes when they choose in turbulent times.

5.6 CONCLUSION

I hope that readers will get four main ideas from this chapter. First, the possible sources of ideas that may or may not be seen fit only for disbelief are diverse. However, depending upon how consumers employ them, these sources may be mutually reinforcing or contradictory. Second, prospects seen in term of a particular construct axis/characteristic scale may be envisaged in a variety of ways: in terms of bounded sets of rival scenarios to which either potential surprise ratings or 'probability weights' have been assigned, as highly blurred images, or as tightly focused single scenarios. Third, choices may be deemed to be crucial in nature if they appear to involve consequent rival prospects for a dramatic closing off or opening up of the chooser's future options. Fourth, and finally, we have added more flesh to the notion of confidence. In the previous chapter it was suggested that confidence can arise from a chooser's failure to envisage possible events which would call into question her ability to predict and control her life. Now we can see other aspects of confidence, namely an awareness of potentially fatal possible obstacles to the taking place of counter-desired events, a lack of awareness of potentially fatal obstacles to the taking place of desired events, and an awareness of possible obstacles to things that might get in the way of desired events. In other words, confidence arises from a mixture of awareness and blindness to different kinds of possibilities. A person's state of confidence will be heavily dependent upon how she gathers together and processes ideas about what might happen. In a world of turbulence, however, new ideas are continuously being generated, so persistent adherence to once 'confidently held' beliefs may require a good deal of self-deception or a failure to think creatively or encounter new pieces of information.

6 How Minds are Made Up

6.1 INTRODUCTION

When we 'make up our minds', we concoct justifications for adhering tentatively to particular bounded images of the future that could lie before us when we choose. Some of the devices that people employ in constructing such justifications were considered in section 5.5, in the light of Steinbruner's (1974) work. However, it would be misleading to say that if we know about people using such devices we know *how* they make up their minds. For a major question is still waiting to be answered, namely why does a decision maker delude herself this way rather than that when forming her mental landscapes of the future? As she constructs single or multiple scenarios it is likely that she will regard some analogies as useful and others as misleading. It is also likely that she will accept the advice of some people and reject that of others, and be selective in the extent to which she takes account of changes in 'the state of the news'. Such inferences of impossibility as she draws may be based on impeccable logic, but logic, however good, is an incomplete tool for making confident assertions; it can only apply to what has already been incorporated in a model of the situation at hand. She could have drawn different inferences on the basis of different partial models that were equally logical in their structures. Inferences of transformation and negative images are by their nature subjective. If the decision maker's mind can cobble together one set of images and partial justifications, what stops it from constructing another set, given a particular set of possibilities?

In this chapter, the primary aim is to answer this question in a way that avoids the conclusion that decision makers' minds generally operate in a 'spontaneous and erratic' manner (the term is part of Coddington's (1982, p. 481) critical characterisation of the beliefs of subjectivist Keynesians). The failure to avoid such a conclusion would be nihilistic in its implications for economics as a predictive discipline. We would be left admitting that choosers might believe absolutely anything that their creative processes or the 'state of the news' threw up as a possibility, and might act upon it; their behaviour would be unstructured and coherent patterns might only be observed by chance in aggregative contexts.

The nihilistic conclusion is swiftly avoided in section 6.2, with the aid of the remaining key ideas from Kelly's (1955, 1963) theory of personality. In my experience, these ideas are rather more difficult to grasp on first hearing than the ones I introduced in section 4.2; hence, in keeping with Steinbruner's way of thinking, I will devote section 6.3 to some clarificatory 'arguments from analogy'. In section 6.4 some techniques for investigating these ideas empirically will be outlined. The next two sections introduce a strategic/structural perspective. Section 6.5 examines differences in the ways in which people organise their ideas to cope with surprises, while section 6.6 investigates why some ideas—including ideas about what one might choose to do—often seem easier to change than others. Section 6.7 is a thread-tying conclusion.

6.2 RULES FOR THOUGHT

We have already seen, in section 4.2, how people may be blind to some possibilities because they do not include appropriate construct axes in their limited repertoires, and how their expectations will be shaped by the reference standards they use and the ranges of convenience they assign to construct axes which they do employ. What we have not so far considered is how people decide whether and how to include possible construct axes in their repertoires or how they adjust their reference standards and construct ranges. These possible means for forming constructs have to be judged themselves—for they too are expectation-laden constructs—before other expectations can be put together. It sounds at first sight as though we are faced with a problem of infinite regress. For example, consider the mental processes of the subject in the following imaginary interview:

Researcher: 'Why did you believe the Canon AE1 Program would be the easiest 35 mm SLR camera to use?'

Subject: 'At the time I bought it, my friend Grahame had one and he told me it was the only one around that you could just focus and shoot, with no need to worry about aperture and shutter-speed settings.'

Researcher: 'Why did you believe him?'

Subject: 'Because he's the sort of person who always does his homework on expensive products before he buys them.'

Researcher: 'How do you know this?'

Subject: 'Because he always seems to know a lot about things.'

Researcher: 'How do you know he's not just bluffing?'

Subject: 'I trust him.'

Researcher: 'Why?'

Subject: 'I've never had reason to doubt what he says whenever we talk; he's not like some people who go about making exaggerated claims that conflict with what they said the previous week.'

Researcher: 'He might be a very clever bluffer, and there might be good reasons behind the surface contradictions in what others say....'

Subject: 'I doubt it.'

Researcher: 'Why?'

Subject: (getting agitated,) 'Look here, is this the Spanish Inquisition or something? I've got better things to do than to sit here and be quizzed like this.'

The stormy break-up of the interview is precisely the kind of thing that tends to happen in real-life situations where a set of questions gets unexpectedly probing and challenges the bases of everyday beliefs. (See Garfinkel, 1967, for some actual examples, or experiment on friends you do not mind upsetting!) But, in any case, I had to employ *some* method of bringing it to a close, for in questioning the subject the researcher appeared to be going round in circles or, rather, along an endless judgemental helix. The subject's expectation about the camera she chose was something she had made dependent on what her friend had to say about cameras. In doing this she was acting upon the expectation that her friend's advice was worth having, a construct that depended on how she chose to construe her friend as a person, which was in turn determined by the way that he was seen as talking about things relative to the way employed by other people who were believed to be unreliable in what they say.

It is by no means intrinsic to the situation in question that *this* chain of expectations has to be used to form the end product, the image of the camera that it would be appropriate to buy. However, it is the chain—which we might describe also as a procedure or set of rules—that our consumer happens to have chosen as a means for making up her mind. She is *allowing* her view about whether a camera is easy or difficult to use to be *determined by* Grahame's opinions, rather than being prepared to take note of what people in general say: in the context of judging cameras that she has not yet tried, she ranks her 'ease of use' construct as subordinate to 'Grahame's opinion', providing he has an opinion in this context. But when she judges the worth of Grahame's opinions in this context against those of people in general, she allows her assessment to be determined by how she judges his opinions in terms of the construct 'moderate/consistent *versus* exaggerated/inconsistent'. That is to say, *if* she has (by some thus far unspecified procedure) judged Grahame's opinions to be 'moderate/consistent', *then* they are deemed worth taking note of; their worth is placed subordinate to their consistency. It should be noticed that if the relationships between constructs are given for the present, and if a higher-ranking construct—the view that Grahame's opinions are 'moderate/consistent'—is also given, then we have no need to be troubled by the infinite regress question. Very simply, a given assessment of Grahame's opinions is being used by our consumer as a *basis* for forming expectations in situations where he makes suggestions about possibilities. Now we know that if Grahame rushed up and said breathlessly to our consumer: 'if you're still looking for the easiest 35 mm SLR to use, don't buy the Canon AE1 Program, since it's just been rendered obsolete by a new model', then she would change her view of the AE1 Program.

This hierarchical, rule-based view of expectation formation seems to be what Kelly had in mind in his theory of personality. His (1955, p. 56) organisation corollary holds that 'each person characteristically evolves, for her convenience in anticipating events, a construction system embracing ordinal relationships between constructs'. The term 'ordinal' suggests that some constructs are subordinate to others, yet may subsume still others, which is precisely what we have just seen in our imaginary interview. In using the term 'evolves', Kelly indicates that he does not believe people generally adhere to unchanging sets of rules in the face of surprises that are judged to have invalidated earlier constructions of events. He elaborates this point with his (1955, p. 72) experience corollary: 'a person's construction system varies as she successively construes the replications of events'. Constructs may thus be reranked, reversed in polarity, used with wider or narrow ranges of application, and newly added to (or discarded from) the person's system. For example, suppose Grahame's claim about the ease of use of the AE1 Program had been discredited when the person happened to mention it in the camera shop and was shown a new model with automatic focusing, winding and film loading. The person would then have needed to consider whether she should change her assessment of the general worth of his opinions and use other criteria (for example, what the person in the camera shop says, or reports in a photographic magazine) when deciding upon subsequent purchases.

At this point, we run once again into the 'strange loop' problem. A person can only judge in terms of her existing construction system whether or not a change in that system may be in order; for a new way of looking at things is itself an event that must be construed before it can make any sense (see Kelly, 1955, p. 79). In order to escape from the loop, we must recognise that a person who changes her way of looking at the world will always make an incomplete break with her past way of forming beliefs each time she adjusts her construction system. She will never 'change her mind' completely; there will always be *some* (and usually very many) constructs that are maintained from her past view of the world. For example, had the consumer been embarrassed by Grahame's outmoded claim whilst in the camera shop, she might have concluded that it is unwise to judge the worth of somebody's opinions by their consistency, and that a better way of judging them might be according to the criterion of whether or not the person expressing them has a strong enough incentive to give accurate advice. But these conclusions would be things that she allowed herself to believe according to other, given criteria, that prevent her from seeing as adequate her original way of judging opinions. (She would now have 'the evidence of her own eyes', a personal demonstration, that Grahame can be wrong; previously she might not even have considered the 'incentive to give good advice' criteria, or she may have considered it before and at the time judged it as a cumbersome rule to employ, compared with the one it is now allowed to displace.)

Kelly addresses these issues formally with his (1955, p. 77) modulation corollary: 'the variation in a person's construction system is limited by the permeability of the constructs within whose range of convenience the variants lie'. Readers may find it helpful to see a construct's 'permeability' as referring to its readiness to allow the admission of new ways of looking at things—that is, how strictly it serves as a *filter*, rejecting wholly or in part some notions that might be taken seriously as possibilities (see 'characteristic filtering', in section 7.4). Suppose that the consumer had actually purchased the AE1 Program after taking Grahame's advice and without discovering in the shop that it was now out of date. Suppose also that *en route* for the shop she had met one of the people she sees as an unreliable source of information, and had been informed by this person that 'there is a 35 mm SLR that is much, much easier to use than the AE1 Program, but I'm not sure what it's called'. This statement may not be something which the person would have seen as exaggerated had she heard it from her friend Grahame, but the way she sees the third person prevents her from accepting it and prevents her from seeing Grahame as someone with outmoded opinions about cameras. So she filters the information from her attention and, as a result of the inflexibility of her way of judging what people say, she ends up purchasing a model that is now obsolete and still quite troublesome for her to use. The upshot could be that the views of the world she captures in her photographs fail to come up to her expectations.

In the case used here, the impermeability of the consumer's construct seems unfortunate, since it causes her to be needlessly left somewhat behind in a world of rapid change. (Canon AE1 Program owners may miss many action shots because they have forgotten to wind manually on to the next frame, whereas owners of the more recent Canon T50 will not suffer such disappointments, for their cameras have automatic film advance and loading; this was something my own friend Grahame did not mention at the time I asked him which was the simplest SLR camera to operate! Still, if we have permeable construction systems and discover new possibilities, we live and learn.) However, it would be a mistake to argue that impermeability of constructs is *generally* a bad thing. On the contrary, it is necessary in *some* degree if the consumer is to be able to form bounded and resilient conjectures of what could happen, when faced with a turbulent mass of mutually exclusive raw possibilities. By virtue of her incompletely permeable construction system, our consumer at least ends up with some kind of camera and some limited ideas about which photographs are worth trying to take; she is not completely bewildered by the enormous range of choices within the present and between the present and future imagined possibilities (see the discussion of the schizophrenic consumer, in section 6.6).

The limited permeability of a person's constructs, and her need to use some existing constructs to judge new ways of looking at things, combine to ensure that, although she may adjust her world-view in the light of her experience, her system is best seen as being in a fairly viscous state. Her mind will not be in a complete state of flux, with each day's picture of the scheme of things differing in a kaleidoscopic manner from that of the previous day. To be sure, she may make some not inconsiderable kaleidic shifts of the kind discussed frequently within Shackle's work, but these will impact only upon particular subsystems of her overall construction system. Even so, such changes may result in behaviour that surprises onlookers. This problem arises from the fragmentation corollary of Kelly's theory: 'a person may successively employ a variety of construction subsystems which are inferentially incompatible with each other' (1955, p. 83). Unless onlookers perceive the broader contexts in which subsystems are allowed to operate, the person's expressed thoughts and actions may seem hopelessly inconsistent. This may mean it is difficult to play a particular desired role—such as successful salesperson—in a social process involving this person (see Kelly's sociality corollary, defined in section 4.2).

The idea that a person forms her expectations by employing an hierarchical system of rules does not preclude the possibility that she may fantasise—by considering, 'what if...?'—as she attempts to form the expectations that she will use as a basis for action. Her system may tolerate loose thinking for a time, as in dreams (Kelly, 1955, p. 484), but its rules of operation will eventually firm up expectations, be they composed of single-point forecasts or sets of potential surprise curves, in ways that label some possibilities as 'inconceivable' and assign them to her mental trashcan.

To illustrate this point it is useful to take an example from Kelly (1955, pp. 19–20) concerning the situation of a person who is about to serve a pie at a dinner party. It is by no means intrinsic to a pie that it be served in wedge-shaped slices with the point always facing the diner. However, if the server feels bound by the rules of etiquette in such a situation, because she has made her view of her 'self' subordinate to whether or not she behaves politely, and if her construction of 'polite behaviour' is subordinate to her construction of what constitutes 'conventional behaviour', then there may be very few ways open to her for action. One possible way (not suggested by Kelly) is that she should tear the pie apart with her bare hands and hurl the pieces at the plates of her guests. If the guests view the world according to 'conventional' rules for construing behaviour at dinner parties, they will be shocked, barely able to believe their eyes, if such behaviour actually materialises. It will not fit into their dinner party constructs; they may find it fits only into those of their constructs that relate to mental disorder.

The pie example may seem trivial, but the point it illustrates is quite general. It relates even to how readers can see this book—a work which commits to paper very many of its author's constructs concerning processes of decision making, purporting to be a contribution to economics. If a reader's set of rules for subsuming contributions to economics does not admit non-mathematical pieces of work that do not contain the use of econometric procedures, and which are not formed according to Cartesian/logical positivist principles employed by mainstream theorists, then she will not be able to see it as economics. According to another reader's set of rules, however, it may be open to being construed as a contribution to economics and she does not have to concoct a case for rejecting it. But whether a reader accepts or rejects it, she cannot know for sure whether its ideas are right or wrong; they are merely admissible or inadmissible according to the set of judgemental rules she uses.

So far, I have sought to keep these complex ideas as simple as possible by writing as though a subordinate construct only has one construct that is ranked directly above it; for example, the person's expectation that the Canon AE1 Program would be the right 35 mm SLR camera for her to buy seems to have been determined solely by her expectation that she could find no 35 mm SLR camera that would be easier to use, an expectation which was itself determined solely by Grahame's opinion. Usually though, an expectation will be subordinate to a group of constructs. For example, which camera might be the right one to buy could be judged to depend not merely on ease of use, but also on how the consumer judged price, availability, durability, weight, picture clarity and so on. Each of these superordinate expectations might in turn be subordinate to more than one construct. For example, picture clarity could be judged to depend on film type ('35mm is fine, 110 film is too small'), lens quality (for which price might be taken as a proxy) and type of focusing ('a reflex system is the only one that lets you actually see if your shot is focused').

Now, of course, once we have an expectation being made to depend on a variety of other constructs, ambiguities and conflicts appear to be in the offing once again. For example, how does an expensive 110 SLR camera compare with a cheap 35 mm SLR camera or a moderately priced 35 mm camera with adjustable focus but with a separate viewfinder; how surprised would our consumer be to find each of them letting her produce pictures of a particular standard of clarity? Likewise, how does the consumer judge that one (or none) of these three cameras could be good enough for her to buy, given that they differ in other respects besides the prospective picture clarity that they are judged able to help her produce? We are back with the initial problem once again, but we can once more note that the consumer has a way out of it if she has, within her construction system, rules for dealing with these puzzles and, if need be, rules for dealing with any problems that the former rules generate or fail to reconcile in a workable manner.

In speaking of procedures for combining potential criteria of appraisal to determine how a person sees various possibilities, I might ostensibly seem to be discussing no more than methods of expectation formation prior to choice. However, I am in reality also discussing how rival action-schemes come to be ranked, for rankings themselves are personal constructs (for example, 'I think camera X could be OK for me but I don't think camera Y is good enough, since ...'). A person's construction system is the means whereby she generates her choices, in the face of conflicting ideas about what she could choose and what could happen as a result of, or despite, her actions. In thinking about what she might choose to do, a person generates verdicts with the aid of the hierarchy of rules that she has tentatively put together as a means of coping with life. As we shall eventually see in Chapters 7 and 8, these rules for choice may take a variety of forms when images of possibilities are seen as directly subordinate to more than one construct. This view of the relationship between expectation formation and action dispenses with any reference to a prespecified, complete system of 'preferences' of the kind that orthodox economists have in mind when they draw indifference curves. I am depicting consumers as if they can only construct and express rankings in respect of possibilities they have actually considered.

6.3 CONFLICTS AND COMPLEX HIERARCHIES

The processes whereby people form constructs may be likened to the processes according to which systems of government and corporations reach decisions. Individuals and institutions alike have to deal with conflicting possibilities. Judicial systems and firms do, of course, involve individuals in their processes of conflict resolution; indeed, they are systems that have been designed by people. Yet their basic workings are rather easier to understand since they can be analysed without it being necessary to understand the thought processes of the people involved with them.

Consider a proceeding in a criminal court. Counsels for the prosecution and defence are in the business of selling ideas to a decision-making body: the jury. By their very nature these ideas include rival possibilities. Some of them, however, are deemed 'inadmissible' by the judge; in other words, they are ruled 'out of court'. Clearly, the jury is only being allowed to reach its verdict within a framework that some senior authority has set up. Once reached, the verdict may be disputed on grounds which allow the case to be sent to the appeal court. Such a body can seek to overrule the original verdict, but may allow it to stand. In situations where the defence still will not accept the verdict, the case may eventually be referred to the highest court in the land. At this level, one might expect that matters would be settled once and for all, but here politicians might get involved. For example, Hofstadter (1979, pp. 692–3) points out that the US Supreme Court very nearly got itself embroiled in a confrontation during the Watergate era, when Richard Nixon threatened to disobey any supreme court ruling that was not 'definitive', all the while claiming that *he* had the legal right to decide what was 'definitive'. In the end the confrontation never took place but, had it done so, the President would have needed subsequently to be able to maintain his implicit claim for supremacy in the face of popular opinion. As Hofstadter comments, 'it is well to remember that, in a society such as ours, the legal system is a polite gesture granted by millions of people—and it can be overtaken just as easily as a river can overflow its banks'. In other societies, dictators use the armed forces to assert their superiority, but even they are prone to be overruled in a military coup staged by army officers who see things differently, *provided* these officers have the support of personnel in the ranks.

The kinds of legal system just described can be depicted formally as if they are collections of rules for making rulings. Some of these rules would concern the circumstances in which other rules can be changed, and whose rulings can be overruled by whom. These rules enable high-level judges to set precedents, for example, and politicians to vote in new laws, including laws that bear upon the powers enjoyed by judges and juries. Ultimately though, judges, juries and politicians are only agents of the people the system seems to control. The masses—in the armed forces or in civilian life, whichever group has the most brute power—have the final say. They will overthrow judgemental systems whose operations produce results that seem to conflict with their expectations; their rules are inviolate, crude though they may seem in comparison with the rules framed by specialists on their behalf. However, since the membership of the population comprising 'the masses' changes through time, the expectations to which agents must conform will not necessarily be static. (I should perhaps add that, in this nuclear age, what I have just said may not strictly be correct: an elected president may get to 'push the ultimate button' and send an automated missile system into operation against the will of the masses, before they have time to band together and defeat him. The possibility of technological failure may then be the only thing left to reverse the president's choice. Here, for those who have imagined the scenario, is a cause for anxiety if ever there were one!)

Corporate organisations, similarly, are hierarchies whose very existence depends on their continuing to conform with externally imposed requirements. They are constrained by the legal framework (though they can try to exert pressure on the systems of government), by their customers' willingness to see their products as they would wish, and by the requirements of their suppliers of finance. These bounds may none the less offer a good deal of freedom for action: there may be many policies which might look as though they could satisfy survival conditions. Different bodies within a corporation will throw up conflicting suggestions as to which policies might be preferred. Unless there is complete anarchy, conflict resolution is achieved by one party being able to exert supremacy over the others. When internal bickering reaches the level of the boardroom, the shareholders may step in and appoint an alternative set of directors. As in systems of government, the extent to which conflicts reach the highest levels can depend considerably upon how conspicuously and persistently certain possibilities are pushed forward; intermediate levels of judgement may sometimes overrule ideas emerging in relation to low-level conflicts, which higher levels would take seriously if only they knew about them. The use of agents and segmented organisational hierarchies economises on the costs of forming judgements and expectations, but at the cost of allowing some inconsistencies to pass by unnoticed. Higher levels will only see good reason to experiment with a change of lower-level elements and organisation when things happen that conspicuously threaten their own positions.

6.4 PERSONALITY AND PREDICTION

The analysis in section 6.2 was constructed with a view to showing that one can adopt a subjectivist view of expectations that is systematic; a subjectivist economist does not have to 'sweep the problem under the carpet' (Tarshis, 1980, pp. 12–13) with vague references to 'animal spirits'. The road to nihilism can be avoided with Kelly's structuralist/subjectivist view of how people think, which opens up scope for anticipating patterns of behaviour. At least, this is the impression I have so far sought to convey by emphasising that a person's pattern of beliefs, and hence her expectations, is determined by the way her mind is organised. But a major limitation is imposed upon our predictive capabilities by the creative processes that operate within a person's mind and by the complexity of the processes whereby she encounters other raw possibilities that might be converted into expectations.

In order for a researcher to be able to anticipate correctly a person's behaviour, she needs to be able to uncover not merely the structure of that person's judgemental system, but also the relevant list of raw possibilities that will emerge as candidates for admission to the person's view of the world. The latter list must specify the order in which the person will consider these possibilities, since the ones she thinks about initially may change her way of looking at things and hence affect the way she judges the remaining ones. The list with which the researcher is going to have to work will inevitably be incomplete. Even in the limited circles within which the researcher's subjects move, there is an enormous volume of information about what was, is and might be that each of them might encounter or create and spread.

Even if subjects have highly restricted construct repertoires, they can potentially create enormous numbers of fresh thoughts; as Shackle (1979, p. 21) reminds us, a small set of alphabetic elements can generate a huge dictionary. The 'Garfinkel problem'—the tendency for people to panic and/or become hostile if one tries to get to the core of their views of the world—also poses a barrier to the discovery of complete judgemental structures as a means of dealing with Kelly's fragmentation corollary. At best, the researcher is probably going to be able to uncover only subsystems from her subjects' mental organisations and then see which possibilities, from a list which *she* has devised, would be admitted by these subsystems. But this, surely, is better than nothing unless the end result of such efforts is that the researcher makes predictions which are no better than those made by lay people—whose own predictive competence is evident in the extent to which they can cope with a social and turbulent world (see Hutchison's (1977, pp. 9–11; 1978) remarks on what should be expected of economists).

As far as discovering cognitive structures is concerned, we can note that there is an extensive technical literature associated with Kelly's own tool, 'repertory grid technique' (see Adams-Webber, 1979, Bannister and Fransella, 1971, Bannister and Mair, 1968, Slater, 1976, 1977, and Stewart and Stewart, 1981). Kelly developed the tool, for use in a clinical context, as a means of helping patients to understand their own views of the world and for helping the clinician to see how less dysfunctional outlooks might be presented to them in ways that could be construed as admissible. One could say that, from the clinician's standpoint, repertory grid technique is a marketing tool, a device to help 'sell' new worldviews. That it might also be a useful tool in market research and the design of sales campaigns is something which has not escaped the attention of the marketing profession. However, before considering the use that marketeers have made of the technique, it is useful to outline briefly how it works.

In its pure form, Kelly's repertory grid technique is unusual in that, unlike most attitude research devices, it attempts not to impose pre-selected dimensions of inquiry upon subjects. Suppose we want to understand how a person looks at cars. Grid technique begins by asking her to consider some (typically about ten) vehicles that she considers personally significant, possibly including her actual and ideal cars. The elements thus elicited are noted down on separate cards. The person will then be given combinations of cards, three at a time, and asked in what senses the cars are different or similar. By this means, constructs are elicited; for example, the consumer might say that 'Z and Y are *front-wheel-drive*, whereas X is *rear-wheel drive*'. When all the possible triadic combinations have been considered, the constructs are listed and the consumer will then be asked to rate all of the elements in terms of all of the constructs, in either a binary or scalar manner. The data matrix thus obtained may be processed, using factor analysis, principal components analysis or a variety of other procedures. (As Adams-Webber, 1979, p. 32, notes, 'during the last two decades there has been a remarkable proliferation of novel statistical techniques for analysing "repertory grid" data'.) With principal components analysis, for example, the *dimensions* that make up a particular subsystem may be identified. In this context, the term 'dimension' means more than just a single construct; it is often the case that some sets of constructs and elements will be particularly closely correlated in the mind of the decision maker, so that they can be thought of practically as separable wholes. For example, the data matrix might produce a strong set of correlations between certain 'performance-oriented' constructs and two particular vehicles, one of which scored consistently at one end of each of these construct axes, and one of which scored consistently at the other end. These two vehicles might well be the ones that the consumer would normally use as 'yardsticks' of good or bad performance when judging a third vehicle. Another strong set of construct/element correlations might concern, say, 'running economy'. But however tight or loose the relationships in the matrix, it will be unusual for there to be more than two or three significant dimensions and ten to fifteen constructs. Many seemingly 'obvious' constructs will often be absent, and repertory grid technique may help pinpoint gaps in a person's world-view.

Basic grid technique tells us nothing about construct rankings and, when used with consumer products, tends to provide 'perceptual constructs that are less representative of the underlying psychological dimensions that serve to differentiate products' (Reynolds and Gutman, 1984, p. 161). (When repertory grid technique is used with people as elements, the subject can be asked to include her actual and ideal 'selves' in the list of elements, and will tend to use more abstract constructs—for example 'cruel *versus* kind'—rather than merely referring to surface features such as 'tall *versus* short'.) To obtain such information, one needs to employ the 'construct laddering' and 'implication grid' techniques pioneered by Hinkle (1965), one of Kelly's graduate students (whose unpublished thesis is summarised in Bannister and Mair, 1968). For each of the constructs originally elicited, the subject is asked to explain which is her preferred pole (if she has not already done so by including her 'ideal' as an element). She is then asked why she prefers it. Sometimes the justification will refer to other 'concrete' constructs that may already be on the list: for example, 'I prefer cars with front-wheel drive because they usually have more room inside and are more economical because they are lighter in weight'. But often new personality-related dimensions are evoked: for example, 'I prefer new cars to used cars because you don't have to worry about whether or not they are roadworthy', or 'I prefer a car with good seats and a quiet ride at high speed because I don't then arrive at the end of a long journey feeling exhausted and irritable, and the family likewise'. The procedure can be repeated until new constructs cease to be evoked: there will come a point at which the laddering can go no higher because the consumer in effect says 'I prefer it because I do'—the limits of her reasoning, or as much as she is willing to reveal, thereby having been reached. For example, the consumer might say: 'I prefer not to get irritable because I end up losing control of myself—it's obvious why I prefer not to do that'. At this point, the researcher who tries to get the subject to go further is likely to run into the 'Garfinkel problem'.

From this enlarged set of constructs, an 'implication grid' can then be constructed, using the following technique. First, the researcher draws up an 'n by n' matrix for all the constructs. (One could envisage it being possible for this to be done automatically by a microcomputer in front of which the researcher and subject are seated, given appropriate software.) This matrix is then filled in by presenting one construct at a time to the subject and asking, 'If you *had* to change from being at one pole of this construct to being at the other pole, on which of the other constructs would a change also be necessary?' As Adams-Webber (1979, pp. 56–7) notes:

In this procedure each construct is paired successively with every other one twice, with any one of four outcomes: (1) a change in Construct A implies a change in Construct B, which is recorded as one 'superordinate' implication for A and one 'subordinate' implication for B; (2) a change in B implies a change in A, which is recorded as a 'superordinate' implication for B and a 'subordinate' implication for A; (3) a change in either construct implies a change in the other, which is recorded as a 'reciprocal' implication for both constructs; and (4) a change in either construct has no implications in terms of the other, in which case nothing is recorded.

Four people could thus possibly include an identical pair of constructs in their repertoires and yet provide the researcher with four different implicational results. To illustrate this possibly, I will have to depart from the motoring theme since, try as I might, I cannot think of a 'motoring' example which could work four ways. Let '*A*' refer to the construct 'fail to finish my doctorate *versus* obtain my doctorate', and let '*B*' refer to 'a non-academic job *versus* a lecturing job (when my research scholarship money runs out)'. Now imagine four people who would prefer to finish their doctorates and get lecturing jobs when their scholarships come to an end. We could then possibly have:

(1) person *W*, who believes that 'if I can't finish my doctorate, I won't be able to get a lecturing job, though not getting such a job wouldn't necessarily stop me from getting my doctorate finished eventually';

(2) person *X*, who believes that 'I'm not going to finish my doctorate before my money runs out and if I don't then get a job as a lecturer I'll never finish it, though fortunately it should not be necessary to have it finished in order to get a lectureship';

(3) person *Y*, who believes that 'if I couldn't finish my doctorate before my money ran out, I'd be stuck in a Catch-22 situation: I couldn't get a lecturing job without having finished my doctorate, but without the time that a lecturing job, unlike a non-academic one, allows for research, I'd never be able to finish it';

(4) person *Z*, who believes that 'if I couldn't finish my doctorate, it wouldn't necessarily stop me from getting a lecturing job, and if I had to try to finish my doctorate while working as something else, I can't see this would necessarily stop me from getting it'.

It should be noted that the wording of the question that is used to fill in an implication grid does not require a subject to specify how much of a change in a subordinate construct would be brought about by a polar switch in terms of a superordinate construct. The aim is simply to discover if one construct has some leverage over another. Of course, if one is dealing all the time with strictly dichotomous constructs, as opposed to scalar ones, a change in a subordinate construct is always a polar one. With scalar constructs, however, it is easy to envisage the technique being adapted to make it reveal the extent of leverage between pairs of constructs. Such a modification could prove very valuable in situations where one construct was subordinate to a group of others, each of which might change only partially at any one time.

Apart from the excellent work with the 'construct-laddering technique' carried out by Gutman and his colleagues (Olson and Reynolds, 1983, Reynolds and Gutman, 1983, 1984, Gutman and Alden, 1985, and Reynolds and Jamieson, 1985), the use of Kellian methods in market research seems hitherto to have failed to encompass the use of Hinkle's methodology. Rather, it has involved the use of factor analysis and principal components analysis of repertory grids, to discover: the distinctive dimensions of choice, whether or not already restricted repertoires of constructs can be further simplified due to some constructs having essentially the same meanings, and where particular products seem to fit into subjects' views in relation to their images of the 'ideal' and rival products. Frequently the main aim in marketing applications of Kellian techniques, aside from that of uncovering categorisation tendencies and the extent of blinkering, has been only to help segment a market into groups of potential customers who share broadly similar outlooks. This activity is known as 'psychographics', and an excellent review of it has been provided —largely in relation to work on US lifestyles—by Wells (1975). Lewis (1982, p. 64) has proposed a similar kind of role for repertory grid techniques in the context of research into attitudes towards state benefit and taxation systems, pointing out that, unlike many other research methods, it 'would go a long way towards shielding the respondent from interpretations imposed by the investigator'.

Although the scope of these consumer-oriented applications of the research methods of PCP looks narrow by comparison with the applications I can envisage, it is most heartening to see the growing interest in these techniques. However, before going on to examine still more of the theoretical territory that such tools open up to empirical exploration, it is important to note that, in the forms in which they are presently used, they leave something to be desired in contexts where subjects perceive uncertainty.

Repertory grid technique somewhat paradoxically attempts to uncover expectations without asking subjects to delimit the extent of their uncertainty in their constructs. Typically subjects are asked to locate each element on a point on each construct scale or on one or other pole of a strictly dichotomous construct axis. It would be more time consuming, yet by no means impossible, to ask subjects if they felt uncertain about how to rate elements in terms of the constructs they had evoked. Whenever they answered in the affirmative, they could be encouraged to define potential surprise curves for the construct axes and elements in question.

Second, we should note the care with which implication grids need to be constructed or interpreted if misleading conclusions are not to be drawn from them. Consider once more the doctorate/lectureship example. Person Z believes that a failure to finish her doctorate will not necessarily mean she cannot get a lecturing job. However, this does not necessarily mean that she believes doctorates and lectureships are unrelated; she could well believe that a failure to finish her doctorate could pose something of a barrier to getting a lectureship, even if it would not necessarily debar her from obtaining such a job. The point here is that the implication grid is not being constructed with reference to a construct such as 'helps *versus* hinders (my *chances* of getting a lecturing job)' but with reference to a construct that concerns the *type* of job. In the 'finished doctorate/chances of a lectureship' construct pairing, person Z might well have in mind a ranking of a deterministic kind, even if she does not see that the possession of a doctorate necessarily determines whether or not she can get a lectureship. Clearly, when constructs are differentiated from each other in this subtle kind of way, the researcher must record and interpret with great care her subjects' comments concerning likenesses and differences amongst elements. It would be only too easy to draw inappropriate inferences from sloppily defined constructs.

6.5 ENVIRONMENTAL TURBULENCE AND MENTAL ORGANISATION: THE EVOLVING CONSUMER (3)

The data contained in an implication grid are useful if we wish to understand how the person in question may feel if she sees her expectations being falsified, and how she might behave as a consequence. A perceived falsification is essentially a construction of a part of reality that is newly admitted by a person's construction system, at the cost of discarding a previously held, mutually exclusive expectation. The implications that the person will see as a result of admitting the falsification will depend on how she organises her ideas.

For example, suppose a person receives notification that she has not been successful in her application for a job she fully expected to get. She might, of course, be totally unable to believe the rejection letter and see it as a mistake or a hoax, continuing for the moment to believe she is going to get the job. But suppose she actually finds the rejection letter perfectly credible, albeit very surprising. Its implications might in some cases be seen by her in a positive manner; for example, not getting the job might be taken to imply no need to continue to suffer the anxieties of moving a long distance or having to play new workplace roles. However, she might construe many implications in negative terms; for example, she may no longer expect to be able to explore an exciting new environment a long way distant from where she presently lives, she may no longer expect to have consumer durables she had hoped to be able to buy, and she may see her self-image and social standing threatened by such reductions in her planned conspicuous consumption. Whether, and to what extent, the rejection letter comes as a relief or as a disappointment will depend on two things:

(1) on precisely how much leverage she allows a particular revised construct to exert over the constructs that she sees as being superordinate to it—for example, a forgone prospect of a particular means towards conspicuous consumption does not *have* to be seen as implying a crushing blow for her self- and social-esteem; for its role is a personal construct too, and she may judge that it is appropriate to see her self- and social-esteem as if they are dependent on a *variety* of things, combined in a particular way;

(2) on how she judges the *overall* implications—both positive and negative—of her changed assessment of her prospects related to the future she had previously imagined for herself.

Both of these issues take us back to the need to consider possible forms of rules for assessing possibilities (in this case: 'how I should see my failure to get the job', which could be seen in a variety of ways) when these have been made subordinate to a complex of other constructs. These rules are examined in detail in Chapters 7 and 8.

Ahead of a discussion of the forms such rules may take, we can presently notice that the consumer has it in her own power to manage her feelings of disappointment (or joy) in a world of surprises. She can determine the spill-over effects of changing any single construct via her choice of implicational *linkages*. Such a choice comes into the 'strategic' category and in considering it we may once again usefully draw parallels with Neil Kay's work on how choices of product portfolios may be taken by corporate planners with regard to the ways in which linkages between product markets affect prospects for corporate disappointments. Many kinds of 'mental strategies' are possible, but two potentially dysfunctional ones seem to serve to illustrate clearly the main dilemma with which consumers must grapple: I am thus going to introduce the 'schizophrenic consumer' and the 'obsessive–compulsive consumer'.

Consider first the case of a person who is disappointed by the fit of her constructs against her experience. She notices that it is the interrelationships between her expectations that are causing her to be particularly upset at what has happened. From the way she looks at things, the world seems a turbulent place that is going to continue to disappoint her unless she does something about her way of forming expectations. She decides that, even if she cannot form expectations that individually match her experience better, she can at least reduce her failure rate by reorganising her ideas in a way which cuts down the linkages between them. A search for new ways of looking at things may also seem likely to help. Such a change of mental strategy is akin to that of a corporation which diversifies in order to reduce its overall dependence on activities in which it had previously sunk resources in an attempt to obtain synergy. It is quite possible that the consumer's new strategy will be an improvement: she may find life much less stressful in prospect and, because any individual disappointment that she suffers is not a disaster for her, she has more time for carefree thoughts from which may emerge ideas that match her experience better than before. However, it *could* be that the strategy still leaves her in a state of confusion; since she has cut down on linkages between ideas and their associated activities, she may be even less able to form a coherent set of expectations. In particular, she may run into problems as a result of trying to acquire new constructs by experimenting in areas that are only loosely related to what she has done before.

In the latter case, it could be a dangerous move to repeat the strategy. Ordinal relationships between constructs are used as means of resolving conflicts and imposing bounds upon one's expectations. If a person removes such relationships, she is discarding ways of making up her mind. For example, suppose the consumer has hitherto made her expectation about whether or not she can engage successfully in particular acts of conspicuous consumption dependent solely upon her expectation concerning a particular job prospect. Now she severs the link. Not getting the job will no longer imply she cannot afford to buy the conspicuous consumption goods. But it will not imply she *can* buy them either. So she would then see that she might be perfectly able to afford them *and* that she might not. That she would then not be able to make up her mind might worry her if she has made her self-image strongly dependent upon the possibility of being able to engage successfuly in such conspicuous consumption. However, suppose she also severs this link. Then nothing would be implied about what kind of a person she is by whether or not she is able to engage successfully in conspicuous consumption. This means that it would not seem to *matter* to her whether or not she could really afford to buy the goods in question without suffering from financial ruin. She could get out her credit card and buy them without worrying about her ability to meet payments, but she would also have no need to engage in such expenditure, since its outcome would tell her nothing about the validity of her self-image construct. She might jump either way, on impulse.

Pushed to the extreme, a strategy of hedging one's mental bets will result in one possessing, not a construction system, but a mere bundle containing a large number of unrelated constructs. It would not seem to matter what one did or believed, so long as one kept one's expectations independent of each other—one would be making everything subordinate to the notion that the key to survival in a world of surprises is to stop single disappointments from having spill-over effects. One could end up being unable to dismiss all manner of 'fantastic' notions that most people would regard as crazy, and hence be diagnosed as suffering from 'thought-disordered schizophrenia'. Someone suffering from this condition finds it difficult to make any consistent, lasting judgements, as ideas flit through her mind. Studies of how such people think do indeed suggest that their minds may be characterised as having unusually large numbers of weakly correlated constructs—see Adams-Webber (1979). The mind of this kind of schizophrenic looks like the prototype of the 'spontaneous and erratic' mind that Coddington (1982) has alleged to lie at the centre of Shackle's (and other 'fundamentalist' Keynesians') analyses of expectations. Someone suffering from this condition needs to be trained to introduce some structure into her construct collection. Otherwise, as Adams-Webber (1979, p. 66, emphasis added) observes, 'The experience of such [a person], in so far as we can imagine it, must seem hopelessly *kaleidoscopic*'.

(Another route to such a state of confusion, which would also involve the victim having unusually large numbers of constructs, might begin with the consumer trying to conjure up or look around for possible consolations—positive implications—that could be made subordinate to negative outcomes of experimentation. It would then be something of a disappointment *not* to be disappointed. The consumer who had a very creative mind could end up being totally unable to rank rival action schemes, just as surely as if she had pursued the linkage-severing strategy. In fact, it is not inconceivable that someone might experiment with both strategies. Being able to think of the good and bad points of rival possibilities is a useful skill to have, unless one is always able to think of a few more 'plus points' as redeeming features of any possibility that is looking relatively difficult to take seriously.)

The polar extreme to thought-disordered schizophrenia is known as the 'obsessive–compulsive syndrome' (see Makhlouf-Norris and Norris, 1972). Here a person gets into difficulties as a result of constructing an overly integrated view of the world; when sufferers' construct subsystems are examined using principal components analysis what is usually discovered is either a single 'monolithic' cluster, in which everything is correlated very tightly, or a series of essentially segmented compact clusters of elements and constructs. The problem is that the sufferer has developed a view of the world in which there are very many reciprocal relationships between constructs, as well as one-way implicational relationships. Hence any failure to match expectations by one construct calls into question most of the person's other expectations in that area. The sufferer cannot rest with anything that is not absolutely in conformity with her expectations; if *some*thing is not 'just right', *every*thing seems a disaster. (The rock group 'The Police' included on their third album a song about precisely such a person, the title of which conjures up neatly the fragility of such a way of life: 'Canary in a Coalmine'.) In order to be able to weather the 'minor' upsets and disappointments of everyday life, and to allow what would normally be regarded as minor 'fires' to burn unattended, such thinkers need to be trained to sever some of the linkages between their constructs and generally loosen up their ways of thinking—in other words, they need to be trained to introduce more permeability into their construction systems (see the discussion of problems with 'conjunctive' choice rules in section 7.4). In the absence of such therapy, someone suffering from this syndrome is likely to find life very difficult. She is likely to make a supremely accurate clerk; unfortunately, she is also likely to be completely unable to get to work on time because her appearance and the house she leaves behind must be absolutely spotless and in order before she can feel secure.

While these two dysfunctional syndromes are rather unusual, they arise from extreme applications of modes of thought that we all tend to employ in some degree as consumers. In section 6.4, I noted how principal components analyses of construct subsystems reveal that people normally tie referential elements and constructs together in a strictly limited number of dimensional clusters. Within these clusters, the invalidation of a particular way of construing things could be expected to have spill-over effects on other constructs—the more so the more closely correlated any of these are with the invalidated one. But so long as a person has other dimensions of thought and other, essentially separate construct subsystems, such an invalidation will not wreck her expectations (her life) completely. Even within a damaged dimension, the correlations are not usually total, so even when a person loses a major reference point or assumption, she may be able to find some starting points for putting the fragments back together again. Moreover, as the work of Makhlouf-Norris and Norris (1972) shows, the construct subsystems of 'normal' people—in contrast to those of obsessive–compulsives—usually each contain some degree of articulation between dimensional clusters. That is to say, some constructs will be correlated with more than one cluster, implying that the person has more than one way of deciding how events should be fitted against such attached 'articulating' constructs; in other words, she has 'another way of looking at things' in the face of disappointments that destroy one of the clusters.

This pattern—of partially correlated groupings of elements and constructs, with tendencies for articulation between some constructs—has an obvious parallel in the mixed synergistic/hedging patterns identified by Kay (1982, 1984) in respect of business themes and activities in corporate strategies. People, like firms, *usually* exploit to some extent the potential for conceptual linkages, but they also partly hedge their expectational bets as they do so. In some construction subsystems they may build up their expectations around a variety of loosely connected themes, yet in others they may integrate their ideas rather tightly—as with the person who sees nothing wrong with letting her house and style of dress look a shambles, yet insists fanatically on keeping up with the 'state of the art' in 'hi-fi' equipment. Or they may be consistent in the degree to which they tie their ideas together. By such choices of ways of looking at the world, people seek to predict and control events; but some people, like some companies, fail to select viable strategies.

It would seem reasonable to hypothesise that, as a result of experiences in different kinds of environments, people may often come to believe that the more turbulent an environment seems the wiser it is to avoid creating large numbers of expectational linkages (especially reciprocal ones), and the more sense it makes to be ready to take life as it comes. Their choices of activities and kinds of household relationships will reflect these patterns of thought. To the extent that people are slow to recognise that some areas of their lives are becoming more turbulent, they may suffer disappointments and stress before they adjust accordingly their strategies for thinking. When they do make these adjustments they will not usually end up in a state of thought-disordered schizophrenia. However, their choices of activities may seem increasingly to lack consistent themes or to be based less upon strongly held values (aside from 'flexibility' or 'independence');

they will seem less obsessive in these turbulent areas than before, less willing to commit themselves. But not all people will conclude that this is how one should face up to turbulent environments that are costly to avoid. Some may see dangers in seeking to avoid disappointments by avoiding forming expectations. In particular, it may seem unwise not to set goals in one's life (a goal essentially being an expectation of what one might achieve in a particular area), since, without something at which to aim, one may avoid disappointment at the cost of simply drifting around. Some people may see themselves as more than usually able to determine what happens, instead of becoming victims of their circumstances. They may therefore be willing to let many of their expectations 'revolve around' a few strong assumptions.

An example from the business history literature may serve not only to illustrate how vulnerable to mugging someone with an integrated, one-dimensional mental strategy may be, but also to provide a bridge to the next section, which is concerned with barriers to changes of mind. It concerns the career of Lee Iacocca, the present head of Chrysler. Having unexpectedly been fired by Henry Ford II, Iacocca found the ideas of early retirement, or life outside the car industry, unthinkable. Moritz and Seaman (1981, p. 213, emphasis added) capture his world-view vividly:

It didn't take Iacocca long to conclude that what he wanted most was to get back to the automobile business. As broadly applicable as his marketing skills might be, they were, for him, built around a love for cars. He was *not a very diversified man*. He'd done some things for the Boy Scouts and was, because of his wife's long affliction, an active member of the American Diabetes Association and related groups; he was a trustee of Lehigh—but almost everything else he did revolved around his family or the automobile business. He lived and breathed cars. Even working for an automotive supply company like Dana or Bendix or Budd couldn't have satisfied him. 'I had to be in the mainstream of the car business', he recalled. 'That's where I'd spend my life.... It's like a guy saying "Gee, you're a good musician—you can play the piano. Why don't you try the saxophone?"'

There is an ironic, but obvious, parallel between Lee Iacocca's reluctance to change direction when Henry Ford II's action of firing him threatened to destroy his expectations, and the reaction of Henry Ford I in the face of consumers whose switch away from the Model T Ford in 1926 threatened to destroy his business. Just as Iacocca had built his life around cars, so Ford had created an integrated production process that was specific to the Model T and which was only reluctantly abandoned. Ford's assembly lines, foundries and machine shops were not suited to the Model A, still less to the annual replacement of entire ranges of products. During the eighteen-month changeover, Ford lost $200m and laid off 60,000 workers in Detroit; 15,000 machine tools had to be replaced and another 25,000 had totally to be rebuilt. Furthermore, as Selzick (1957, p. 110) notes, 'even this did not bring about the changes in orientation, with attendant upward revisions in the status of sales and public relations activities, that were required. Only after World War II was a reorganisation in depth completed'. If Iacocca had not been able to get back into the mainstream of the car industry, the effect of losing his job with Ford would have been similarly traumatic for his personality. It was his good fortune that Chrysler's top management were having trouble making their own expectations come true in the turbulent world of the automotive industry.

6.6 RESISTANCE TO CHANGE

When a person is surprised by an inadequate match between her expectations and her impressions of reality, she might be expected to be receptive to new ways of looking at the world—ways that offer the prospect of an enhanced ability to anticipate events. Bannister and Mair (1968, p. 211) have hypothesised that the elaboration of new constructs and construct relationships is initiated—as was suggested in respect of the problem of thought-disordered schizophrenia—by attempts to understand inconsistencies generated by existing patterns of thought. Likewise, Adams-Webber (1970, p. 39) argues that people restructure their construction systems in attempting to accommodate ambiguities. However, such changes of outlook and of associated activities may often be resisted, even if they are being suggested by helpful friends and media sources and not by seemingly biased salespersons. In this respect, the inertia of consumers parallels that identified in academic science when new paradigms emerge (see Kuhn, 1970) and in large corporations when major organisational restructurings or changes of activity are proposed in times of difficulties (see Chandler, 1962, and Earl, 1984, Chapter 5). Such resistance can be understood in a variety of ways.

When her expectations are falsified, the consumer's first task is to decide what kind of problem she is up against. This initial decision may take her a good deal of time to reach, since she has to deal with something known to philosophers of science as the Duhem–Quine problem (after Duhem, 1906, and Quine, 1951). She cannot simply say that *one* of her beliefs has been refuted, even if *its* predictions have not materialised, for she is always testing a complex of theories: her assumptions may involve the use of further theories, while her test techniques and interpretations of results certainly will. Thus the Duhem–Quine thesis holds that, if a particular idea is apparently contradicted by events, there may be nothing wrong with it as such; it may merely be that part of the theoretical apparatus used to test it is not behaving in the expected ways. For example, suppose our consumer keeps finding that her car requires expensive repairs. This does not mean that she must necessarily revise her view of it and construe it as a 'lemon'. It could simply be that she is unknowingly allowing it to be 'fixed' by an incompetent or dishonest garage. Like an academic scientist, an inquiring consumer can only say that a particular *set* of theories she holds is or is not inconsistent with a particular body of evidence framed in the light of some of the theories in this set. There is no way of knowing for sure which part of her world-view needs to be reconstructed, or whether the whole (sub)system is obsolete. Our motoring consumer might simply need to change her favoured garage, but she might really have a lemon, or even a lemon whose performance is made worse than need be by the garage she uses.

In order to avoid letting this problem paralyse her, the consumer will sooner or later bring into play her self-imposed rules for resolving inconsistencies in her construction system; for example, she may conclude that 'I think my car is the problem, not the garage, because the latter has serviced all my previous vehicles, and many owned by my friends, without there being trouble on such a scale; I can't believe the garage's standards have suddenly slipped, since it's still the same old family business'. Here we might note that this way round the Duhem–Quine problem, embodied for 'man the scientist' in the organisation and modulation corollaries of Kelly's theory of personality, is very similar to the analysis put forward by Lakatos (1970) in respect of the behavior of academic scientists. Lakatos argues that the scientist is not driven back to first principles by each new anomaly she discovers. Rather, she operates according to a 'scientific research programme', divided into two sections: a 'hard core' and a 'protective belt' (Lakatos, 1970, pp. 132–7). The former is a set of propositions and procedures which the scientist makes a dogmatic methodological decision not to lay open to empirical challenges. The latter is the body of 'auxiliary' hypotheses which she is prepared to modify in the face of empirical observations or perceived logical difficulties. If necessary, she is prepared to make *ad hoc* modifications to auxiliary hypotheses, though if this is the best she can do, Lakatos (1970, p. 118) would describe her research programme as 'degenerating'. Remenyi (1979) has taken these ideas further, postulating that scientific subdisciplines, existing within the main core's protective belt, will have their own 'demi-cores' and associated protective belts of auxiliary theories—these are the analogue of Kelly's construct subsystems. Thus the Lakatosian view is of research programmes as hierarchical groupings of theories, with their users proceeding on the basis that their ways of looking at things are not rotten to their hard cores if things appear not quite to fit. The protective belt serves as a buffer against changes in its respective (demi-)core. Reality may dent the belt by forcing adjustments to auxiliary hypotheses but it is not allowed to challenge core notions.

A second source of delay in the consumer starting to become seriously interested in new ideas is that even once she has decided *what* is in doubt, she may still believe that she has not yet got an adequate basis for concluding that things are *bad enough* for her to be well advised to consider alternatives. What might be seen by an obsessive-compulsive as a major source of alarm might come well within the bounds of tolerance of another thinker. For example, a rapid succession of automotive repair bills might be taken as symptomatic of enormous potential for future bills; or such a collection of bills might come as only a moderate surprise to the consumer and, having incurred them, she might judge that she is now very likely set up nicely for a period of trouble-free motoring. But it is by no means easy to decide how brittle to make one's expectations. An 'obsessive-compulsive' motorist may lose thousands if she switches her car at the first sign of trouble or (by way of insurance) the moment its warranty runs out; yet, at the other extreme, one can equally lose a fortune by motoring in the belief that one's present car is not a lemon and is worth investing in to keep it in good order. The latter strategy is one which it is particularly difficult to demonstrate to have been a failure. Between the beginning and the end of a motoring year, the consumer may end up spending more on repairs than it would have cost her to switch at the outset to a vehicle guaranteed to be free of repair bills. Members of her reference group may point this out to her and argue she has made a mistake. If her construction system does not admit the idea that she could be fallible in this respect, then she can try to demonstrate her decision-making competence by continuing her policy for a further year; it may *then* become apparent that the total cost of repairs would have been less than the total cost of guaranteeing repair-free motoring for two years. If she is still down by the end of the second year, she can still try to demonstrate that her policy is cheaper than an 'obsessive one', by spending yet more (see Wolf, 1970, 1973). (Both extremes of behaviour might seem 'crazy' to someone who employs the policy of buying a three-year-old car each year and keeping it for only a year, regardless of the bills—which in some years may be very high—incurred in the year of ownership.)

A third reason for resisting new ideas, when existing ones are being called into question, is that new modes of thought and possible action-schemes cannot be costlessly evaluated or assimilated, even when pertinent information is 'freely' available. There are a number of sides to these costs. First it should be recognised that, if a person is busy trying to change herself, she is forgoing opportunities to devote her attention to problems that still seem amenable to control with the aid of procedures from her imperfect construction system/research programme. There is no point in trying to learn about a superior way of coping with the future if one's life disintegrates in the interim. The significance of this barrier to change will depend upon how brittle one makes one's expectations and upon how many negative implications would seem to follow from their disconfirmation. An 'obsessive–compulsive' will see alarming 'fires' forever breaking out in her life. She will thus not feel able to stand back and try to work out a more fireproof way of forming expectations; she will not even feel free to examine the extent to which it is the inadequacy of her present way of seeing how to fight the fires of everyday life that enables them to keep flaring up afresh. (For parallels in corporate behaviour, see Radner, 1975, and Sir Michael Edwardes', 1983, especially pp. 75, 282, account of his stressful life at British Leyland.)

A second feature looming large in any consideration of the costs of changing one's mind is the possibility that one could end up investing a good deal in a new way of looking at the world, only to find that it, too, has weaknesses as a way of anticipating events. This is something that Lakatos (1970, p. 155) neglects in setting out conditions under which a new research programme will be adopted. He suggests that this will happen if the new way of proceeding can offer excess empirical content (in Kellian terms: 'a wider range of convenience') while also explaining how the past successes of the old one were achieved. The trouble is that it is not obvious that the research programme which has seemingly fitted events best in the past will continue to do so in the future; science has a tendency, not unlike that in fashions of dress, to go round in circles as old research programmes in somewhat revamped forms acquire seemingly improved explanatory powers (see Robertson's, 1956, p. 81, famous analogy between high-brow opinion and a hunted hare, and note also the end of section 9.2). Such considerations may mean that potential for 'excess empirical content' remains undiscovered. For although her current research programme is not entirely satisfactory, a decision maker may feel justified in devoting her philosophical energies to examining how it might be made to perform better, rather than to exploring radically different alternatives: better 'the devil you know' than to 'jump out of the frying pan and into the fire'.

As a person assesses possible costs of changing her ways of thinking, she might not unreasonably be expected to see them as positively correlated with the number of subordinate expectations that she has attached to the construct(s) currently being called into question. If so, she would be more likely to invest in trying to see a way of making a superordinate construct fit reality—instead of looking for an alternative way of forming constructs presently deemed subordinate to it—the more subordinate implications she has attached to it. In other words, we should expect to find that resistance to change in respect of a particular construct is a function of the number of expectations it carries. Precisely such a finding emerged in Hinkle's (1965) original work with implication grids. As well as using the 'implication grid technique' to uncover the number of findings that would result from a polar change for each construct, Hinkle elicited from each of his subjects a 'resistance-to-change ranking' of constructs. The method involved presenting each subject with all the possible pairs of constructs from the larger sets they had evoked, and asking, 'on which of these two constructs would you prefer to remain with respect to, if you *had* to change in terms of only one of them?' (For example, 'you say you would prefer to be kind rather than cruel, and generous rather than mean, but if you could be only one of these, which one would you prefer to be?') Constructs were then ranked from lowest to highest according to the number of times they had been designated for 'no change'. Support for Hinkle's results is to be found in the work of Crockett and Meisel (1974), which combined implication grid technique with experiments that provided subjects with bogus feedback against their expectations. As Crockett and Meisel (1974, p. 298) point out, on more than one occasion subjects faced with inconsistencies to resolve were heard to remark, 'if I change this, I'll have to change practically everything'.

Lee Iacocca's view of what he *had* to do after being fired from the Ford Motor Company is a particularly dramatic illustration of how people may resist ideas of change when they lack suitable constructs to replace those they would be giving up. However, implicational linkages between constructs may quite often be such that seemingly 'minor' changes of expectations would have all manner of spill-over effects and involve a great need to restructure one's life. A strategically minded consumer of the kind discussed in the previous section might not always be aware of major assumptions around which she has allowed her life to revolve. This is because the social processes whereby people acquire ideas may often work in such a way that people pick up expectations without realising what these *could* imply and the constructs to which they *could* be subordinate within the rules of their construction systems. Only in the face of anomalies may they have such possibilities brought to their attention. As they consider them, they may be horrified by what they see.

For example, many people expect that, in their main meal of the day, they will normally eat meat, despite the fact that this is by no means intrinsic to the nature of such a meal. Now let enter the strict vegetarian, who refuses to consume meat as well as any other animal products. Most people find such a person's behaviour quite perplexing, all the more so once they have made the deviant give justifications for her actions. The vegetarian may point out that (1) the conventional picture of a meal is based on the tacit assumption that it is entirely acceptable to exploit and slaughter animals for human gratification; and (2) that she does not see herself as someone who can eat food prepared at such a cost when it is (a) *unnecessary* for humans to consume animal products, (b) *technologically inefficient* and (c) *selfish* to do so, given the low vegetation/animal conversion ratio and the millions who are starving in a world which would comfortably give all an adequate vegetarian diet. For the vegetarian to behave in the conventional manner could therefore be seen by her as an act which would call into question her view of herself as someone who is not selfish and respects the right to life. If omnivorous consumers also see themselves as non-selfish people who respect the right to life, we might expect them to be swift converts to the vegetarian lifestyle. However, a consideration of the implications of such a change may lead them to see that they could suffer other kinds of self-image confusion and the opening up of all manner of gaping holes in their abilities to cope with the world. For example, their possible choices of restaurants, clothes, shoes, shopping routines, cosmetics, cars (no more 'luxury' hide interiors and leather-bound steering wheels), holiday accommodation, and so on, will be greatly constricted, whilst their existing knowledge of cookery will be rendered largely obsolete (even 'beans on toast' isn't as simple as all that, since most bread uses animal shortening!); they may also envisage a shrinking social life (fewer dinner party invitations, for example) and the need to be able to deal with frequent demands for self-justification.

Thus having started with a simple, 'minor' matter involving a challenge to a construction of the nature of a meal, we now find the omnivorous consumer considering things that matter to her a good deal. She essentially has to ask herself whether she finds it either (1) easier in prospect to suffer what she presently sees as damage to her self-image owing to forgone luxuries, and to suffer anxiety whilst learning how to be a vegetarian, or (2) easier in prospect to suffer guilty doubts about her view of herself as a someone who is not selfish and respects the right to life. Caught thus on the horns of a dilemma, she might choose either way, depending on the rules of her system. Experience suggests that in situations where the omnivore elects not to change, she either refuses to justify her position to inquisitive vegetarians or cultivates the skill of putting forward anti-vegetarian arguments that are often *ad hoc* and include the following: 'at least *I'd* never stoop to ordering lobsters that are cooked live, and *I* don't waste a scrap of meat, since I put all the leftovers in soups'; or 'but if I give up eating meat and dairy products, the animals won't be bred and get to live even for a short period'; or 'what about the rights of a farmer to a livelihood: how can you say that her happiness and that of her customers is not increased by more than the happiness animals lose in factory farms and slaughterhouses?'; and 'don't plants and agricultural pests have rights too?' Thereby such consumers seek to avoid feeling guilty as they resist the costs of changing their lifestyles.

These arguments are not without their practical implications for those involved in marketing. It would appear that, if a seemingly minor change of activity could actually require a consumer to make a major change of mind, it will be difficult for a marketing strategy to produce such a change unless:

(1) the consumer's attention can be kept away from considering implications that she has not yet construed yet which she would be liable to see as destructive (once the person has committed herself to the new way of thinking, and the products it entails, she may *then* wake up to problematical implications and yet carry on with her new philosophy because a reversion to her original one would carry even more difficulties);

(2) it can be demonstrated to the consumer that a failure to change her way of thinking will cause much greater damage to her subordinate construct groupings than she would suffer by changing;

(3) the consumer can be provided with a comprehensive new way of looking at things, which repairs the damage which

an initial change of outlook and behaviour would trigger off via linkages amongst constructs and construct subsystems.

My earlier (section 4.4) arguments about the use of marketing ploys that relate to guilt and anxiety may now be seen to have substantial theoretical underpinnings.

6.7 CONCLUSION

In this chapter I have attempted to show that although the world with which consumers may have to contend may be highly fluid, they usually attempt to think about how to deal with it in ways that are systematic. With the aid of self-constructed networks of rules for forming expectations and for amending them in the light of experience, they come to 'see' that some actions are preferable to others. These networks of rules effectively serve to ensure that, no matter how carefully they think about what they do, their choices are, in an important sense, programmed. People run their lives according to different programmes because they started out with different elementary principles and in different environments, with different capacities for handling interdependencies and making connections (one might say: 'different mental hardware'), and because, partly as a result of how they started, they have had differing histories, which have impacted upon the outlooks they have evolved. They will thus differ in their expectations, including those concerning which activities they can safely and profitably undertake—just as firms with different histories, self-perceived capacities and planning departments will evolve different strategies for coping with the world of business. These differences, which encompass differences in capacities for originative thought, will mean that, at best, the resource-constrained market researcher is only going to be able to attempt approximately to anticipate the behaviour of broad groups of consumers comprising individuals whose judgemental systems have a good deal in common. However, the researcher's task owes its very feasibility to the resilience of judgemental rules that competent decision makers select as means for thinking about choice environments that are often highly turbulent. As Heiner (1983) has argued, prediction would be impossible if people did not employ simplifying rules for coping with change and instead always adapted perfectly to each new situation.

The arguments in this chapter may also enable us to see more precisely what Kelly had in mind in suggesting that it may be useful to see people as if they were trying to 'predict and *control*' events. Until now, I have not explicitly noted that, according to Kelly (1955, p. 525), a person is 'in control' if she is able to extend the range of convenience of her predictive system while maintaining its essential features intact. The discussions of implicational relationships between constructs reveal what is meant by 'essential features': a person is losing control when, in order to preserve her highest-ranking ideas, she finds herself having to admit expectations that destroy fairly high-ranking constructs (rank being dependent on the number of superordinate implications a construct carries), yet which do not bring with themselves admissible new ways of theorising about the events whose previous images have been demolished. In such a situation, she will suffer from anxiety and will attempt to avoid admitting such possibilities; that is, she will behave in a hostile manner, seeking to reconcile them with her expectations by contorting them if need be, until things get so twisted and/or complicated to hold together that she crosses a self-imposed threshold of tolerance and recognises (is converted to) the idea that it is easier to reorganise her system of thought than to prop it up with *ad hoc* arguments.

The more a consumer is able to envisage losing control in her present environment, the more she will seek to develop a predictive system which may enable her to establish control in new territories. Even if the imagined difficulties do not materialise, such experimentation at least enlarges her experience, her knowledge. In deciding quite where and how to experiment, the consumer faces a problem similar to that which confronts a firm when it cannot take it for granted that its products' lifecycles will not suddenly be truncated; on the one hand, it can be dangerous to pin many expectations on only a few ideas, or to make them highly interdependent, but on the other the costs of avoiding integration by compartmentalising ideas and activities may be a loss of insight and a failure to achieve control. However, the consumer, like the firm, needs *some* principles for thought if she is not to become overwhelmed by a raging sea of seemingly believable but forever kaleidoscopically changing thoughts.

The scope for empirical work in relation to the ideas expressed in this chapter seems considerable, especially given that the theoretical ideas are so closely bound up with the techniques of repertory grid and implication grid analysis. I would strongly urge readers to examine the pioneering studies by Gutman and his colleagues, referred to in section 6.4. It would be interesting to go beyond these to see how far mental attempts to hedge or exploit scope for linking expectations are associated not merely with anticipated environmental turbulence, but also:

(1) with the degree of environmental turbulence that a consumer has experienced in the past (other things equal, people with stable backgrounds would be expected to be less likely to be 'mental hedgers');

(2) directly with hedging and synergy at the level of physical choices. Here one might conveniently investigate, for example, the relationships between the structures of university students' construct subsystems pertaining to their record collections and the degree of diversity in these collections. People with 'obsessively' structured collections would be expected to have more tightly correlated sets of constructs than others with similarly sized but 'schizophrenic' collections that sample a wide variety of artists and styles of music. Investigations of such subjects' 'record subsystems' and physical collections over a number of years, or the study of their own accounts of how they evolved them, might also be revealing in strategic terms and could shed some light on (1) above. Records are a particularly interesting product to investigate from this standpoint, since the record market is highly turbulent and pervaded by fashions and peer pressure amongst consumers.

If the second kind of research involved the compilation of implication grids as well as repertory grids (preferably repertory grids enlarged via the construct-laddering technique), resistance to change could be studied in relation to cognitive structures. For example, if studying 'record-collecting strategies', one might seek to explore why some people vehemently resist opera, and others avoid rock, reggae or 'new wave'. One might even use implication grids from samples of university economists to test my (1983a, especially pp. 102–3) analysis of the reasons for resistance to behavioural theory amongst the bulk of the economics profession. Instead of starting out with repertory grids for consumer products, one could begin by getting economists to compare and contrast the seven economics research programmes mentioned in section 1.2.

7 Complexity and Tests of Adequacy

7.1 INTRODUCTION

Having studied the nature of consumer motivation, the kinds of choices that may be undertaken and the origins of expectations, we are at last ready to consider how deliberating consumers come to rank mutually exclusive action schemes in order of attractiveness. There is an obvious sense in which, after venturing outside the normal realm of the economics of consumer behaviour, we are back on familiar ground and are about to produce an analysis comparable with that discussed in Chapter 2. However, orthodox economists would be unwise to permit themselves a sigh of relief at this prospect, for they are about to have their core tenets challenged from two new directions.

As in the previous chapter, we are going to be concerned essentially with judgemental processes: I want to uncover the rules—the choice heuristics—that deliberating consumers use to reach verdicts concerning the actions they should undertake. These rules should be seen as devices for handling confrontations between the consumer's theories predicting particular possible properties of rival action schemes, and her theories predicting what it is appropriate for her to expect to be able to obtain. The rules are members of the set of expectation-forming judgemental rules according to which she organises her life, which was outlined in Chapter 6. However, although we already understand how rule-hierarchies determine verdicts concerning degrees of disbelief in possible events (for example, 'could scheme X be better for me than scheme Y?'), the analysis from Chapter 6 is insufficient to explain how rankings are worked out. The deficiency is simple to see: while I have argued that expectations are assigned degrees of belief by the consumer's hierarchy of rules, I have not considered the *forms* that these rules might take. In terms of our analogy with the judicial system, the point is still more obvious: the appeal court may be superordinate to the criminal court and hence able to pronounce on whether disputed verdicts of the latter are to be accepted, yet there are many different forms the two ruling bodies could each take. A criminal court jury, for example, might contain twelve members, with unanimity being required for each verdict; but it might be constituted in a different manner, with a different number of members, a simple majority of whom could determine the verdict. In the present chapter I will examine the possible shapes of rules that determine a person's preferences, and suggest why some shapes might be more easily disbelieved than others.

The rest of the chapter is structured as follows. Section 7.2 sets out the nature of the evaluation problem in relation to the decision maker's evolving construct system. Section 7.3 considers possible choice heuristics that are variations on the ideas discussed in Chapter 2, and notes some of their problems. Section 7.4 then examines rules that do not involve the notion of compensation amongst attributes. I am by no means the first to make this departure from neoclassical notions of substitution in order to discuss choice in terms of 'priorities'. However, these previous attempts have not met with widespread acceptance, so in proposing this kind of analysis once again I have the task of doing so in a different, more convincing way. Therefore, in sections 7.5 to 7.7, I will consider some refinements to the basic ideas of section 7.4. The conclusion, section 7.8, may come as something as a surprise after my spirited attempts to develop non-compensatory rules, for it suggests that it may be unwise to argue in favour of any *one* rule, compensatory or otherwise.

7.2 THE CHOICE MATRIX AND ITS IMPLICATIONS

Once a consumer has formed her expectations about the nature of her options, we might usefully see her task consisting in processing information underlain by what might be called her 'choice matrix'. This matrix may actually exist on paper—for example, as a data chart in a consumer magazine in front of the decision maker—or it may exist only in the consumer's mind, as something which could be uncovered through an application of repertory grid technique. The columns (or rows) are headed with the characteristics the consumer sees the action schemes to possess, and one row (or one column) is assigned to each scheme. For purposes of this chapter, we may keep things simple and imagine that the consumer does not have in mind any uncertainty as to the characteristics associated with each scheme; rules for dealing with uncertain prospects are considered in Chapter 8.

Brick versus weatherboard
Tiled versus tin roof
Western shore versus eastern shore (of the Derwent estuary)
House versus apartment
Three versus two bedrooms
Separate laundry versus laundry in bathroom
White goods included versus white goods excluded
Built-ins versus need to buy wardrobes
Detached versus semi-detached
Wood/coal versus oil heating
Mountain versus water views
Ergonomically sound kitchen versus cluttered kitchen
Striking versus dull styling
Large versus small
Good versus tasteless/tatty decorative order
Well-developed versus neglected garden
Well-drained versus prone to dampness
Expensive versus cheap

Figure 7.1: House-buying constructs

In order to provide a focus for the analysis, I would like readers to consider a choice matrix from my own experience—the task of house hunting on my arrival in Hobart. In all, I visited twenty-five properties in the space of two weeks, and the eighteen constructs in terms of which I evaluated them are listed in Figure 7.1. There are several things to be noted here. First: an eighteen by twenty-five matrix is a very demanding information structure for a boundedly rational consumer to be able to handle. I have an excellent memory, yet as my search progressed I was becoming increasingly confused and driven to take notes on what I was seeing; also, the whole process became very stressful and tiring, even despite the fact that I had already pruned down my list of options to twenty-five by rejecting many properties as 'not worth looking at', purely on the basis of a paper evaluation. Such problems arose because I was trying to flout Miller's (1956) empirical rule, that people can keep in mind at once only seven, plus or minus two, things, and because this was my second time in the business of house-purchase, so there was much I knew I must look for. Often, consumer choice matrices will be much more restricted—for example, ten characteristics and half a dozen options.

Second, it should be recognised that even a restricted matrix exists within an hierarchical context. Quite often, the constructs in Figure 7.1 actually concern other elements (construction materials, cupboards, water views, and so on) which are themselves complex configurations of constructs. Quite a few of the constructs are actually superordinate to common constructs not on the list: many are constructs that in my mind determine how time consuming it could be to own a particular property (because they determine how much time I will need to spend on travel to work, gardening, decorating, getting the place warm in winter, and so on); many seem to affect how much it could cost in pecuniary terms to live in a particular property, or how easy it might be to resell. Some of the constructs are superordinate to several others, but not all such constructs are superordinate to the same sets: for example, which side of the river a property is located affects my travel time to the university, while my time is also affected by the state of the decor; however, the state of decor does not in large measure determine whether or not it is possible to enjoy a sunny aspect along with a good water view *and* a good mountain view, but location on a particular side of the Derwent river certainly does.

On the surface, it would appear that some characteristics related to constructs in my choice matrix are intrinsically uncommensurable (how can one compare time savings and views, for example?). This will frequently appear to be so, and in my earlier work I have used this observation to argue against choice rules, of the kind discussed in the next section, that involve the aggregation of values. In the context of a car-purchase decision, for example, I could imagine a consumer being able to compute overall running costs, using estimates of depreciation, and insurance, fuel and maintenance costs. All of these economy related characteristics could be dealt with on paper, or with a calculator, in terms of money. I could also imagine the consumer being able to aggregate elements of style, such as interior decor and outward appearance. I found it rather more difficult to admit the possibility that the lay consumer might try to add together features that would have some bearing upon a vehicle's ability to provide driving excitement, if this happened to be desired. (I was quite prepared to concede that, the greater the consumer's expertise as a driver, the more likely it is that she might appreciate how elements such as acceleration, road-holding and braking interact to shape the overall performance of a car.) But I could not see how these different dimensions' scores might meaningfully be compared unless the consumer could ultimately reduce them all to units of what, for want of a better word, might be called 'utility'.

But now I can see a better word, a common unit: this unit is 'the implication', as discussed in section 6.4, in Hinkle's (1965) use of the word. I have depicted the consumer as trying to build up a system which she can use to predict and control events in a satisfactory manner. Her choices matter to her because, and in so far as, they seem to have constructive or destructive implications for the system of expectations she is trying to develop. In deliberating, she will try to assess the consequences of committing herself to a different consumption pathway from that around which she has thus far constructed her expectations. Compared with this 'no change' reference point, she may construe possible new courses of action as having arrays of implications—usually both positive and negative for each scheme—for the development of her system for coping with life. In so far as she construes schemes differently, she will have attached different patterns of implications to them. Given our analysis of motivation, it is natural to argue that, *if the consumer can see these overall patterns of implications*, she will rank her perceived options according to their net (that is, constructive minus destructive) implications relative to her 'no change of pathway' point of view, and she will be indifferent between schemes that she construes as having identical 'net implications' scores even if the patterns of their implications are very different. We could use the research methods described in section 6.4 to gather data from which we could infer not merely these implicational tallies but also relative total scores of rival options, and attribute weightings, in expectancy value models of the kind examined in section 2.6. Such arguments raise two key questions:

(1) Given the ways in which a consumer has construed the implications of rival action schemes, can she in practice see each scheme's overall implications?
(2) If, on occasion, the consumer has in mind a choice matrix of sufficient complexity as to prevent her from seeing overall implications, how, then, might she come to rank rival action schemes?

7.3 COMPENSATORY RULES

The procedures according to which a boundedly rational consumer *might* evaluate rival action schemes could take many forms, yet they will have a variety of things in common. They must, for reasons earlier explained, involve satisficing rather than optimisation, with choices being made from restricted agendas of options. They will also each imply terms upon which one kind of characteristic yield will be willingly compromised to obtained another. In this section, I will consider rules that enable schemes with poor performances in some respects the chance of dominating because they offer adequate or exemplary performances in other respects.

(1) A Satisficing Expectancy Value Rule

This is essentially a trade-off approach to evaluation, of the kind discussed in Chapter 2 and alluded to in section 7.2. It only involves satisficing in the sense that, after requiring that the decision maker works out a set of overall (implicational) scores for the schemes on her agenda, it involves her in asking whether the highest of these scores is 'high enough'. If the answer is 'yes' she is not prompted to engage in search. For such a rule to be practically applicable, the decision maker must have:
(a) the ability to assign options to expected places on performance axes;
(b) the ability to transform the impacts of having more or less of a particular characteristic into scalar ratings in terms of a common numeraire;
(c) adequate computational powers.

In some contexts, these conditions may certainly all be present. The example of choices in design engineering makes this clear, as Steinbruner (1974, p. 104) points out:

A ship designer is aware of the characteristics of water which make it necessary for him to increase the power he designs into his ship as a cube of the increase in its speed he might desire. This involves him in complex trade-offs with cost, range, fuel consumption, displacement, etc., which he constantly juggles with the aid of very explicit calculations.

The discussion at the end of section 7.2 should make it clear that I do not see condition (b) as an insuperable requirement; but the other conditions are by no means guaranteed. At best, a person's choice matrix is going to be only as detailed as her limited repertoire of her constructs and their limited ranges of convenience will admit. *This* is not a problem as far as being able to reach a decision is concerned; but a real difficulty arises when the decision maker 'hasn't got a clue' as to how she should construe things in certain dimensions. Here, condition (a) is violated and it can only be reinstated if the consumer can employ a subsidiary procedure (see section 8.6) to assign scores to each of the problem dimensions, or if she is prepared to disregard dimensions where she cannot make *some* kind of assessment. As far as condition (c) is concerned, the quotations at the end of section 2.6 would seem to serve as ample warnings that quite often the overall ramifications of possible action schemes may be 'beyond' the decision maker; if we recognise the fact of bounded rationality, we must admit the possibility that the consumer's mental 'hardware' could prevent her from seeing net implicational impacts. For reasons of computational workability, rule (1) might often be replaced by another form of 'software'. So let us now consider some less demanding heuristics.

(2) An Additive Differences Satisficing Rule

As the process of search continues, a consumer might ask herself how the most recently investigated possibility dominates over, or is dominated by, the 'best' of the options she has hitherto investigated. If the sum of these differences (in implications) is greater than zero, the 'new' option then becomes the reference point against which the next option investigated will be evaluated. Otherwise, the option is removed from the list of possibles and the previous reference scheme is kept. Search stops when allotted search time runs out, or when the consumer fails to encounter better and better prospects and judges, in terms of some other rules, that she is insufficiently likely to discover anything better in her allotted search time. This kind of rule (discussed in Payne, 1976) makes smaller demands upon a person's memory than does rule (1) (which envisages total scores being worked out independently before a comparison of options is made). Evidently, if this rule is being employed, the choice matrix is continually being up-dated (unless it exists already in printed form), and it should never consist of more than two lines of data. The use of this rule could be investigated in a laboratory setting, in relation to a supplied choice matrix, by employing sophisticated eye-position-sensing equipment (see Russo and Dosher, 1983, for a discussion of related work on eye-fixation patterns and evaluation techniques). Evidently, something is amiss if the consumer's attention in any short period does not flit only between two rows of a matrix in which her options are represented in rows, or if she works down single columns, or if she comes back to rows that had formerly ceased to hold her attention. Certainly, in my house-buying experience, I recall having more than two properties in mind as serious candidates for much of the evaluation period.

(3) A Characteristics Cut-offs Expectancy Value Rule

An alternative way of simplifying a trade-off task is to assess the overall rating of each option by asking oneself a series of questions with 'yes/no' answers, whose results are then added according to some system of weights that reflects one's judgement of the implications, for each characteristic, of a 'yes' or 'no'. Thinking dichotomously is less demanding than making assessments in scalar terms, but this rule also works for bipolar scales where the consumer has in mind particular aspirational cut-off targets (for example, 'at least three bedrooms', or 'no more than twenty minutes' drive from work'). The last two compensatory rules that I wish to consider are even less demanding.

(4) A Simple Averaging Rule

Here, the consumer is thought of as if she rates schemes in respect of each of their attributes (in, for example, marks out of ten) and adds the scores together in an unweighted manner. To be 'satisfactory', a scheme must achieve a particular average score; if no such scheme is in her initial choice matrix, she may engage in search activity. She chooses the highest scoring of those schemes she evaluates. Evidently, this rule avoids the weighting demands that still afflict rule (3), but its use of score scales makes it less easy to envisage being applied where satiation or inherently dichotomous evaluations are involved. Certainly, one can sometimes see consumer magazines noting average scores of rival products in this way, but this method of evaluation looks somewhat questionable when set against everyday observations of people arguing over the relative importance of various decision criteria.

(5) The Polymorphous Satisficing Rule

This variant on the satisficing theme (inspired by the work of Lea and Harrison, 1978) admits a scheme as satisfactory if it offers the prospect of meeting a sufficient number of unordered characteristics targets. Clearly, this rule requires a much smaller capacity for processing information than do the first four rules and, like rule (3), it involves satisficing in a dual sense. But, like rule (4), it seems to suggest that one views decision makers as if they lack well-thought-out value structures and are not concerned with 'importance' or with the implications of a failure to meet particular aspirations. Furthermore, its unordered view of targets means that it breaks down if several schemes tie as least bad options.

7.4 NON-COMPENSATORY RULES

With rules (4) and (5), we were beginning to see the consumer increasingly losing sight of the overall implications of the choices she might be making. Given the benefit of global rationality, the consumer who applied either of these rules might well regret her choices. Similar possibilities arise if the consumer uses either of the rules considered in this section.

(6) The Conjunctive Rule

The obvious alternative to trading-off one characteristic for another is to try to 'have one's cake and eat it'—that is, to seek a scheme of action that is satisfactory in *all* respects, and only to stop searching when such a scheme is discovered. This is what the conjunctive rule entails and the process it embodies is essentially akin to a search for a scheme which will fit into a *mould*, whose shape is determined by: (a) the characteristics the decision maker has in mind as relevant to the choice at hand; and (b) the decision maker's aspirational targets in respect of each of these characteristics. And the search is carried out in the belief that something exists which will fit this shape, which will 'fit the bill'. However, if a person has carved a very intricate mould, involving many different and highly demanding characteristic targets, and if she insists on meeting them all, her expectations may be sorely disappointed. Kelly's (1963, p. 121) characterisation of women thinking about the possibility of marriage, from an implicitly conjunctive standpoint, makes this very clear. Potential husbands exist initially only as the intersects of mental construct dimensions. Where a woman has only a few dimensions in mind, it may not be long before she encounters someone who conforms with her expectation. She may thus end up marrying young, not long after meeting the man. By contrast, the 'old maid' is, in Kelly's picture, someone who has imagined a husband as the intersect of very many conceptual dimensions and 'nobody ever lands on the precise point where all of them converge'. Unless she revises her expectations, she will very likely remain a spinster.

The 'old maid' in Kelly's example might have fared better if she had set herself a 'closing date' by which time she would cease searching or 'waiting for her prince to come', and if she had worked out how to choose amongst potential marriage partners who could not match her mould in every respect, yet who differed in their mis-match tendencies. If the conjunctive method of choice leaves one incompletely satisfied, one needs a conflict-resolving tool that makes it possible to select the 'best of a bad bunch'.

(7) A 'Characteristic Filtering' Rule

If the aggregation of values is possible, rule (3) would serve well as a conflict-resolving device in situations where a conjunctive rule breaks down. However, the use of an hierarchy of characteristics targets as a filtering device enables conjunctive conflicts to be resolved without undue demands being placed on the consumer's computational powers. Rule (7) thus involves subjecting rival action schemes to a series of tests, in a particular order of priority. Only those schemes which pass the first test are subjected to the second test, and so on down the ranking until only one scheme is left. Of course, it could be the case that all schemes fail the first test, but do so in different degrees, and the decision maker does not anticipate that search could be fruitful. According to the characteristic filtering rule, the decision maker will, in this situation, select the scheme which comes closest to passing the first test, regardless of other considerations. She will behave similarly when she sees herself faced with an absence of satisfactory schemes in respect of lower priority tests. However, where no schemes pass a test but several tie as 'least bad failures' the schemes that tie, but not the more dismal failures, are allowed on to the text test, unless the decision maker believes she can discover other schemes which will pass this test (and *all* the higher priority tests).

The characteristic filtering rule provides a plausible means of explaining why people often explain decisions to reject particular action schemes as being 'because' of a *single* failing. Such 'fatal flaws' are difficult to explain in terms of the application of any one of the first six rules we have considered; according to these rules, it makes no sense to 'single out' a particular fault—unless in all other respects the rejected scheme is treated by the rule in question as if it is identical to the favoured option.

One might well infer that I applied a characteristic filtering rule in my house-buying decision. For I did not look at properties above a particular price (fortunately plenty were 'within my budget'), or which were not on the western shore. Nor did I seek to inspect homes listed as having less than two bedrooms or which were listed explicitly as having other than brick and tile construction. By such means, I was able rapidly to reduce my choice set to the twenty-five properties I actually inspected. Amongst these were many that were subsequently rejected on the basis of particular failings. For example, two were 'ruled out' because they were adjacent to large and unsightly concrete water tanks, even though these properties were in many other respects more than adequate. The presence of the water tanks conflicted with my world-view as far as a desirable residence was concerned, and I felt they could jeopardise resale prospects as far as buyers with similar views to my own were concerned.

Another obvious example of characteristic filtering at work concerns appointments' committees in many American universities that immediately reject applications from candidates who lack doctoral qualifications. If one is snowed under with applications, and if one believes that somewhere in the pile is a *curriculum vitae* which would survive a conjunctive test, one dimension of which is the doctoral degree requirement, there is the prospect of saving considerable information-processing efforts by setting up a series of priority screens. To begin with a conjunctive procedure could involve much time being spent in examining sequentially (though only partially, since each examination is halted once one failing is discovered) many applications that fail to offer the desired all-round adequacy, before a satisfactory one is discovered. Should no such candidate exist, it would then be necessary to backtrack and re-examine all the partially considered applications. By starting with priorities such a backtrack is avoided, along with the need to give more than a cursory examination to many of the applications. Of course, if there is no perfectly adequate candidate, the applicant who survives the most filters may leave the committee with a long list of prospectively unsatisfied goals. In priority terms, the operative question then becomes: 'have enough tests been satisfied in order of importance, or is it worth searching (via a readvertisement) for a candidate who could pass some more tests and get further down the checklist without any failings?'

Disgruntled would-be house-sellers and academic appointees might well wish to challenge the wisdom of people who employ a characteristic filtering evaluation procedure. They would surely concede that, unlike rules (4) to (6), rule (7) accommodates observed tendencies for people to assign differing degrees of importance to particular characteristics, and it also avoids the information-overloading problems potentially associated with the weighting rules (1) to (3). However, they might justifiably argue that characteristic filtering is a procedure which is by no means guaranteed to result in a consumer selecting from her agenda the option that is least bad as far as the overall implications for the development of her world-view are concerned. Depending on how demanding are the consumer's high-priority targets, the use of this procedure could well involve her in filtering out schemes with much higher 'net implications' scores than the one she actually selects.

It would be natural for the consumer to accord top priority to the characteristic goal which, if she *failed* to meet it, would present the biggest barrier to the development of her construct system along the lines she presently anticipates. (This developmental blow could actually take the form of a shrinkage in the range of convenience of her system.) The second priority would be accorded to the goal whose failure to be met would imply the second biggest barrier to the development of her system, and so on for successively lower-ranking characteristics (see the discussion, in section 6.4, of empirical work with 'resistance to change' rankings of constructs). Given a long enough list of characteristics, it is obvious that a scheme which failed to meet the top priority could have a better overall implicational score than one which is actually selected because it is the only option to pass, say, the first five priority tests. The favoured scheme might well be utterly deficient in respect of a long list of less important characteristic tests: it is, so to speak, favoured 'at all costs' by virtue of its ability to pass the high-priority tests. If the consumer can *see* this at the time of her choice, her rationality is not so bounded that she cannot use a compensatory rule. However, the longer that the characteristic list would have to be for a rejected scheme to be able to dominate in principle in terms of its overall implications, the less likely it would appear that the consumer in practice will be able to comprehend that the application of the characteristic filtering procedure is inconsistent with her aims in life.

But it is by no means inevitable that the application of a characteristic filtering procedure will *necessarily* result in the consumer making choices that are suboptimal in terms of her overall predictive system. The implicational score attached to the first priority test alone could in principle be so great as to swamp the combined scores of all the remaining pertinent characteristics. If this were the case, and if there were only one scheme which came anywhere near to passing the first test, yet which happened to be dreadful in most other respects, it would be perfectly appropriate to choose this scheme on the basis of rule (7). The choice is precisely that which she would make if she were able to count up the overall implications seemingly attached to each of the schemes she considers. None the less, to an external observer it could seem a hopelessly irrational choice, since the observer may not see the same set of implications arising out of a failure to make the selection.

Although a characteristic filtering procedure may sometimes generate choices radically different from those which would be dominant in a counting-up of implications, I must emphasise that I do not see the typical user of this procedure as someone blindly pursuing priorities at all costs. A consumer may not be able confidently to say to herself that she can sum together with tolerable accuracy the net implications associated with many different dimensions of choice. But she may certainly be smart enough to see that, if she sets a target, the number of implications directly associated with meeting it will depend on the size of that target. She may also be not unaware that the pursuit of a demanding high-priority target is *possibly* going to have *some* kinds of cost in terms of forgone advantageous implications associated with other characteristics which she will suffer if she fails to moderate her high-priority requirement. However, if she cannot see the overall implications of moderating one aspiration and making a number of aspirations more demanding—not necessarily in identical degrees—her awareness of opportunity costs among characteristics is too fuzzy for her to employ a compensatory rule. In such a situation it seems entirely reasonable to choose, as a means to choice (yet another of the 'strange loops'!), a set of priorities and associated aspirations which, it is hoped, will select schemes in a manner which *approximates* to the unworkable procedure of counting up overall underlying implications. The characteristic filtering procedure is certainly non-compensatory, but its rationale lies in ignorance of the magnitude of opportunity costs, not in ignorance of their existence in 'broad' terms.

A set of characteristic filters—or, for that matter, any other decision-making heuristic—should be seen as a personal construct, tentatively selected and potentially open to revision if it does not match up to expectations. A consumer's first priority may indeed be that which, by virtue of the aspirational requirement assigned to it, has the highest implicational tally. Such a priority may also filter options by treating slight under-attainments as identical to large ones, despite the fact that the target is personally selected rather than intrinsic. This in turn means that a scheme which nearly passes the first test and which would have dominated in subsequent tests—had it been allowed to take them—is dismissed without any weight being given to the fact that it 'nearly' passed. However, the consumer is setting up her filters in the hope that the results—in terms of the number of priorities met, and their associated implications—will be good enough. If she *does* see her personal development suffering as a result of the particular characteristic filtering procedure she has constructed, she will have reason to redesign her priority rankings and/or her aspirational requirements.

In such a situation, it may be obvious to the consumer that, for example, her first priority test is 'too tough' *and how* 'near misses' can be compensated for by exemplary performances elsewhere. If so, she is not suffering from so much bounded rationality that she cannot switch to using an efficient compensatory choice heuristic. But it may merely be obvious that the first priority test is too tough, and not obvious *how* failures could be compensated for on disparate other tests. If so, how far to lower the target, or whether to lower the ranking of the characteristic, or both, will not be easy to decide upon. The consumer must therefore experiment. (This argument has been made with respect to the top priority, but it can be made with respect to any characteristic filter, of whatever tentative ranking, which seems to stand out as excessively intolerant and holding up the development of the consumer's world-view.) On some occasions, the consumer's mould-reshaping experiment will be a personally crucial one; we should make no presumption that gradually, by repeated choices, she will stumble across a set of priorities and targets that will guide her to make choices which are optimal in terms of their overall implications.

7.5 SHORT CUTS WITHIN PRIORITY SYSTEMS

In this section I am going to make some refinements to the characteristic filtering idea, in order to show how a priority-based choice rule can accommodate modes of thought that would seem on the surface to be inconsistent with rule (7) yet not at odds with compensatory choice rules. A critic might well argue, from introspection, that she does not feel people always look first at the 'most important' characteristic desired in a scheme of action, or evaluate choices matrices one characteristic at a time rather than one scheme of action at a time. On this basis the critic could reasonably contend that everyday talk of 'priorities' or 'orders of importance' (such as those elicited by market researchers) could relate, not to priority rankings, but to sizes of various weights consumers have in mind as they choose according to compensatory procedures.

To refine the characteristic filtering idea, I will merge it with some other behavioural findings on how people simplify the process of decision making. My starting point is Simon's (1955) original satisficing model. This was notable not only for its satisficing nature but also for its introduction of the notion of sequential search. Simon suggested that, to economise on the costs of evaluating action schemes in situations of uncertainty, decision makers investigate the most promising, nearby solutions first of all and only expand their search 'nets' if these fail to appear satisfactory; that is to say, they try out obvious options they already have in mind, or generate potential plans of action one at a time. Loasby's (1967; 1973) empirical studies of firm relocation decisions produced findings not inconsistent with this view: when firms were prompted by problems to seek new factory sites, they only troubled to look outside their existing localities if their initial investigations failed to find a satisfactory local site. This idea meshes very obviously with rules (1) to (6), where one scheme is evaluated at a time, and the choice matrix possibly built up *as the evaluation proceeds*. Evidently, if the consumer has reason to believe that a particular scheme of action could well be adequate in a conjunctive sense, she stands to save herself some information-processing effort if she focuses her initial attention on it alone. If her conjecture is well founded, she will have no need to investigate other promising options unless she is afraid she has set some of her targets unnecessarily low. Even if she ends up having to explore several schemes in detail, she may still incur smaller evaluation costs than those which she would incur if she applied a series of priority tests to all thus-far-uneliminated options. By evaluating individual schemes according to her priorities, she comes to see how far down her checklist they get without failing. If soon she comes across one which gets to the bottom, all is well and good; but if there is actually no scheme which would pass a conjunctive test, she has at least avoided the need to backtrack which would exist if she carried out individual conjunctive appraisals, applying aspirational tests in no particular priority order. In the context of screening job applicants, for example, much time could be saved by looking at candidates who are rumoured to be strong contenders, for the choice matrix embodied in the pile of applications initially exists largely as a set of unknown quantities; the rumours may efficiently bias the screening process, for until shown to be wrong they are pieces of information that have already been processed, possibly without error.

A particularly important example of decision making (though not in the context of consumption) which illustrates a combination of sequential search and priority ideas concerns Soviet planning with material balances. The time limit under which the planners must operate, and the huge scale of their problem, means that their rationality is bounded even though they can make extensive use of computers. The input–output nature of their problem means that it is natural to try one plausible plan first and see how it performs in respect of all the relevant targets, instead of asking the computer to assess a variety of plans in respect of a single-valued utility function. Iterations can then be attempted to improve the fit, after changing the demands that will be placed upon enterprises. But when time runs out, or it seems unlikely that more can be asked of enterprises, priorities have to be used to define a plan solution. Priorities are similarly applied when shortfalls occur during the operation of the chosen plan (see Ellman, 1973). The parallels between this example and my discussion (in section 3.3) of the budgeting problem in the context of household production systems should be so obvious as not to require elaboration.

Sequential search is a possible short-cut way towards a decision. But it is not necessarily the best short cut to take during complex processes of choice. An alternative short cut is sequential screening, discussed by Gallagher (1971) in relation to problems of research and development in the chemicals industry, and by Loasby (1976, pp. 50–5). Instead of trying the most obvious solutions first, the decision maker begins by attempting to eliminate the least likely solutions on her agenda of possibilities. This makes eminent sense if the 'promising' but as yet uncertain 'solutions' require a great deal of investigation and if the less-promising options are easier to decide upon. The second refinement I wish to make to the characteristic filtering idea is a short-cut procedure that essentially lifts this idea from the product/ goods space to the characteristics space. The essential point to bear in mind is that, especially in situations where the choice matrix is not given but has to be constructed, the appropriate sequence for a set of screens depends on conjectures of evaluation (construct-forming) costs as well as on underlying orders of priority.

Suppose I have reason to believe that very many schemes may meet my top priorities. If my conjecture is well founded, I can reduce my decision-making costs by starting my evaluation process some way down my priority ranking and finding out from this basis which scheme is implied as the winner; that is to say, I begin with a test that I believe a good many of the options will fail and, having thus reduced my agenda, continue on down the ranking. I may even apply this short cut more than once if I have a very long list of attributes that are relevant to the problem at hand; that is to say, I jump down the list in stages, stopping off at those characteristic targets which seem likely to be powerful discriminators. By these means I arrive at a preliminary choice, whose performance I can then assess against the higher-ranking aspirations that were missed out in the short-cut process. If the 'preliminary choice' meets all the remaining tests with no gaps, I have achieved a considerable information-gathering and processing economy. And I may still achieve this if I am forced to look again at the scheme which reached second farthest down the preliminary filtering list (or even at the third and fourth schemes), owing to some high-level failing becoming apparent in my preliminary choice. In terms of our academic screening example, it could be the case that the 'doctoral degree requirement' is by no means the top priority. However, it may usually serve as a good proxy for other desired attributes, and act as a powerful screen against many conjunctively inadequate candidates (for example, ones who are still writing their dissertations and are running out of money, who might be less prone to give their attention to teaching, or who might be people who will never complete and publish research projects).

The use of this kind of short cut offers a way of explaining observed tendencies for decision makers to neglect paying attention (since attention has its costs) to 'objectively important' characteristic targets when evaluating schemes of action. For example, a questionnaire investigation by researchers at Cranfield Institute of Technology (reported in the *Financial Times*, 19 May 1981) revealed that buyers of new cars tended to focus on economy and reliability and neglect safety-related features; only 3 per cent claimed to look for good brakes when buying a car. Few of these motorists, I suspect, would knowingly have purchased reliable, cheap-to-run cars with very poor braking systems, but many would surely have felt it rather trying to carry out emergency stop or 'brake fade' tests, particularly with a salesperson beside them. But it would not be unreasonable to suppose that car buyers typically assume that all cars on sale have been forced to undergo stringent tests before they reach the showrooms (for example, government 'type approval' tests for new cars and compulsory roadworthiness tests for second-hand cars beyond a certain age). Such 'commonsense' knowledge might lead many decision makers to neglect this sort of feature *entirely* unless something happened to make them question the adequacy of particular vehicles on their agendas (for example, they might be surprised and alarmed about how far they had to depress the brake pedal to elicit a response in Volkswagens and Fords designed by heavy-footed German engineers).

In so far as choices are prompted by problems encountered with existing activities, it seems natural that a decision maker's attention may locate first on attributes in respect of which she is failing to meet her aspirations. For example, suppose rising petrol prices are causing havoc with my budgeting because my existing vehicle is not very economical. In this situation it would be illogical for me to begin to seek a solution by examining alternative cars for, say, their road-holding capabilities rather than their economy, *even if* I accord road holding a higher priority. If my existing car has adequate road-holding properties, I will only want to check the road-holding capabilities of those cars that seem likely to solve my economy problem. It is a waste of time for me to start at the top of my list and test drive an assortment of cars selected without prior reference to fuel economy, or to begin by reading test reports of how cars within my budget range hold the road—especially when fuel economy is something I can usually assess simply by inspecting a column of figures in a motoring journal.

It should be becoming apparent that, once theory formation

and validation are recognised to be a costly exercise, the idea that the consumer puts together a choice matrix to which she *then* applies tests of adequacy may at best be a useful theoretical simplification. Often, tests of adequacy of one kind or another will be applied during the expectation-forming stage, with only a limited number of schemes surviving to make up a choice matrix of the kind outlined in section 7.2. In some situations the nature of the search and evaluation environment is such that the decision maker is pretty well forced to adopt sequential search and there is then no chance of going back to select an option once rejected as less than adequate. A likely example of this concerns the choice of marriage/cohabitation partners in societies where serial monogamy is the custom. Here, too, back-tracking priority appraisal methods may be used. For example, a person may accord a much higher priority to being able to live with someone in a satisfactory manner (a notion which might be simplified into several subpriorities concerning 'different' types of behaviour), than she does to matters of physical appearance. But to evaluate in detail whether or not any *one* partner is likely to be satisfactory in this respect could take a good deal of experimentation. Cultural norms prevent her from being able to perform such experiments with several partners simultaneously, while a partner she initially rejects may subsequently be unavailable, having entered into another relationship. She must either forgo such experiments and arrive at a decision on the basis of her initially hazy impressions—evidently at considerable risk—or she must search sequentially with a series of trial cohabitations. If she has no idea about how it might be to live with any of her prospective marriage partners, she can only make a trial decision on the basis of criteria that have implications in respect of her lower priorities, and then see whether or not the partner fits into her high-priority mould.

The arguments in this section may help to show how difficult it may be to judge, merely on the basis of casual introspection, which decision-making procedures are most popularly used. A tendency for decision makers to evaluate schemes of action as wholes and/or start making up their minds by looking at relatively unimportant attributes seems, on the surface, to lie most easily with a view of choice that sees 'importance' from a compensatory perspective. But the procedures appended in this section to non-compensatory rules offer a new perspective on what may be happening. And these procedures are not *ad hoc*, arbitrary amendments to save the notion that very often deliberative choices depend on a series of tests of adequacy in a particular priority order. The procedures actually involve a greater recognition of the problem of bounded rationality and of the possibility that some means of gathering and processing information in a world of complexity may be more efficient than others.

7.6 TIE-BREAK TECHNIQUES AND THE RESOLUTION OF DILEMMAS

The next theoretical refinements relate to my suggestion that it may often be appropriate to view the boundedly rational consumer as ideally seeking a scheme of action that will fit into a conceptual *mould* in a satisfactory manner. I suggested the characteristic filtering procedure as a device for dealing with the possibility that there is no option which will fit a mould defined only by a set of characteristics and their associated aspiration levels. A priority system further defines the shape of the mould and determines how far the prospective schemes of action can be made to fit. (Inadequate high-priority attainments prevent a scheme from being pushed very far into the mould; it is rather like trying to put a ring on one's finger and finding that it gets stuck at the first joint.) But in some situations it may be the case that several schemes on a consumer's agenda fit her mould of tolerance. She is, in common parlance, 'spoilt for choice'. She needs a means for breaking the tie between schemes that her choice procedure labels as equally satisfactory.

These possibilities come to mind as worthy of serious consideration. The first is due to Kornai (1971, pp. 108–9). Whereas I have been assuming prior to this section that the consumer is normally forced to choose to meet some characteristic targets at the expense of others, Kornai presumes that people use a conjunctive choice procedure that usually generates several adequate options. He therefore proposes that ties are broken by *random* decisions. One could most readily accept this suggestion where the consumer had arrived at a tie after making *overall* assessments of rival schemes using, say, rule (1) or (2)—for then she would be truly indifferent. But a general belief in random choices seems to imply a belief that the mind will generate random impulses instead of trying to reason things out. By contrast, the other two ways of breaking such ties, which I will now propose, involve attempts to apply reason; my belief is that if one perceives activities as different one cannot rest happily with a mould of tolerance that, in effect, labels some of them as identical. In order that a 'conjunctive tie' may be broken, the mould of tolerance must be modified.

One obvious modification is for the decision maker to deepen the mould, that is, to add to her list of sought-after characteristics. Consider, for example, the comment of motoring journalist David Taylor ('Peugeot 205 road test', *Punch* 11 April 1984, p. 46):

all these contenders are so finely matched in the supermini sector that really there are only hair-splitting differences. The choice is so bewildering on merit that what it'll come down to is a subjective decision that this one looks a bit different from next door's or that the other one happens to be recommended by the local garagiste or yet another is there in the showroom in the colour you happen to fancy. It may seem a bit reckless to spend £4000 in quite such a cavalier fashion, but can it matter a damn when there's truly so little in it?

In fact, the number of occasions when consumers find themselves in this sort of situation will tend to be limited by the natural tendency for them to become connoisseurs in some degree during the process of search—they will be gathering information from friends, salespersons and published sources about 'things worth looking for'. Where characteristics are ordered in terms of priorities, new attributes may be added to the list at the bottom, or may be slotted in elsewhere among pre-existing targets. (The addition of new characteristics to her priority ranking may sometimes cause the consumer to rerank some of her pre-existing priorities if these relate to the new characteristics and have come to be seen in a somewhat different light; for example, an executive who is introduced to the possibility of purchasing a luxury car with an antilock braking system may become more safety conscious than hitherto and raise other safety-related features in her ranking. Of course, such rerankings may occur during the process of search, even if no new characteristics are discovered, for people may become aware of the broader implications of not having certain characteristics. Such rerankings may affect the stage at which certain schemes get filtered out, but if a tie would have occurred anyway they will not of themselves do anything to break it.)

A second modification—which neither excludes nor is excluded by the first—is to tighten up the mould in respect of pre-existing characteristic targets. Where a tie has occurred, it is unlikely that the schemes in question have each happened *barely* to meet all the original aspirations. Generally speaking, schemes that are seen as other than identical will tend to perform beyond the minimum targets in different ways; for example, one house might have a much more than adequate view, yet only just be big enough, while another might have a view that was just about satisfactory but be much more than adequately spacious. Several schemes are rattling around in the mould, but they are making different noises as they do so. To revise some aspirations in an upward direction in accordance of what now seems attainable has the effect of tightening up the mould and eliminating the slack that allowed the tie to result.

The idea of a mould of tolerance being refashioned in the light of changing perceptions of what is possible is a notion concerning individual mental processes that is an analogue of the firm-level analysis of the uptake of organisational slack in the work of Cyert and March (1963, pp. 36–8; see section 3.5). How much slack there is in a firm at any moment depends upon how the rival coalition members have adjusted their aspirations in relation to potential attainments. The distribution of slack payments to coalition members is shaped by the degree of moderation in the demands made by other coalition members with different goals. The presence of slack in the Cyert and March model makes determinate outcomes difficult to predict. Slack payments arise because ignorance of the minimum payments that rival coalition members would accept, combined with the uncertain costs of attempting to discover their bounds of tolerance, makes members in some degree moderate their own demands. It will therefore not be obvious which personnel in the coalition have hitherto been earning a return that they are prepared in some degree to sacrifice, or who will most rapidly lower their aspiration levels and thereby create some room for manouevre.

A similar problem of indeterminacy looms threateningly when we extend the idea of slack uptake into the realm of the individual's mind: how can we predict which aspirations will move most rapidly into line with potential attainments? In my original (1983c, p. 88) attempt to deal with the tie-break issue, I unwittingly offered a pair of possible solutions that involved slack uptake, both of which have a certain a priori appeal, despite the fact that they are poles apart. On the one hand, I suggested that the consumer might break a tie by opting for the scheme that she expected to perform best in respect of the lowest-ranking characteristic on her list. This would seem not unreasonable if the consumer has come to set a low aspiration for this characteristic as a result of the past experience of her failure to be able to meet high requirements in its respect, given the demands she makes in respect of high priorities. We might imagine the housebuyer who in the past has got used to the idea of uninspiring views, though ideally she would like a panoramic spectacle, for in the past she has never been able to find an inspiring view in a property whose selection would not involve her in compromising higher-priority wants such as the number of bedrooms. In her new environment, however, she may discover that such compromises do not have to be made, and break a tie by choosing the house with the best view.

The implicitly polar alternative that I suggested was that, in choices involving monetary transactions, a tie could be broken by choosing the cheapest option. Implicitly, I was suggesting that the decision maker was redefining her budgeting filter ('I wish to spend no more than $....') in order to take account of information she had acquired following her initial budgeting choice. This is a 'polar' act of redefinition since, in monetary choices, the budgeting filter may often be thought of as the first hurdle that schemes on an agenda must cross. This tie-break procedure makes sense if the budget strategy that the consumer had previously chosen involved the expectation that attainments would be compromised in respect of priorities that rank lower than those catered for by the act of buying a house. For example, the consumer may be pleasantly surprised to find she can have a perfectly adequate house at a price which leaves her in a position to be able to meet lower-ranking goals, such as 'having $... cash/unused borrowing power "for a rainy day"', or 'running a second car'.

However, *satiation* in respect of top- or bottom-ranking characteristics could arise in some cases, and thereby ensure that tie-breaks centre on the raising of intermediate-ranking thresholds of tolerance. Satiation is here taken to mean a situation where 'ideal' requirements, and not merely previously defined constructs of 'adequacy', seem open to realisation. Three possible causes of satiation come to mind within the analysis of motivation I have proposed. First, some characteristics might be strictly dichotomous; for example, in some societies, people considering potential marriage partners might make unquestioned virginity their top priority. Clearly, this could not be a characteristic of use in breaking a conjunctive tie between rival marriage partners!

Second, further movements along a scalar construct might, beyond some point, begin to carry more negative implications than positive ones. For example, consider a consumer in her working environment as a top-level decision maker, whose first concern is with her own self-image. Up to a point, she will be concerned with the safety of the decisions she makes, for the loss of her job as a result of an error could have disastrous implications for her self-esteem (see section 8.4). However, if it seems that quite a few options look safe enough, she may not opt for the safest of these in the event of a tie, for the implications of being seen to pursue safety beyond a certain point might harm her self-image ('too cautious'). For this reason she might be much more interested in displaying an enhanced span of control over other personnel. But satiation could also set in at some point with respect to the latter goal; the implications of being seen to be 'power mad' might detract from the implications positively attaching to a dramatically widened span of control. With this second view of satiation, we effectively have a situation where the priority test for a characteristic is double edged: to be satisfactory, an action scheme must fall within a particular range, in the midst of which lies the 'ideal' attainment position.

A third kind of satiation may be said to occur if there comes a point at which further movements along a scalar construct cease to have any implications (other than those concerned with opportunity costs, however vaguely perceived and computed) for the consumer's predictive system. For example, a point may come when, although 'objective' differences exist, the potential buyer of a hi-fi sound system cannot distinguish between the reproduction qualities of rival combinations of equipment. Having an 'objectively' better quality of sound reproduction may not enhance her ability to make sense of the (seemingly undistorted) music of composers whose works fascinate her. All she may see implied is that the pursuit of 'objectively' superior sound quality may have some kind of cost attached to it—for example, in relation to the aesthetic appeal of the sound equipment, adequate though the supposedly better-sounding system may appear as a piece of furniture.

It would seem on the arguments considered so far that if we accept the mould-tightening idea, we are faced with indeterminacy; it is by no means a priori obvious that *either* high-*or* intermediate-*or* low-priority aspirations will *generally* be the most likely ones to be adjusted when it is discovered that all pre-existing targets seem likely to be met. It is here that advertisements may stand to exert a good deal of leverage in so far as they can focus attention on particular characteristics and the levels of attainment that their respective products can offer.

Two possible procedures to determine how moulds of tolerance are tightened up come to my mind at present; though there could well be others, just as the seven basic choice heuristics considered in sections 7.3 and 7.4 were by no means the only ones possible. First, it might be the case that satiation tests are already embedded in the shape of the mould of tolerance in respect of many of its dimensions. If so, and if only a few options have reached the tie-break stage, it may not be beyond the consumer's computational powers to bring an additive differences procedure into action. That is to say, she will look at the overall implicational differences involved in choosing one option rather than, say, either of one or two rivals. The application of such a procedure at this late stage in the evaluation process is by no means guaranteed to result in the choice that would have been made had the consumer attempted initially to employ rule (2) rather than rule (6/7). For many possibilities may have been long since ruled out of court for *particular* failings, despite possible differential advantages.

Second, the consumer might be unable to compute totals for implicational differences, but she might none the less be able to form some picture of the overall difference between her present 'adequate' mould and her 'ideal' one. If so, she might tighten up all presently unsatiated tests by amounts that are functions of the proportionate differences between actual and ideal ratings on the scales in question. Adequacy targets that had hitherto been set a long way from ideal notions would be raised more than those that were already close to ideal, with the distances serving as *proxies* for the implications of less-than-ideal attainments. Schemes in the tie-break could then be re-examined in terms of the new priority mould. The tightness of the mould could be adjusted until only one scheme survived in conjunctive terms.

Related to the question of how a consumer breaks conjunctive ties between schemes is the question of how she behaves when she finds herself on the 'horns of a dilemma'. In the present context, I will consider the nature only of those dilemmas that concern choices between *known* characteristics. If no scheme is adequate in all respects, and if the characteristics of rival schemes are clearly defined, the decision maker ought to be able to reach a decision using a characteristic filtering rule; so how, one might ask, can she find herself paralysed by indecision?

An inability to choose in a straightforward priority-based manner, when the properties of rival schemes are not perceived as uncertain, is something that I see as resulting from uncertainty about what constitutes an *appropriate ordering* of priorities in the context at hand. The consumer knows she cannot have everything, but because she is unsure of the implications attaching to the known characteristics she does not know what she should try to sacrifice and which aspirations she should continue to try to meet. If she can choose one priority ordering rather than another, her choice is defined, but she hesitates, asking herself, 'is characteristic X more important than characteristic Y?' Her task, then, is not so much to choose between the competing schemes, but to choose the mould into which she is going to attempt to fit them. Her task, quite literally, is to '*make up* her mind', and the choice between rival moulds is an example of the general problem of choice under uncertainty discussed in the next chapter.

To conceptualise the task of resolving dilemmas in this way is to move still further from the orthodox idea that decision makers choose in respect of a fully specified preference ordering that they possess at the start of the decision process. The orthodox view leaves room for advertisements merely to serve the function of aiding the decision maker as she attempts to decide which characteristics are possessed by rival schemes. If one sees the consumer as approaching an act of choice with a partially open mind, the possibility emerges that advertisements (or, in non-market contexts, other attempts at persuasion) may shape her view of what she is looking for, and not merely affect what she sees.

7.7 RULES WITHIN RULES

As this chapter has proceeded, it has become evident that the process of choice is by no means as simple as I initially depicted it to be. We have run up against various problems that may make some rules unworkable, and have identified risks that it *may* be worth taking to simplify the task of decision making. In practice, the consumer, too, is likely to find that she initially attempts to process information with heuristics that sometimes break down due to information overload, that fail to generate unique solutions, and that involve the pursuit of 'red herrings' rather than the realisation of successful short cuts. During a complex evaluation task, we should not be surprised to find that many different heuristics are employed, in a contingent, problem-solving sequence (for a similar conclusion, and some relevant empirical work, see Payne, 1976, Bettman, 1979, and Svenson, 1979). Some examples may help to clarify this important idea.

A manageable preliminary choice matrix may be created from a potentially unmanageable set of possibilities via the use of a filtering procedure, applied to only a limited number of characteristics. We saw this in my house-hunting example; it is also conspicuous in 'multiple tests' in consumer magazines which compare 'front-wheel-drive family saloons', 'hot hatchbacks', 'programmed 35 mm SLR cameras', 'top-loading automatic washing machines' and so on. However, if possibilities are restricted by the scarcity of available types, such a characteristic filtering procedure may not be necessary. (For 'example, when compact disc players were launched in the UK, only two models—one from Sony, the other from Marantz—were available. However, note that some prior filtering—compact disc versus other ways of improving the quality of one's audio system—could *still* have been going on.) In this latter case, the consumer may be able immediately to apply a compensatory rule without too much bother.

An initial filtering procedure might narrow down the number of options sufficiently to permit an evaluation of those that survived the preliminary appraisal in terms of an additive differences rule. For if many of the powerful initial filters were dichotomous in nature, the differences between the schemes that survived might not relate to many scalar dimensions. On the other hand, as with the house-hunting example, the choice matrix that emerges from the initial filtering process might still be so complex as to preclude the immediate application of a compensatory procedure. A major reason why this could be so is that, although the option set has been pruned down, a subsequent detailed evaluation could involve many more characteristics, so the choice matrix thereby constructed could actually have more elements than did the potential matrix that was subjected to the filtering procedure. In such a situation, the next procedure to be employed might be a conjunctive one. Then, if no scheme passed in conjunctive terms, the consumer might be driven back to characteristic filtering (though, this time, the filtering will concern information discovered after the initial pruning-down of the list of possibilities).

Alternatively, a conjunctive procedure might result in a tie, and the prospect for breaking this by trying to see which other characteristics might be worthy discriminators might look stronger than that for resolving the matter simply via an additive differences procedure. But if no new worthwhile characteristics are uncovered (characteristics with zero implications for the person's construct system will not serve as discriminators), the additive differences rule might then be tried. Failing that, and failing the procedure of tightening the mould of tolerance according to relative ideal/adequate distances, the consumer might end up tossing a coin. Alternatively, she might conclude that the real problem is that she *does not know* what it is best for her to select, because she cannot see the overall implications of the rival choices. In this case, having thus reframed her problem, she might apply one or more of the procedures discussed in the next chapter.

In my house-hunting experience, three serious contenders eventually emerged from the twenty-five options that survived the initial filtering process. The intermediate filtering process was clearly non-compensatory, but mould tightening proceeded apace *during* the process of search. I began to see that, even if I reduced my budget by 20 per cent, I still ought to be able to *find* a nearly new, detached three-bedroom house with an acceptable water view; originally I had been prepared to consider two-bedroom apartments, but that was before I had a chance to see that, out in the suburbs but within an acceptable driving time from work, much more could be had. The house I ultimately purchased was slightly smaller than its two rivals, less well decorated and with a barely adequate kitchen layout, but it was cheaper than both its rivals and had better views. This all sounds like a final three-by-five choice matrix, which should have been amenable to evaluation with an additive differences rule. However, my *impression* is that my chosen home was selected because it passed a conjunctive test, when the other two did not; in the other two cases I kept having doubts about whether I would be satisfied with the views—in one case there were trees partially blocking the view; in the other, telegraph wires got in the way—and I felt I could do better without compromising any of my requirements. The chosen house was the last I went to see.

Evidently, one could simulate possible complex contingent networks of choice heuristics in the form of computer programs. It would then be possible to examine which contingent system correctly predicted a consumer's ranking of options on the basis of constructs elicited from her. But this would by no means be an easy simulation task, particularly since there is an additional sense in which rules may be networked together that I have so far not discussed explicitly.

Most of my attention in this chapter has been devoted to procedures for appraising ratings on rival characteristics scales. I have sometimes mentioned that several characteristics may often relate, in principle, to other characteristics. On some occasions, complexity may prevent or deter a consumer from aggregating their related implications. However, this need not mean that the potentially related characteristics are not in *some* way grouped together. It is possible that the consumer may apply a conjunctive test in respect of a group of characteristics, in order to determine whether any schemes are adequate in respect of a subordinate characteristic. For example, the consumer may judge whether a car could be sufficiently economical to run by asking herself whether it promises a particular target fuel consumption figure, whether it comes within a particular insurance category, and whether its major service interval is after no less than so many thousand kilometres. Only if it passes all three tests is it deemed adequate in terms of economy. On other occasions the consumer may be able and inclined to apply a compensatory test to a grouping of characteristics—in which case we may have expectancy value procedures being employed within conjunctive or characteristic filtering procedures.

In this connection I would like, finally, to come back to the 'simple-averaging' and 'polymorphous' rules that I criticised, in section 7.3, as being at odds with the willingness of consumers to assert that some characteristics are particularly important. But it could indeed be the case that the consumer does lack an ability to order some characteristics, since she is not sure of their implications. In such a situation, she may find herself faced with a dilemma which she revolves by grouping the features together as if they were a single dimension of choice, and then applying to the group a satisficing rule with a simple-averaging or polymorphous form. (Something akin to this procedure is employed in Shaw's (1984) hedonic study of the market for cassette decks. In order to reduce the number of dummy variables and the total number of variables in his equations, Shaw pooled seemingly minor features, such as memory-rewind facilities and automatic head demagnetisation, and then counted up, for each cassette deck, how many of these features were offered. These scores (out of a maximum of twelve) were then treated as if they referred to a single characteristic in its own right.)

7.8 CONCLUSION: NO GENERAL RULES

It should be evident from this chapter that I am very favourably disposed to the idea that, for reasons of bounded rationality, consumers will very frequently employ non-compensatory filtering procedures during deliberative decision-making processes. This is a major challenge to the mode of thought of the orthodox economist. However, in *this* book, I am not going to claim that deliberating consumers are *always* forced to employ non-compensatory filtering procedures. Here, readers may construe a change in my position since I wrote *The Economic Imagination*; for in that book I attempted to argue that consumers in the process of deliberation generally use a characteristic filtering approach to choice, and not an expectancy value one. Some reviewers did not challenge this view, but John Hey (1984, p. 207) suggested that I was 'going too far'. He pointed out that 'just because people are not transcendent geniuses, does not mean they are morons; just because they cannot trade-off a large number of commodities, does not mean they cannot trade-off a few'. (Note that Hey's remarks are expressed in commodity terms, with no mention of characteristic trade-offs, and that they beg the question of how the 'few' get selected.) Of course, I was indeed going too far. In seeking a general model, I was displaying a behaviour tendency that, as Skinner (1979) has shown, is a long-standing one amongst scientists. My argument that the characteristic filtering procedure *is* the only one used in deliberative decision making was without doubt flawed; yet, as an 'as if' generalisation, it might be less misleading to assume that characteristic filtering is used rather than an expectancy value approach to choice. Now I do not wish to propose, as a description, that one particular choice heuristic is used; instead, I wish to assert that deliberative choices are generally rooted in sets of contingent procedures, which may take many forms. A single example of such a set, and perhaps one which Hey might find it easy to envisage being fairly commonly employed, would be: first, characteristic filtering—to select a sufficiently simple choice matrix—and second, the application of an additive differences procedure to resolve the trade-off between the limited number of distinguishing characteristics associated with the restricted set of possibilities that survived the first round of tests.

If economists are interested in anticipating patterns of consumer behaviour, then they will have to investigate seriously the kinds of contingent rule systems according to which consumers reach their decisions. Some sets of rules may be more commonly employed than others (I would expect characteristic filtering sequences to figure very often). However, it would be a mistake to take the most common of these as one's 'general' set of predictive heuristics. Rather, predictions should be constructed by segmenting the population of consumers according to the choice rules they use as well as according to normal psychographic criteria. Simplifications may have to be made to make this procedure workable; for example, it might be necessary to look at how well single rules, rather than sequences of rules, predicted choices, so that some consumers might approximate more closely to one rule than to others. The researcher could then employ the methodology developed by Bruno and Wildt (1975) for discovering predictive complementarities between rival heuristics that seem to fit rival market segments in different degrees. The suggestion that economists should bear in mind that consumers make up their minds in different ways, depending on the contexts and on the workable information-processing strategies they have evolved, does not carry the implication that economists should cease trying to anticipate patterns of choice. It is a suggestion that should open up the possibility of improved predictions.

8 Rules for Evaluating Uncertain Prospects

8.1 INTRODUCTION

If a person's expectation-forming processes admit that an action scheme is an uncertain prospect in respect of a particular dichotomous or scalar characteristic, she is admitting that its selection has *rival* sets of possible implications attached to it in respect of this characteristic. In the event, only one set of implications will come about and this set may be one which is neither precisely defined (it may not be clear what has actually happened) nor one which the consumer has thought of as possible for the characteristic in question. Rules for dealing with uncertain prospects must somehow deal with the mutual exclusivity amongst those sets of implications that the consumer does not reject as totally unbelievable prospects. It would be natural to expect these rules to be variants on the rules considered in the previous chapter, for those rules were also devices for dealing with rivalry amongst sets of implications. Thus one might expect neoclassical theorists to want to assume that consumers somehow 'weigh together' the implications of rival outcomes for a characteristic, just as these economists assume consumers weigh up overall scores for the various characteristics a scheme might contain. Similarly, one might expect an economist like myself to prefer to think of consumers as if they subjected a scheme's set of rival possibilities to a non-compensatory 'mould of tolerance' test, each individual possibility for a characteristic being treated rather as if it were a characteristic in its own right. In fact, this is precisely what one finds in the literature—though it is noteworthy that almost all the literature on choice under uncertainty is concerned with single-characteristic outcomes (for example, bets concerning gains and losses in terms only of money).

Like Chapter 7, this chapter explores first the most-commonly-proposed choice rules and then gradually departs further and further from them in the light of points of criticism that are raised. Once again, I do not intend to propose that in practice any one rule is always employed by consumers.

8.2 THE EXPECTED UTILITY RULE AND SOME RECENT VARIANTS

In Chapter 5, I argued that it would be most logical for decision makers to think about possible outcomes not in a probabilistic manner but in relation to the ease or difficulty they have in disbelieving them. However, the vast bulk of the literature on choice under uncertainty is set in a probabilistic framework, and in section 5.4 I noted possible lines of thought by which a set of potential surprise conjectures *might* be recodified in probabilistic terms. In this section, let us presume that such a recodification has indeed been undertaken by the consumer, who has attached fractional probability weights to each rival outcome she associates with a scheme in respect of the characteristic in question. These weights sum to unity and their sizes reflect the extent of the difficulty the consumer has in dismissing them as possible outcomes. The question at issue is then: how does she rate the scheme as a prospect in respect of this characteristic dimension?

Following Von Neumann and Morgenstern (1947), most economists would argue that the consumer should be thought of as working out on overall rating by multiplying each 'probable' score on the characteristic scale by its respective 'probability' rating, and then adding all of these subtotals together. The score thus obtained might be equal to that obtained on the same dimension by another scheme for which no uncertainty was perceived. If so, and if the consumer were, other things equal, indifferent between the two schemes, an orthodox theorist would describe her as 'risk neutral', and would expect her to adopt this attitude consistently. However, if the consumer rated the 'risky' scheme as more (or less) desirable, other things equal, than a 'certain' scheme with an identical score, then she would be described as a 'risk lover' (or 'risk averter'). Where the consumer is not risk neutral between identical total scores that are underlain by differing risk factors, it might be inferred either that she is employing a subsidiary rule for comparing similar scores with different risk connotations, or that she is employing a subsidiary procedure for scaling gains or losses down or up prior to the aggregation process. (Orthodox theorists have to need to mention such subsidiary rules being employed as means for coping with uncertainty, since they just assume choosers have utility functions that are shaped according to their love of, or aversion to, risks.)

This 'subjective expected utility' (SEU) approach has been subject to extensive empirical investigation (for an excellent review of this literature see Schoemaker, 1982); consumers' attitudes to risk are revealed in betting experiments that present them with well-defined probable outcomes and associated odds. Unfortunately, many of the subjects in these experiments do not behave as if they have well-behaved utility functions of the kind assumed in simple SEU theory. It seems that subjects are commonly risk averse for gains (for example, they will often value a 60 per cent chance of winning $100 above a 30 per cent chance of winning $200) but are risk lovers when it comes to trying to avoid losses (for example, they will often value a 30 per cent risk of losing $200 above a 60 per cent risk of losing $100). It also seems that, even when odds are precisely known, people give small probabilities higher ratings than one would expect, given the first finding: as Maital (1982, p. 211) notes, 'large majorities *accept* a one-in-a-thousand chance to win five *thousand* dollars rather than take a sure five dollars, and they *reject* a one-in-a-thousand chance to lose five thousand dollars, preferring to lose a sure five dollars'. These and other findings led some theorists to conclude that, if one is usefully to suggest thinking about consumers dealing in an aggregating manner with uncertain outcomes, one needs to suggest a rather more complex aggregation formula. I have room only for brief discussions of two of these recent variations on the traditional theme, namely prospect theory and regret theory.

The central idea in prospect theory, proposed by Kahneman and Tversky (1979), is that, when faced with an uncertain prospect, an individual works out its overall value with reference to some fixed point, such as where she stands right now in respect of the characteristic (for example, her present wealth). Changes in this reference point can alter the relative values she places on particular options, whereas in SEU theory this will not happen. Prospect theory then assumes that the decision maker's cognitive processes will edit according to a variety of principles the probability scores used in the adding-up process. The editing procedures mean that, relative to the chosen reference point, the decision weights (that is, the edited probabilities) are twisted in a concave manner for gains and a convex manner for losses. This idea is consistent with the observed tendency for people to make apparently risk-seeking choices when trying to avoid losses and risk-averse choices when faced with rival 'probable' gains, while the concavity and convexity either side of the reference point accords well with the tendency people have to see the difference between 0 and 100 as much greater than the difference between 1000 and 1100. Kahneman and Tversky (1979, p. 279) further argue that the editing process involves loss values of particular amounts falling off faster, relative to the reference point, than gain values of identical amounts increase, since 'the aggravation that one experiences in losing a sum of money appears to be greater than the pleasure associated with gaining the same amount'.

Although prospect theory accommodates evidence from betting experiments that causes problems for SEU theory, Loomes and Sugden (1982, p. 817) have criticised it for its 'complex and somewhat *ad hoc* array of assumptions' (only some of which are mentioned in the previous paragraph). Instead, they have proposed the much more straightforward regret theory, which is also consistent with Kahneman and Tversky's anti-SEU empirical findings. This theory rests, according to its proponents (1982, p. 820), 'on two fundamental assumptions: first, that many people experience the sensations which we call regret and rejoicing; and second, that in making decisions under uncertainty, they try to anticipate and take account of these sensations'. Loomes and Sugden have in mind the type of consumer who recognises that if a poor outcome arises, she will feel disappointed not merely because of its low score in terms of the characteristic scale in question. The consumer will anticipate feeling further aggravated to the extent that she can see she could have avoided letting herself in for this outcome by selecting some other option at the time of her choice. Such an anticipation—that she will be 'kicking herself' on discovering 'what might have been'—will make her revise downwards her valuations of conceivably avoidable poor outcomes, the more so the more regret she would expect to feel if they eventuated. On the other hand, such a consumer may anticipate feeling she would have some cause to rejoice if a good outcome—which she would have 'missed out on by playing safe'—actually eventuates and demonstrates the quality of her judgemental skills. If so, her valuation of a good result of a gamble would be higher than that implied by multiplying its characteristic score by its probability of occurrence. If these adjustments of expected utilities with reference to anticipated feelings of regret and rejoicing are not made according to a linear function of the distances of imagined outcomes from 'what might have been', the decision maker may well end up making valuations of rival strategy pairings that would clash with the transitivity assumption of SEU theory. Changes in the list of options that might have been chosen will clearly affect feelings of prospective rejoicing and regret associated with probable outcomes of any particular choice. Again this contrasts with SEU theory but has something of a similarity to the reference point aspect of prospect theory.

Regret theory is still in its early stages of development and investigation, but the fundamental idea behind it has a certain appeal here, given my attempts to understand consumer motivation in terms of ideas from PCP. Sugden and Loomes are placing at the centre of their theory the decision maker's skill in anticipating events. The results of a choice have implications for the chooser beyond those which are directly contingent on the level of attainment—for example, a host of negative implications may arise from a general failure of property prices to rise, but it will be far more 'soul-destroying' to have purchased one of the few properties that fails to appreciate in value at a time when house prices generally rise. In the light of the discussions in Chapter 6 concerning implications, one might suggest that there is an even easier way of incorporating this aspect of choice in the formation of expected values. Instead of suggesting that a consumer takes each of a scheme's 'probable' scores on the characteristic scales and multiplies them according to their respective probability and regret/rejoicing factors to compute their expected values, it would seem much more intuitive to say simply that the expected value a consumer places on a particular outcome may depend on the net implications she attaches to it, times its probability rating.

Expected values thus obtained for each of a scheme's probable outcomes on the characteristic scale could then be aggregated to obtain the scheme's total score for that characteristic, just as in SEU theory.

The fact that the recent ideas of Kahneman and Tversky, and of Loomes and Sugden, appear to be consistent with betting experiments that call into question the postulates of SEU theory does not mean we need not examine other possible procedures for dealing with uncertain prospects. It is noteworthy that the betting experiments deal with (usually hypothetical) *simple, pairwise* choices with a one-dimensional outcome. Subjects in such experiments are not being tested to see whether in practice they behave as if they compute and then aggregate several, or quite a few, expected values for each scheme to obtain its rating in respect of dimensions where its performance is an uncertain prospect. In reality, one may be able to envisage quite a few sequels to a choice in respect of a particular dimension, which may vary considerably in the extent to which they seem open to disbelief (though see section 5.5). Aggregating this information could prove a very demanding task, particularly if anticipated feelings of regret and rejoicing had also to be dealt with. Quite separate from this issue of informational complexity is the question of whether or not a decision maker will consider it to be rational to aggregate all, or even some, of the scores of rival outcomes that might be the sequel to a particular choice. These two considerations have led several theorists to make a variety of proposals which depart significantly from the ones just considered.

8.3 'SAFETY FIRST'

John Blatt's (1983, pp. 253–7) recent criticism of SEU theory calls into question the idea that probabilities of very poor attainments can always, in principle, be swamped by suitably large and seemingly probable prospects of good attainments. To illustrate his contention, Blatt considers an illegal gamble, importing heroin into Singapore, which will result in a death sentence if one is discovered, but which otherwise is very profitable. He then argues that, although it is rare for a would-be criminal to be deterred by a one-in-a-million chance of 'being hanged on the gallows', most such people *are* deterred:

> when they reckon that the probability p of hanging is *too* high; that is, once p becomes *large enough* (larger than some p_{max}), then no amount of money m will induce them to take the gamble.... For some people, p_{max} may be ½. For others, the gamble is still accepted (given sufficiently large incentive m) for p up to 0.9; even more reckless ones might be induced to gamble with their lives even when p is as large as 0.99. But sooner or later, the probability of survival, $1 - p$, becomes *too small* for the game to be worth the candle (Blatt, 1983, p. 254, emphasis added).

Such behaviour violates the first axiom of formal SEU theory, for it denies that 'everything has its price'; no amount of money in prospect can make the would-be criminal take the chance, if the prospect of being hanged is unacceptable. The clear implication is that a fully additive view of choice under uncertainty may be unrealistic, so Blatt (1983, pp. 279–82), following Roy (1952), proposes a two-stage approach: first, exclude projects with an excessive probability of disaster; second (and there he adheres to the additive methodology), rank non-excluded projects in terms of their expected returns calculated by a weighted averaging technique. This approach is clearly akin to a characteristic filtering/additive differences hybrid procedure of the kind discussed in section 7.7, except that it all takes place with respect to a single characteristic outcome scale. The procedures discussed in section 8.5 take Blatt's approach much further, for they are wholly non-additive within individual choice dimensions. Before we consider these, however, it is appropriate to examine Shackle's non-probabilistic analysis.

8.4 PROCEDURES THAT COMPARTMENTALISE GAINS AND LOSSES

Shackle (1949, 1955, 1958, 1979) has questioned the rationality of adding together mutually exclusive expected values that might be the sequel to a particular choice. He argues that as someone considers the possibility that the sequel to a particular choice may be a dismal failure, she will not expect to have her feelings of disappointment reduced by the thought that things might have turned out much better. A failure is a failure and in many cases there is no (or at least no low-cost) way of repeating an experiment to see whether, sometimes, it succeeds: put a foot wrong now in your choice of lifestyle or in many of its component activities and you may have to suffer the consequences hereafter. And even when people can expect to have another try at something following an initial disappointment, they are often difficult to console with soothing remarks about 'another time'—as Shackle (1955, p. 65) puts it, 'we live in the present moment'. That is to say, although people often run parts of their lives according to methodologies that make it difficult to decide when their experiments have failed (see sections 6.5 and 6.6), they often run other parts of their lives according to methodologies that categorise things as crucial experiments when they need not be, and consequently they end up 'jumping to conclusions'. Shackle applies a similar line of argument in respect of successful outcomes: the gloss is not removed from one's success by the thought that things might have turned out much worse, and success is not dulled the more so by the thought that things might have turned out much, much worse. If, in the event, things are successful, thinking about what could have happened instead will not change the level of attainments on the characteristic axis in question. Possible outcomes are conceptually separate rivals and, in Shackle's way of thinking, it makes no sense to add them up.

As well as voicing these philosophical concerns, Shackle argues that in practice people do not add together all of each scheme's rival outcome/potential surprise ratings. Rather, he argues that their minds focus on particular pairs of attention-stealing pairs of gains and losses, either side of a reference point which he calls a 'neutral outcome' (which he (1958, p. 48) defines as 'a hypothetical outcome whose realisation would leave the decision maker feeling neither better nor worse off than he does at present'). The ability of a hypothetical outcome to attract the consumer's attention will depend a combination of two things: (1) how far distant it is from the neutral outcome (large potential gains or losses will be much more attention arresting than small ones—an idea which is clearly compatible with my suggestion that the consumer is choosing with a view to the possible number of constructive and destructive implications her action might have for her expectation-forming system); and (2) how difficult it seems to disbelieve (outcomes that are easily dismissed as seeming 'practically impossible' will be less able to capture a person's attention, other things equal, than ones in whose way seem to lie few obstacles). The pair of potential outcomes upon which the consumer's attention is fixed for a particular scheme in respect of the characteristic in question is called 'primary focus outcomes'; they will not, in Shackle's own analysis, normally be identical for each scheme. Focus gains and focus losses will often be associated with different degrees of potential surprise for a single scheme of action as well as between rival schemes. This possibility is illustrated in Figure 8.1. The neutral outcome is labelled A_N (I would prefer the term 'neutral aspiration'). Potential surprise curves for two schemes, YY and ZZ, are shown as bold lines. The other curves on the figure are indifference curves that represent what Shackle calls an 'ascendency function', in other words, the ranking of potential surprise/gain and potential surprise/loss combinations in the order of their ability to attract the consumer's attention. The attention-attracting power of a

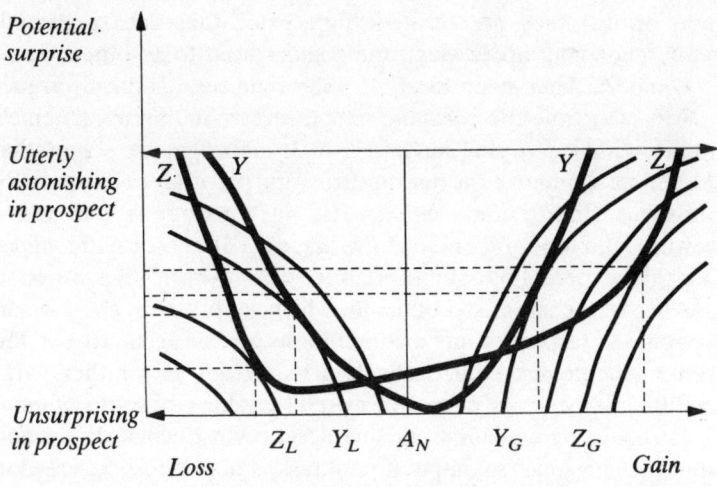

Figure 8.1: Focus outcomes for a pair of options in respect of a single characteristic

possible outcome increases as we move away to the bottom-right or bottom-left of the diagram from the point of intersection between the maximum surprise line and the line linking it in a perpendicular manner to A_N. The most attention-attracting outcomes are those where potential surprise curves are tangential to these 'ascendency' indifference curves (or 'isoascendency lines').

The next stage of the consumer's problem is somehow to compare these rival pairings and rank them. In Shackle's theory this involves the consumer in converting each of the primary focus outcomes into 'standardised focus outcomes'. His idea is that we should think of the decision maker as shifting her focus from the primary focus outcomes to hypothetical outcomes that are similarly attention arresting but which would not be a cause for surprise. These are found on Figure 8.1 by following each of the isoascendency lines to which the potential surprise curves are tangential, until one comes to the 'unsurprising in prospect' line at the bottom of the diagram. Scheme YY has Y_L as its standardised focus loss and Y_G as its standardised focus gain. Scheme ZZ's standardised focus loss and gain are, respectively, Z_L and Z_G. These standardised focus outcomes are then supposed to be examined in relation to the consumer's 'gambler preference map', and are ranked according to gambler indifference curves upon which they are located. Figure 8.2 illustrates a gambler preference map upon which the standardised focus outcomes for YY and ZZ have been located. The origin on this diagram is the neutral outcome the consumer has in mind, and all points on the indifference curve that passes through the origin are seen by her to be as attractive as an unsurprising neutral outcome is in prospect. Indifference curves rise in ranking as one moves towards the top-left corner of the diagram. In the case drawn, the consumer ranks both gambles above an unsurprising prospect of staying where she is (an outcome which, in practice, she *may* not imagine in respect of any of the options on her agenda). She also ranks scheme ZZ below scheme YY, though with rather flatter gambler indifference curves this would not have been the case.

It should be evident from this description of Shackle's theory that the consumer's computational task is in one respect eased by comparison with SEU theory; she focuses on only two of a possibly wide range of each scheme's imagined outcomes. However, what follows the 'primary focusing' is by no means simple (I

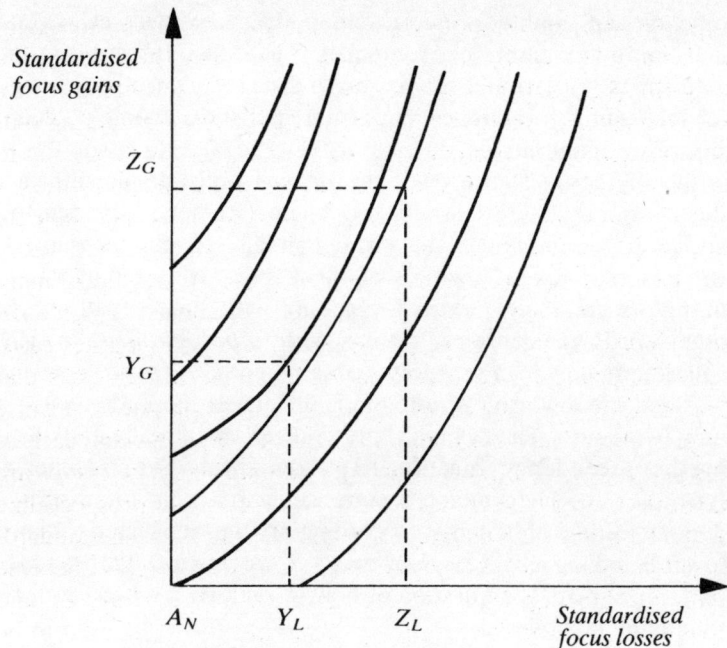

Figure 8.2: A gamble preference map

can recall finding Shackle's precise description very hard to grasp the first time I encountered his theory). Indeed, it looks decidedly neoclassical in its use of indifference curves, although one could take these as conveniently smooth approximations to the consumer's underlying mental ordering procedures. The most curious thing, however, is that despite Shackle's philosophical arguments about it being inappropriate to weigh together rival possibilities, the Shacklean consumer ultimately (on the gambler preference map) does effectively weigh gains and losses (albeit only one of each for each scheme) together. They are only kept in distinct mental compartments for part of the story, and while Shackle does not call a scheme's location on the consumer's gambler preference map its 'overall expected value', the fact that it is a single point formed from a gain and a loss does without doubt imply an aggregation of rival values.

As Ford (1983, Chapter 4) has noted, Shackle's ascendency

function and gambler preference map ideas have been called into question by a number of economists. The difficulty, and it is one with which Ford cannot see reason to disagree, concerns the need for the gambler preference map. Characteristic outcome/potential surprise configurations do not attract the attention simply by virtue of their distance from the neutral outcome/the difficulty the consumer has in disbelieving them. Rather, they demand attention to an extent that is dependent on the consumer's willingness to take chances, a willingness that is rooted in her set of judgemental procedures for coping with such situations. In other words, the consumer's stance with respect to taking chances will determine which two points on a potential surprise curve she will find most worthy of attention—if indeed she does focus on only two points. Her 'gambler preferences' are already embodied in the ascendency function. To have both the ascendency function and the gambler preference map seems to involve a double testing of schemes according to the consumer's stance towards taking chances. However, if we discard the gambler preference map, the question of how to rank rival schemes seems to remain unanswered.

One obvious possible way of getting by without the gambler preference map is to argue that precisely how attention arresting a particular primary focus outcome is to the consumer is a direct function of the implications she attaches to it. If so, we are have a cardinalist basis for the indifference curves in Shackle's ascendency function. We might then envisage the consumer as ranking schemes according to their net (implicational) primary focus outcomes. Net standardised focus scores would not have to be calculated, for they would be *ex hypothesi* identical to the net primary focus scores (see Ford, 1983, p. 106). In fact, although his work lacks the 'implicational' perspective I have incorporated from PCP, Shackle does formally define his ascendency function in cardinalist terms. But, when other theorists have proposed using the ascendency function directly to rank rival schemes, Shackle has continued to assert that his more complex view is valid; he sees his ascendency function not as a ranking device but as a theoretical construct that encapsulates how a consumer reduces complex conjectures to manageable pieces of information (that is, the pairs of gains and losses that make her stop and think); the role of the gambler preference map is to encapsulate how the consumer comes to rank the pairings that make her stop and think. From my own, 'implicational' standpoint, I feel inclined to side with Shackle's critics on this issue and discard the gambler preference map. My reasoning is as follows: a consumer's attitudes to gambling are personal constructs (which may differ from subsystem to subsystem) to which she may attach certain general implications; for example, the more of a gambler she construes herself to be, the less worrying she may find a low potential surprise rating for a particular possible loss, or a high potential surprise rating for a particular possible gain. Thus the implications she potentially attaches to a particular point on a potential surprise curve may depend not merely upon the characteristic output in question but also, given her view of risk taking in this area, upon its potential surprise rating. The ascendency function would therefore seem to embody her 'gambler preferences'.

Ford (1983, Chapter 5) wishes to amend Shackle's analysis even more by discarding the ascendency function as well as the gambler preference map. Ford is disturbed by the idea that rational decision makers might focus their attention in the manner implied by Shackle's ascendency function, for how can it be rational to discard some of the information one has at one's disposal, prior to reaching a decision? As Shackle (1961, pp. 176–7) sees it, the focusing process does involve the consumer in scanning all the information, and it is only *after* the ascendency function has done its work that part of the available information is left aside. Ford finds this argument of Shackle's unacceptable and he argues instead that 'if all the information at the disposal of the individual is to be utilised then there is no escaping the fact that an index has to be found through which the quintessence of an action scheme can be portrayed' (1983, p. 156). However, Ford approves of Shackle's idea that, during the process of making up their minds, people keep potential gains and losses—their hopes and fears—in separate mental compartments. His own proposal is something that he sees as combining Shackle's work with the additive, non-focusing approach of SEU theory. He suggests that decision makers first recodify potential surprise conjectures into a probabilistic form, to compute expected values for each possible outcome. Second, he assumes that, for each scheme, decision makers aggregate separately gain values and loss values on either side of the neutral outcome. Finally, they combine the utilities they attach to these overall gain and loss values into a single index from which rankings can be inferred. The end result of all this looks hardly different from that implied by the procedures of SEU theory: as Hey (1984, p. 206) remarks, 'what is this other than the expected value of some (utility) function of the prospect's payoffs? As such, it is open to questions similar to those raised at the end of section 8.2.

8.5 MOULDS OF TOLERANCE FOR UNCERTAIN PROSPECTS

If the 'Fordian' and 'net primary focus outcomes' amendments to Shackle's model seem unlikely to be employed by those decision makers who, for philosophical or computational reasons, wish to avoid adding ratings of rival gains and losses, we need to uncover other procedures by which they might be able to rank or select schemes in situations where overlaps amongst potential surprise curves makes their relative orderings far from obvious. In an early constructive critique of Shackle's work, Carter (1954, p. 59) argued that people might employ one of the following, very simple rules when they are not immediately able to reach unequivocal conclusions:

One is to look for a third course of action which can beat the other two.... Another is to delay action, if that is possible.... A third possibility is to do *both* the actions...; this is surely the origin of hedging. A fourth is to trust to chance, to toss a coin.

It will be observed that these rules may generate solutions to the problem of choice under uncertainty without any need for reference to ascendency functions and gambler preference maps. The first is clearly an example of problemistic search, whereas the fourth is reminiscent of Kornai's (1971) approach to conjunctive choices (see section 7.6). The third may frequently be ruled out due to indivisibilities, but the second seems eminently plausible, should the first fail.

Carter's rules are simple, but they look to me more like the kinds of procedures people will keep in reserve for those occasions on which other procedures leave them with indeterminate conclusions and a dilemma of a rather different kind from that discussed in section 7.6 (in that section, uncertainty centred on which combinations of characteristics would be appropriate choices, not on how to rank or select uncertain prospects in relation to a single-characteristic scale). From the standpoint of satisficing theory, one would expect the decision maker to be concerned, in the first instance, to discover which schemes look like being good enough gambles in respect of characteristics where their potential performances are open to doubt. If a consumer is employing a characteristic filtering procedure, it would seem likely that she might naturally think of employing one or both of the following two procedures whenever it is unclear whether a scheme will, in the event, pass an aspirational test she has set. It she is cautious and/or if there are many options available to her, she might adopt the rule of excluding schemes whose least-bad imagined outcomes fell short of her aspiration level (her neutral outcome/aspiration), and if no scheme survived this test she could employ the subsidiary procedure of choosing the least-bad failure. (In the case of Figure 8.1, this would mean that *YY* ranked above *ZZ*.) But she might recognise that this rule could be prone to result in needlessly poor outcomes. Therefore, she might adopt the alternative procedure of setting specifications for 'satisfactory gambles' and allowing through any schemes that could meet these, even if they were schemes that had some believable prospects that fell short of her aspiration; the schemes that survived such a test would thus be those upon which she felt a chance might be worth taking in respect of the characteristic in question. (My original (1983c, pp. 102–3) analysis mixes together these two possibilities in a way that I now regard as too demanding.) The question that naturally follows in relation to this second procedure is, 'what kind of specifications may a consumer set up as constituting a satisfactory gamble?'

In seeking to answer this question I find it useful to begin by considering a gamble in respect of a characteristic that the consumer sees as strictly dichotomous. Her aspiration is to be at one particular pole of the construct but it is not clear to her whether, if she selected a particular course of action, it would take her there. The potential surprise curve for such an option in respect of this construct must clearly comprise only two points, one potential surprise rating for each of the construct's poles.

One scenario we need to consider is where the consumer is presently open-minded and believes either outcome is perfectly possible; neither outcome would surprise her in the slightest if she chose the scheme. On the gainside, things look as good as they possibly could for this scheme in respect of this construct, so her attention is naturally directed at the seemingly perfectly possible downside outcome. This latter outcome she hopes to avoid, but recognises that she may not succeed in doing so if she selects the scheme. Any rule which demands that this counter-desired outcome should look at all surprising in prospect is going to class this scheme as an unsatisfactory gamble, even though the decision maker thinks that, if she chooses the scheme, it is perfectly possible for things to turn out just as she hopes in respect of this construct. This somewhat peculiar result makes it difficult for me to believe that such a rule would be very common in this situation. Rather, I would suggest we should not be surprised to find the consumer simply considering, in the light of her higher-level judgemental rules, whether or not she could live with the (net) implications of a downside outcome. If she judges that such an outcome would be unbearable, then she will reject *any* scheme of action in respect of which she can imagine no obstacles to both of the possible outcomes for the construct in question. If all of the options she has in mind fail such a test, then this construct cannot play a decisive role in the choice process and matters are referred to the next characteristic filter.

An alternative 'dichotomous' scenario would involve a situation where the consumer allows her degree of disbelief in one polar possibility to affect the degree of disbelief she assigns to its polar rival. For example, consider a woman thinking about using alternative contraception technologies that could leave her either pregnant or pregnancy-free (and which, one might note, will vary in respect of scalar characteristics such as convenience of use or extent of side-effects). If she would be exceedingly surprised to find herself pregnant if she used technique A, then she would be hardly surprised at all to find herself avoiding pregnancy; whereas if she anticipated feeling relatively little surprise at finding herself pregnant if she used the statistically less reliable technique B, then she would be quite surprised to find herself escaping pregnancy. With these kinds of conjectures, neither outcome seems perfectly possible and it is easier to imagine the consumer using a decision rule which works with reference to her assignments of potential surprise.

The logic of this second situation seems to be that the consumer only needs to focus her attention on one pole of the dichotomous construct in question (in this case, *either* on 'get pregnant' *or* on 'escape pregnancy'). This is because the 'either/or' nature of the rival possible outcomes means that the implications of ending up at one pole are simply the reverse of those she has attached to ending up at the other pole. The situation contrasts with that for scalar constructs and outcome possibilities either side of an aspiration level, decision rules for which I will consider later in this section. In the scalar case the problem is that when a particular outcome eventuates, one of its implications is that more than one rival set of implications has failed to arise: by definition, a range of alternative possibilities, each of which has its own set of implications, has been precluded. From the Shacklean standpoint, it would make little sense to say that the reverse of the eventuating set of implications is to be inferred from some kind of weighted average of these forgone implicational sets.

For whichever pole of the construct the consumer chose to focus upon she could set herself a threshold of tolerable potential surprise, within whose boundary her uncertain conjectures would have to fall. One would expect the height of the threshold to be correlated with the implications the consumer had associated with the outcome in question. In the case of desired outcomes, the height of the threshold would be taken by its distance from *maximum* potential surprise, whereas for counter desired outcomes the height of the threshold would be taken by its distance from minimum potential surprise. This is because one would prefer *not* to be surprised by good outcomes and prefer to be surprised by bad outcomes. Thus the consumer in our example either might ask herself, according to her own standards of tolerance, 'if I choose this method of contraception, does it look sufficiently potentially *un*surprising (likely) that I'll escape getting pregnant?'; or she might ask herself, 'if I choose this method of contraception, does pregnancy look sufficiently potentially surprising (unlikely) for me?' But she would have no obvious need to ask herself both questions. If no schemes seemed satisfactory gambles, the consumer could employ the subsidiary rule of selecting the least bad failure. Where several schemes tied as least bad, the rule could be to allow the tied schemes on to the next characteristic filter.

The analysis just outlined can be extended in two ways to cover uncertainty in respect of scalar constructs. One way is undemanding in information-processing terms and has an obvious parallel with Shackle's focusing ideas—which means that it would seem irrational to Professor Ford; the other way is rather more complicated but does not presume the consumer engages in any focusing. The former I call the 'two-point adequacy test' and the latter may be called the 'loss-gain potential surprise curve test'.

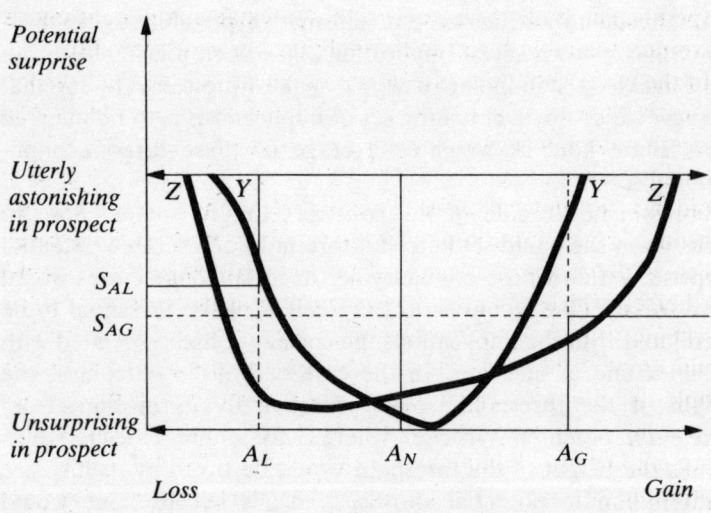

Figure 8.3: A 'two point test' filter for rival potential surprise curves

The 'two-point test' idea is most easily understood with the aid of Figure 8.3. Once again, we have potential surprise curves for two schemes, YY and ZZ. The neutral outcome A_N may be taken to represent the consumer's target for this characteristic. Any potential surprise curve whose left-most portion hits the maximum potential surprise line at or to the right of A_N has passed this characteristic filter test even if it is recognised to be an uncertain prospect. For schemes that do not pass in this simple manner, the consumer has a second, two-point test. Such schemes must seem sufficiently likely not to produce a result as bad as A_L, her loss-avoidance aspiration for this characteristic. The test of whether they seem sufficiently likely not to produce such a bad result is the ability of their potential surprise curves to avoid coming into the region that is left of and below the boundary defined by A_L and by S_{AL}, which is the consumer's minimum tolerable surprise threshold for her loss-avoidance aspiration. Schemes must also seem sufficiently likely to produce a result at least as good as A_G, the consumer's gain-aspiration level for this characteristic. They fail this part of the test if their potential surprise curves do not cut the unbroken lines that are perpendicular both to A_G and to S_{AG}, which is the consumer's maximum tolerable surprise threshold for her gain-aspiration.

In the case of the schemes shown in Figure 8.3, neither scheme passes both tests. ZZ passes the gain aspiration test, but looks altogether too likely to produce an outcome equal to the loss-avoidance aspiration. On the other hand, YY passes the loss-avoidance test but seems insufficiently promising in respect of the consumer's gain aspiration. The consumer must then discover which is the least unsatisfactory gamble. In doing so, she could ask herself which of the tests she regards it as more important for a scheme to pass (and if no schemes have passed either test she could employ the subsidiary procedures discussed in relation to simple dichotomous constructs): if she attaches more importance to passing the loss-avoidance test, YY will win; if she attaches more importance to finding a scheme that will pass the gain-aspiration test, ZZ will win. Without a knowledge of this consumer's way of organising her ideas, we cannot judge which scheme she would prefer. We should also note that the consumer might instead employ one of the procedures suggested by Carter (though tossing a coin is difficult to use if there are more than two schemes between which to choose).

The 'two-point test' idea just described is without doubt open to Fordian objections, in that the consumer does look only at a pair of 'gambler aspiration levels' once she has found that a scheme seems in doubt in respect of her neutral aspiration for the characteristic under consideration; she does discard information in trying to reach her decision in a manageable way. Recognition of the dangers of doing this may make the consumer try to employ a 'tolerable loss–gain surprise curve test' (an idea that Shackle himself first suggested in a personal communication to me—see Earl, 1983c, p. 107). The idea here is that, for each possible outcome on the characteristic scale under consideration, the consumer sets a target: for maximum tolerable potential surprise for outcomes in excess of her neutral aspiration, and for minimum tolerable potential surprise for outcomes less than her neutral aspiration. Hence, instead of a pair of gambler adequacy tests, we may have as many tests as there are points making up the potential surprise curves. Such a set of tests could be depicted graphically as a curve defining the boundaries within which satisfactory potential surprise curves could move. For possible outcomes less than the neutral aspiration, a potential surprise curve could only be deemed satisfactory if it never passed to the left of the test boundary; whereas for possible outcomes in excess of the neutral outcome, a scheme seen as a gamble would only seem satisfactory if its potential surprise curve always passed to the right of the test boundary. One would expect that, the greater the possible loss, the less plausible the consumer would have to find it for it to seem acceptable as a prospect; whereas, the greater the possible gain, the less demanding a test of plausibility a potential surprise curve would have to satisfy. (In other words, near disasters would have to look pretty incredible in prospect, but fairly small prospective gains would have to have little seemingly standing in their way.)

Such a set of gambler adequacy tests could be thought of as defining the consumer's mould of tolerance for schemes that do not seem to be guaranteed to meet her neutral aspiration for the characteristic in question. To be acceptable in *that* dimension, a perceived gamble must pass *all* the relevant tests; a scheme which seems excessively likely to produce a particular loss will not be let through by virtue of its apparent ability (if it has one) to offer a more than necessarily plausible prospect of an outcome in excess of the neutral aspiration. However, if the consumer can find no schemes which fit the mould of tolerance or promise to meet her neutral aspiration, she may judge which is the least-unsatisfactory option in respect of the particular characteristic scale by seeing which one passes the most gambling tests in a priority order.

Where two or more schemes tie on this basis, the best scheme is the one which comes closest to passing the next-highest-ranking gambling test, in terms of its degree of potential surprise for that particular outcome.

The parallels should be obvious between the procedures I have just outlined and the characteristic filtering procedures discussed, for multicharacteristic choices, in the previous chapter: their intolerance may look irrational from the standpoint of orthodox analysis, and yet they do not involve the decision maker in adding up rival outcomes in a manner that is either philosophically questionable or which assumes an excessively implausible ability to process information. Evidently, the more difficult the consumer finds it to think in terms of scalar possibilities, the more her mould of tolerance for a particular characteristic scale will tend to collapse to the two-point test filter, or even to a strictly dichotomous way of looking at things. However, the fewer the possibilities with which she tries to deal, the less computationally imperative it will be for her to adhere to a Shacklean philosophy and avoid adding together a scheme's rival possibilities as a means towards reaching a decision about whether or not to select it.

8.6 RULES FOR WHEN 'WE SIMPLY DO NOT KNOW'

The decision-making procedures discussed so far in this chapter all presume that the consumer is not in a worrying situation where she feels she 'hasn't a clue' and 'simply does not know'. All of these procedures break down if the consumer cannot assign degrees of disbelief, or 'probabilities', to rival potential outcomes in respect of pertinent scalar or dichotomous construct axes. If such situations arise, what can consumers do to try to predict and control events? To avoid anxiety they need *some* kind of 'recipe for success'.

Experience as an examiner of undergraduate students operating in one of life's brutal environments (see my comments in section 9.6 on laboratory experimentation in economic psychology) is most instructive in respect of the kinds of procedures people employ when they feel they lack knowledge or the ability to store and process it. When they set out for the examination hall, many

of the examinees will have taken precautions such as the following:
(1) see what 'their stars' have to offer in the way of advice;
(2) make sure they get out of bed from 'the right side';
(3) make sure that they have not forgotten the 'lucky mascot' that accompanied them on their past successes;
(4) desperately spend many hours not in revision but in attempting to spot, on the basis of past 'patterns', the questions that *will* eventuate, even though their examiners may assure them that they select topics at random from amongst the topics on the syllabus.

The stakes may be high, but the preparatory procedures are likely to be essentially *superstitious* in nature; the examinees rely on beliefs that certain events are causally linked even though they would be hard pushed to explain precisely how. One might hope that people would grow out of such 'unscientific' modes of behaviour once they have graduated (and graduate they often will, even after 'wasting' their time on 'question spotting' and so on). But Gimpl and Dakin (1984) have recently argued most persuasively that, in the turbulent and unpredictable world of business:

management's enchantment with the magical rites of long-range planning, forecasting, and several other future-oriented techniques is a manifestation of anxiety-relieving superstitious behaviour, and ... forecasting and planning have the same function that magical rites have. Anthropologists and psychologists have long argued that magical rites and superstitious behaviour serve very important functions: they make the world seem more deterministic and give us confidence in our ability to cope, they unite the managerial tribe, and they induce us to take action, at least when the omens are favourable (1984, p. 125).

Maital (1982, p. 230) has come to a similar conclusion concerning the means by which people seek to arrange their savings in portfolios of securities which trade in that most random of markets, the stock market. The idea that people use superstition as a device for facing up to unpredictable events may seem highly unscientific, and to run at odds with the 'man the scientist' theme that pervades this book. However, we should take note of Feyerabend's (1975) study of how academic scientists behave in practice: they are much more sloppy and willing to jump to questionable inferences of causation than they typically claim to be, and it is far from obvious where one should draw the dividing line between science, storytelling and magic or mythology.

Having followed superstitious preparatory procedures and having tried to force random events into predictable patterns, the student, like any other decision maker, may find that, in the event, she does indeed 'not have a clue' about what her examiners expect of some parts of the questions they have laid before her. Among the procedures she will employ for dealing with this source of anxiety are:

(1) flee from the examination hall at the first possible opportunity;
(2) attempt to copy the answers of her peers at nearby desks;
(3) write down absolutely anything that comes into her head that seems even vaguely related to the questions that she attempts (a practice that can produce a script which looks for all the world as if it has been produced by someone suffering from thought-disordered schizophrenia);
(4) attempt questions despite knowing nothing about certain parts of them, and answer as if these parts did not exist at all (often after having impulsively chosen the questions in the belief that she will be able to remember pertinent material before running out of time);
(5) hedge what she says in her answers with a non-committal approach;
(6) answer multiple-choice questions with random guesses, or according to some deterministic procedure that relates her ignorance-based selections to her confident answers (for example, 'the last two were definitely option (4) answers: they wouldn't have set three in a row...');
(7) sit and wait for inspiration.

Most of these procedures should not appear surprising in the light of earlier sections: (1) and (4) are foreshadowed in section 4.4, while the procedure of *ignoring* things about which we know nothing was also mentioned by Keynes (1937) in his discussion of the problem of decision making when 'we simply do not know'; (3) fits in with section 6.5; (5), (6) and (7) are basically variations on the ideas of Carter, listed at the start of section 8.5, though of course (5), the hedging approach, is a consistent theme in this book. Procedure (2) is, one hopes, fairly rarely employed in examinations, but in life generally it may be exceedingly widespread. Keynes certainly gave great emphasis to the role of crowd behaviour in his (1937) article: after discussing how people ignore phenomena they cannot anticipate with any confidence, he suggested that they often choose in conformity with the majority, in the belief that others are better informed than themselves. To the extent that people who recognise their own ignorance copy the behaviour of those whom they see as good judges, firms would do well to identify the kind of people who are used as reference points by the others, and then concentrate their selling efforts upon shaping the behaviour of these opinion leaders or producing goods and services that will be acceptable to them. Market research may therefore need to encompass not merely consumer psychology but also sociological inquiries to uncover the structures of the community and cultural networks within which people attempt to predict and control events (see Marris, 1964, Chapter 4).

8.7 CONCLUSION

After presenting many chapters outlining the challenges and complexities of the decision problems that face consumer, I must doubtless have disappointed many non-specialist readers of this chapter by informing them what they knew all along: consumers will often try to avoid taking chances with things that they see as 'too risky' on the down side and/or 'insufficiently attractive' on the gain side, or that they will often use superstitions and pretty crude rules of thumb in order to deal with situations into which they lack much insight. For this, I apologise. However, what may seem altogether familiar to lay readers may none the less disturb economists brought up according to the principles of SEU theory—particularly since I have not asserted that any one rule will have universal currency amongst decision makers or in respect of all the diverse situations that any one consumer may confront. All the variously shaped rules considered in this chapter *could* belong to the set of judgemental procedures that a consumer might try to employ to cope with life. But this is not to say that all consumers include all of them in their repertoires or that all consumers would find them equally easy to employ in 'similar' situations. Nor is it to say that these are the only procedures some people might employ sometimes when they perceive uncertainty; I would not be at all surprised to find that there are others. Such an admission may seem shocking to economists used to assuming that decision makers behave 'as if' they have well-defined preference orderings over all possible states of the world and that they can attach probabilities to these states. If so, they might do well to pause and consider how they themselves have come to favour one particular tentatively proposed theory of choice under uncertainty—namely SEU theory—over all others.

9 Non-Compensatory Choices in Retrospect and Prospect

9.1 INTRODUCTION

It would be very gratifying to discover that most economists who encountered Chapters 7 and 8 found themselves easy converts to the analysis contained therein. Were this the case, I would have brought about a peaceful but revolutionary change in their attitudes; for they would be jettisoning the *general* principle of 'gross substitution', a core construct in the neoclassical economics research programme. Their minds would admit the possibility of non-compensatory and often priorities-based choice heuristics. They would also recognise the possibility that seriously erroneous policy recommendations could be the sequel to analysis conducted with the aid of choice models into which substitution effects have been built via the assumption that preferences are always convex. (We shall see in Chapter 10 that my alternative analysis does indeed have distinctive policy implications.) The kinds of research they wished to undertake, and/or the notions they wished to teach, could change dramatically.

Unfortunately, the omens are not encouraging. As I have already pointed out, much of what is contained in Chapters 7 and 8 is not unprecedented, but previous attempts to propose non-compensatory analyses of choice have not succeeded in bringing about a revolutionary change in outlook amongst consumer behaviour scholars in general. The aims of this chapter are therefore: to provide converts with more ammunition to justify to sceptics their acceptance of the ideas I have outlined, and to try to open further the minds of at least some of those readers who, as yet, remain incompletely convinced of the plausibility of the present analysis. The plan of this chapter is to explore some of the previous contributions (section 9.2), examine how orthodox theorists have reacted to them (section 9.3) and consider some additional arguments to show how non-compensatory notions are not as easily disbelieved as some theorists might like to think (section 9.4 and 9.5). The chapter ends with a consideration of new possibilities for empirical work (section 9.6).

9.2 ANTECEDENT ANALYSES

The first thing to note about many of the forerunners to the present analysis of non-compensatory choices is that they are not 'behavioural' in spirit, since they do not involve satiation or the setting of aspirational cut-offs. In particular, they pertain to choice procedures usually described as 'lexicographic', owing to their resemblance to the process of looking up a word in a dictionary (a 'lexicon'). One only looks at the second priority (proceeds to find the second letter) if there is a tie in respect of outright attainments for the first priority (if one has found the first letter). Some neat examples of this procedure are to be found in Linder (1977, p. 145) and Hawkins *et al.* (1980, p. 454), while Fishburn (1974) has provided a very thorough and formal technical review. I prefer to call such a procedure by the name 'naive lexicographic', and to class characteristic filtering as a 'behavioural lexicographic' rule, in order to contrast the two approaches.

It is certainly important that characteristic filtering procedures are not confused with the more widespread expositions of 'naive' priority approaches to choice. The adjective 'naive' may sound somewhat derogatory; but in many cases it would indeed be a foolish consumer who followed a strict lexicographic procedure. A 'naive lexicographic' procedure is far more *obviously* likely to result in a consumer choosing action schemes that are needlessly inferior as far as the development of her construct system is concerned. Most consumers will at least be able to see why the 'naive' procedure is likely to result in error, even if they cannot confidently sum together net implications associated with different dimensions of choice. Such a procedure, that is to say, may not appear a rational one to employ even if one is suffering from bounded rationality. By contrast, a particular characteristic filtering procedure that has been chosen as a means of approximating compensatory choices in complex situations seems to have a decidedly rational basis (see section 7.4).

Having attempted to make clear how my approach differs from conventional lexicographic procedures, I must now try to make sure it is not instead confused with the 'elimination by aspects' procedure proposed by Tversky (1972) and for which Payne (1976) and Svenson (1979) have identified a good deal of empirical support. With this procedure, aspirational cut-offs are set and rival schemes are examined in respect of them, one characteristic at a time, just as in characteristic filtering. However, the filtering procedure embodied in elimination by aspects involves no particular ordering of desired characteristics: as Hawkins *et al.* (1980, p. 445) put it, 'there is an equal chance of any attribute being considered at each stage of the choice process'. With this rule, the scheme that wins passes a test that no other scheme still on the agenda can pass. The victorious scheme *may* be the only one to possess the characteristic in question, but it may have been possessed by a scheme that was eliminated at an earlier stage. The scope for misidentifying elimination by aspects as characteristic filtering—particularly as some of the short-cut variants of the latter (section 7.5)—seems considerable: not everyone is as careful as Hawkins *et al.* to mention the absence of a specific ordering of characteristics. I can recall how I failed to see the difference when I first encountered elimination by aspects in a paper by Johnson (1979), and it is interesting to note that although Hawkins *et al.* and Johnson each consider 'naive' lexicographic rules and elimination by aspects neither considers a priority-based procedure involving cut-off targets.

Yet more scope for confusion arises because of the variety of contexts in which the priority idea has so far been discussed. It has been applied to:

(1) the characteristics space without necessarily having to apply to the goods space;
(2) the characteristics and goods spaces simultaneously;
(3) patterns of choice in the goods space, though not to preferences;
(4) preferences in the goods space, with no consideration of how they relate to preferences in characteristics space.

Approach (1) is the one that I have adopted (see also Ironmonger, 1972, pp. 23–35); but let us now consider some examples of the other approaches.

Approach (2) underlies the emphasis that Post Keynesian

authors such as Canterbery (1979) and Pasinetti (1981, Chapter IV) give to the role of income effects, rather than substitution effects, in explaining changes in the structure of production. The idea that consumers have a hierarchy of wants is argued to fit in well with observations of Engel curves with kinks: having satisfied their basic nourishment wants, consumers do not buy ever-larger volumes of food as their incomes rise; rather, they use their extra incomes to help satisfy their second-most-important want, and so on. Engel curves that depict behaviour in the aggregate will gradually flatten out as affluence trickles down to the relatively poor. However, these authors do not appear to have given a great deal of attention to the complications caused by the possibility that particular wants may be satisfied by a variety of different goods in different combinations. If one is to observe kinked Engel curves for all commodity classes (as Canterbery, 1979, pp. 85–7, seems to expect), then this only seems compatible with each class of commodity having at least one want which it alone is capable of satisfying. Otherwise, we should expect to observe that inferior goods are very common. How important an objection this is to the idea that priorities over wants imply priorities over goods depends on the level of aggregation—for example, potatoes may be an inferior good, while food as a whole is not.

Approach (3) is used in the work of Paroush (1965, 1973) who uses theoretical models based on, respectively, conventional n-dimensional indifference analysis and Lancaster's characteristics approach to analyse the tendency for consumers to acquire *indivisible* durables in well-defined sequences. Paroush emphasises that priority patterns of consumption in a world of indivisibilities and complementarities may be technologically determined and very largely independent of underlying willingnesses to make trade-offs. He notes, for example, that: 'the usefulness of an electric mixer for making a pie cannot be exploited in the absence of an oven to bake it in and a refrigerator to preserve it' (1973, p. 92). It is thus easy to see why someone might purchase goods in the order: stove, refrigerator, mixer—even if her underlying preferences, in either the goods or characteristics spaces, were such that she would ideally be keen to perform trade-offs. Approach (4) is what advanced neoclassical consumer theory texts usually have in mind when they mention lexicographic orderings as preference systems that violate the axiom of continuity (see Deaton and Muellbauer, 1980, p. 27, and Malinvaud, 1972, p. 20). The empirical work carried out by Pyatt (1964) on the acquisition of consumer durables could also be listed as following approach (4), even though Pyatt (1964, pp. 4–5) does briefly consider the possibility of wants being satiable. It is irrelevant to Pyatt 'whether or not consumers have weakly or strongly ordered preferences or if they are rational or irrational in their behaviour' (1964, p. 10). For he begins with observations concerning: (a) the orders in which samples of individual consumers have made their purchases of durables in the past, (b) how fast they moved along these orderings, and (c) what they say they plan next to purchase. With this data he moves to a probabilistic, differential equation model which enables him to derive short-run estimates of the overall patterns of demand for the household durables that different groups are accumulating *in* different orders and at different rates. These estimates—made at the market, not the brand, level—can be derived without trying to decide which underlying wants households are trying to satisfy, or how these wants might be structured (see also Pickering, 1977, Chapter 1).

Within the literature of the behavioural theory of the firm, one finds a decision-making procedure that has a good deal in common with characteristic filtering, namely the procedure of giving 'sequential attention to goals' (Cyert and March, 1963, pp. 35–6; 118). It is suggested that an organisation attempts to deal first with the most important failure to meet aspirations and, having seemingly done this, moves on to fight the next fire (see also Radner, 1975). Attempts to solve one problem seem to succeed for a time, but cause other problems to arise, with the result that the organisation seems constantly to be 'going round in circles'. I have observed this happen in university student assessment systems—even in those designed by academics who have read Cyert and March! Coursework part-assessment is phased out owing to the administrative complexities and marking burdens it imposes; examination-only assessment then results in the defection of potential students to departments that offer coursework assessments; the crisis of numbers leads to the reintroduction of coursework assessments; and so on.

Two conditions seem to promote such behaviour: a sudden

perception of a *crisis* of attainments (that is, a kaleidic shift of view which admits all manner of disturbing implications associated with allowing the present state to persist), and possible remedies that involve spill-over effects that are too complex to assess properly. The crisis heightens the decision maker's awareness of the bad implications of the choice she has made, which have put her in the situation she now construes; it also adds a pressure to come up rapidly with a solution. Under pressure, however, it is not easy to develop the lines of thought that may be necessary for seeing spill-over effects of potential solutions. All that the decision maker can do is go 'from the sublime to the ridiculous', to switch her preferred pole on an existing construct from one end to the other (see Kelly, 1955, pp. 128–9, and, for a similarly spirited view which also involves an application of catastrophe theory to the analysis of curriculum cycles, see Thompson, 1979, Chapter 8).

In the context of consumer behaviour, the practice of giving sequential attention to goals may be illustrated, in the light of this discussion, with a scenario concerning a consumer who superficially sees cars in terms of a 'performance *versus* economy' construct. The latest repair bill and weekly petrol bill combine to form 'the last straw' as far as her research programme of running an old 'gas-guzzler' is concerned; she swings impulsively from the 'performance' pole to the 'economy' pole of her construct and trades in her vehicle as part-payment for a brand new mini. She fails to construct the appropriate channels for thinking in depth about the real economy potential of her forsaken car: for example, whether or not the new car's lower running costs might be swamped by the higher depreciation costs and interest charges/forgone interest on capital that she now incurs. Subsequently, she may suffer another crisis, but one of performance, not economy (for example, an overtaking near-miss), which makes her admit that her small-car experiment has failed. She then embarks upon another attempt at running a successful research programme with a different, old, high-powered car.

In the light of my analysis of the choice of aspirations and priorities (section 7.4) it is appropriate to note that such extreme gyrations of behaviour—where goals are attended to via sequentially separated choices rather than *within* a single filtering procedure—may not be repeated if the consumer starts to see that a fairly new, medium-powered car might do the trick. Even so, it could be the case that over a number of years the consumer's preferences oscillated between different mixes of performance and economy before she stumbled upon a 'happy medium'. And it should not be forgotten that changes in income and technological possibilities could prevent the consumer from ever settling on one particular mould of tolerance for the commodity category in question.

9.3 ORTHODOX REACTIONS

The literature just considered—which is by no means the total output of its kind—should represent a cause for discomfort amongst mainstream neoclassical economists, for it suggests that there are quite a few people who are willing to dispense with continuous, differentiable utility functions. To assume preferences are ordered in terms of priorities not only precludes the use of a simple mathematical technique such as calculus in the formal analysis of choice. It also poses serious questions in respect of attempts to analyse convergence and stability in economic systems from a general equilibrium standpoint. This is because the utilities enjoyed by decision makers with lexicographic preferences may break off or change direction sharply with movements along some paths in their consumption sets (see Green, 1976, p. 82). Thus, as Ironmonger (1972) has emphasised, stable market level connections between changes in price and consumption depend on consumers differing in their tastes, incomes and awareness of consumption technologies. Remove these differences, and markets populated by 'representative' priorities-oriented consumers become prone to discontinuous kaleidoscopic changes, not incremental adjustments.

That the priority idea should pose such a threat to the overall methodology of the modern neoclassical theorists is rather ironic, since it was on the principle of an hierarchy of needs that Menger's (1871) initial explanation of the Law of Diminishing Marginal Utility was based. This point is emphasised in the work of Lutz and Lux (1979, pp. 44–5)—work which is strongly influenced by more recent writings on priorities, and on hierarchies of needs, by Georgescu-Roegen (1954) and by the psychologist

Maslow (1970). Menger illustrated his idea with the example of an isolated farmer with a poor harvest. The farmer's most urgent need would be to keep himself and his family alive. If his harvest exceeded this subsistence level, he could move on to allocate the surplus to meet his other needs, in the order of their decreasing importance—first, seeds for next year's crop; second, food for the farm animals, and so on. The one commodity—grain—could satisfy a *series* of needs ranked according to their diminishing importance. Lutz and Lux suggest that Menger's idea of a hierarchy of needs was swept aside in the flood of mathematical contributions that the marginal utility idea provoked; the idea of a list of needs did not mesh with the original marginalists' treatment of utility in cardinalist terms.

Despite only using an ordinalist approach to preferences, modern-day marginalists show little inclination to examine the literature on non-compensatory preferences either critically or in detail as they proceed to define the axiom of continuity. Even in 'state of the art' graduate texts, one only finds very brief discussions of lexicographic orderings, which are included merely as vehicles for demonstrating the analytical convenience of convex preferences. Deaton and Muellbauer (1980, p. 27) devote a paragraph to a 'naive' lexicographic example set in the goods space. They then say merely that it represents 'a perfectly reasonable system of choice', but one that it is 'convenient' to rule out. It is quite clear that Deaton and Muellbauer are utterly unconcerned with the empirical significance of lexicographic orderings; it is as if their first priority concerned mathematical tractability. Noteworthy, too, is their total failure to consider a satisficing priority model in characteristics space: this would be even more inconvenient as it would conflict with the axiom of non-satiation. Its omission is, perhaps, hardly surprising since only one of the fourteen chapters of the work in question deals with choice in terms of characteristics. Malinvaud's (1972, p. 20) example of lexicographic preferences is similar, though aided by a diagrammatic presentation. He asserts that 'it is hardly likely to arise in economics' and that its elimination involves little loss 'in the way of realism'. But Malinvaud does not seem to pause long enough to consider the events in everyday life where people apparently attempt to achieve some goals, or pursue some activities, 'at all costs'. Nor does he apply his skills as a casual empiricist to a 'behavioural lexicographic' choice system; like Deaton and Muellbauer, he moves on without further ado to propose the axiom of non-satiation.

Kelvin Lancaster (1971, pp. 146–56) is the only neoclassical theorist that I have discovered displaying a good awareness of the earlier literature on hierarchies and on the satiability of needs and wants, in both characteristics and goods spaces. His analysis is both tantalising and infuriating to a behavioural theorist, since his neoclassical upbringing seems to lead him to want automatically to examine satiation in terms of indifference curves, with only one characteristic depicted in his two-dimensional diagrams as being prone to satiation. Had he drawn diagrams where all characteristics were satiable (see Figure 9.2 in section 9.4 below), he might naturally have come to think in characteristic filtering terms. Unfortunately for the profession, though not for the present author, he did not do so.

Priorities-based choice heuristics also fail to receive major attention in most marketing texts. In my earlier work (1983c, p. 91) I highlighted the methodological sloppiness of the third edition of the market leader written by Engel and Blackwell. Their fourth edition appeared while my work was in the press; it is hardly less cavalier in its treatment of non-compensatory choice heuristics. For the first time, Engel and Blackwell (1982, pp. 422–3) introduce a 'sequential elimination' heuristic but they do not explicitly say whether this involves elimination by aspects or whether it is a behavioural version of the (naive) lexicographic heuristic that, citing Tversky (1969), they briefly mention. They have edited out any reference to the discussion paper by Reilly *et al.* (1976); hitherto, they had noted this as a study in which a majority of a sample of car-buying subjects said a lexicographic decision rule sounded most like the one they used and in which only about a third professed to employ a compensatory heuristic. (These findings have since been published in Reilly and Holman, 1977. In this investigation, the lack of empirical support for a conjunctive procedure may merely reflect the fact that, as far as the subjects in the sample were concerned, none of the options would survive a conjunctive test.) Instead, in relation to the sequential elimination heuristic, Engel and Blackwell note the study by Weitz and Wright (1979) as suggesting that this rule 'is used when people must make relatively hasty judgements and imagine that a final product decision is imminent' (1982, p. 423). They do not note that this study is built around potentially crucial choices of family-planning techniques, as they go on to profess a casual preference for compensatory heuristics (despite their later (pp. 454–9) newly cautious approach to Fishbein's model in the light of recent empirical work that has been conducted in the field as opposed to the classroom). What they *do* say is this: 'It is important to note that there is a growing consensus that compensatory strategies are used under high involvement. Most likely there is a relatively large set of evaluation criteria, and product attributes are then combined in a compensatory fashion' (p. 423). And then, briefly, they suddenly recognise the possibility of contingent sets of rules being used; citing the findings of Lussier and Olshavsky (1979), they add the throw-away comment that, when the number of alternatives is large, 'a non-compensatory conjunctive strategy often is used to eliminate unacceptable alternatives, followed by a shift to compensatory assessment of the remaining acceptable alternatives'.

The minimal justification offered by Engel and Blackwell for their preference for compensatory approaches to choice looks particularly curious when set against the somewhat more open-minded and cautious approach of Green and Srinivasan (1978) in a major survey article on conjoint compensatory models (actually cited in Engel and Blackwell, 1982, pp. 427–8). They note that research aimed at discovering whether consumers actually use compensatory methods, or conjunctive or lexicographic simplifying procedures (for example, Russ, 1971, Wright, 1975, and Hansen, 1976) seems to suggest that different consumers prefer different decision methods, though there is a general preference in the direction of those requiring simpler processes. These findings ultimately do not prevent Green and Srinivasan from proposing to continue to use compensatory models as *general* theories of decision making—but at least they offer a reasoned justification for doing so.

First they argue that the lexicographic procedure is 'a special case... where the weight for the most important attribute is considerably larger than the second most important attribute' (1978, p. 107). This seems to fail to grapple with the potential for outright intolerance in priorities-based procedures, which means that schemes knocked out in a high-level test are not even evaluated at lower-level filters (see Blatt's (1983) critique of expected utility theory, discussed in section 8.4, which implies that formally it is inappropriate to represent breaches of the principle of gross substitution in terms of extreme skewness of weights). Second, Green and Srinivasan make out an instrumentalist case, that 'the compensatory model of conjoint analysis can approximate the outcomes of other kinds of decision rules quite closely' (p. 107), and they suggest that the conditions under which this can happen are not implausible. The conditions involve tendencies for: (a) attribute ratings to be correlated, (b) consumers with differing perceptions to make errors in rating attributes, and (c) preference functions to be monotonically increasing or decreasing over increasing ratings of an attribute if other attribute ratings are held constant (implying an absence of satiation). In many cases, this instrumentalist methodology might generate satisfactory market-level predictions, even if underlying individual choice processes were lexicographic in nature. However, one should be alert to the possibility that *better* results might be achieved by policy makers who formulated strategies in the light of the distinctive implications of the characteristic filtering analysis—as I hope to demonstrate in Chapter 10.

The rarity of carefully considered instrumentalist justifications for adhering to compensatory models, and the brevity of axiomatic pure theorists' dismissals of priorities-based models, serves to suggest a widespread ignorance of the extent of the literature on non-compensatory choice. For such ignorance would remove the pressure from theorists to offer detailed rebuttals of foundation-threatening, priorities-based notions and make them seem easily dismissed as oddities. This ignorance is particularly easy to understand in respect of economists, since they are unlikely to be led by cross-references to the marketing and behavioural science journals wherein lie most of the recent sources (see Earl, 1983a), as well as likely to be misled into thinking that Ironmonger's (1972) work is simply an extension of Lancaster's approach, despite its prior origins as a 1961 doctoral thesis, and despite its emphasis on priorities over wants. However, my experience is that when one freshly confronts an orthodox economist with the possibility that choices may often be made in a non-compensatory manner, the reaction usually involves some attempt to demonstrate that *all* choices can be fitted into the orthodox framework (see my remarks about 'general' models in section 7.8). In the next section I want to show how two may play at this academic game.

9.4 THE VALIDITY OF THE NON-COMPENSATORY PRINCIPLE

On more than one occasion, the neoclassical opening gambit has been to remind me of a joke that is both old and terribly sexist:

Man: Will you sleep with me?
Woman: No.
Man: Will you sleep with me for $100?
Woman: No. I'm not that kind of woman.
Man: Will you sleep with me for $1000?
Woman: Look, I said I'm not that kind of woman.
Man: Will you sleep with me for $100,000?
Woman: Yes.
Man: I've only got $100.
Woman: I'm not that kind of woman.
Man: We've established that you *are* that kind of woman; now we're just haggling over the price!

The woman's position seems to suggest that she is willing to make a trade-off between remuneration and self-esteem despite her protestations to the contrary, providing that enough remuneration is offered. The suggestion, implicitly, is that 'every woman has her price'. However, *even if* this is the case, it can still be fitted into my characteristic filtering framework, for it is very easy to misconstrue the nature of preferences when they are only partially revealed. Two kinds of defence may in fact be offered against the 'everyone has their price' objection to priorities-based choice models.

The first defence takes us back to a basic idea in household production theory, namely, that different activity combinations—different production technologies—may be used to produce similar outputs of characteristics. Now, while the behavioural use of this idea denies that people are *always* able to sum together scores in respect of seemingly different characteristics, it does not deny that people may aggregate the contributions that a variety of activities can make in respect of a particular characteristic. In fact, such aggregation possibilities are actually central to my analysis of budgeting. Thus, computational problems may force the decision maker to treat the prospective state of her image—in her own eyes and in those of the rest of the world—as a separate feature, to which she attaches a particular aspiration and a very high priority ranking. However, once she has made this simplification, she may be perfectly able to estimate the overall image-related implications of the various choices she might make. Some activities would involve her in humiliation and embarrassment; others would fill her with pride. But what ultimately concerns her is the sum total of these ups and downs. To sell one's body may involve a very big humiliation, but it may 'set one up for life' against further humiliation and offer the prospect of self-enhancement through conspicuous consumption. And the bigger the remuneration, the less guilt the person would be likely to feel, since she would find it harder to disbelieve the possibility that people she construes as similar to herself would accept similar offers.

For my second defence of the characteristic filtering idea against the claim that it founders if 'everyone has their price', I would like to use a somewhat more complex (imaginary?) example as a basis for discussion.

Suppose I have allowed a neoclassical proponent of the characteristics analysis of choice to extract the following information about my attitudes towards some academic employment possibilities. (The numbers 1 to 4 refer to ranking, with 1 at the top and 4 at the bottom.)

Academic position	Overall rating	Remuneration	Research reputation
A: Lecturer, University of Stirling	3	4	2
B: Lecturer, University of Cambridge	1	3	1
C: Principal Lecturer, Oxford Polytechnic	4	2	4
D: Lecturer, University of Tasmania	2	1	3

This information seems to suggest that, if I cannot get a post in my ideal university, I may be willing to trade the reputed quality of my research environment for higher remuneration, even if I profess to be horrified at the idea of working in a department that is not a hot-bed of research activity. An onlooker might conclude that, if the price were right, I would even work in a polytechnic rather than a university. From a neoclassical perspective, it would seem quite natural to represent this information with an indifference diagram such as Figure 9.1.

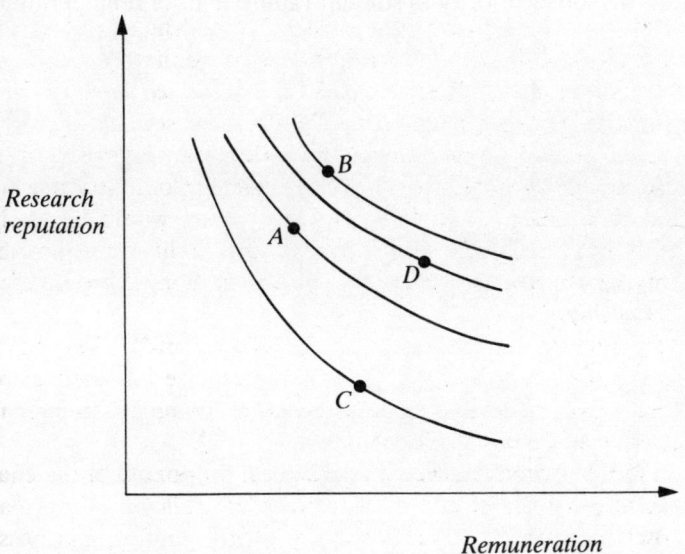

Figure 9.1: Academic employment preferences: a neoclassical view

Things look rather different from the behavioural perspective shown in Figure 9.2. Here, my target for the research reputation is shown by the horizontal dotted line, and my remuneration target by the vertical dotted line. I happen to rank departmental research reputation above remuneration. In terms of these two criteria, positions B and D are both acceptable, but I prefer B, if it is available, on the basis of other criteria not included in the attitude investigation and which can be ranked above, below or in between the two criteria represented in the data. For example,

I *might* rank the calibre of the students above the quality of the research environment, because of the implications of being able to teach 'high-fliers'. Such an élitist attitude to students might lead me to rate students in A, C and D as equally *un*satisfactory; so if I cannot get position B I must feel frustrated in my teaching and choose on the basis of lower-priority criteria, such as research reputation and income. With such an attitude to student calibre, I will rank the four jobs in the same order even if I accord a lower priority to student calibre than to remuneration.

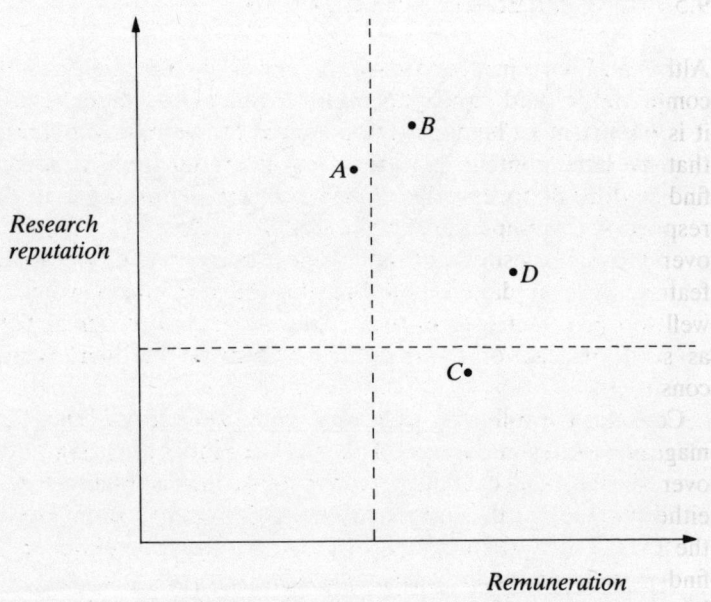

Figure 9.2: Academic employment preferences: a behavioural view

But suppose I rank student calibre above remuneration but not necessarily above research reputation. Once again, I will favour position B even if it actually offers insufficient remuneration (that is, even if my remuneration target lies some way to the right of the one shown in Figure 9.2). In this last case, I will be somewhat frustrated to be in position B, though less so than if I could only get position A. However, it is likely that I will attempt to *console* myself with arguments that deny the existence of a trade-off between student calibre and remuneration (see Steinbruner, 1974, pp. 106–7). One line of argument which could come to mind and not be ruled out of court is that, by occupying position B, I have obtained the best way of ensuring that I will meet my remuneration target, without making any compromises, *in the long run*, as many previous holders of such a post have become professors in universities with high-calibre students.

9.5 PRINCIPLES—AT 'ALL COSTS'

Although I have just been showing how easily one might confuse compensatory and non-compensatory choice procedures, I think it is important to highlight the potential for outright intolerance that the latter contain. There are very many situations in which I find it difficult to envisage that a brilliant performance in one respect will compensate for a failing elsewhere. Prejudice, overwhelming desires and inviolable principles are widespread features of everyday life, and neoclassical economists would do well to open their eyes to these phenomena and recognise them as such, instead of trying to bend them to fit their existing constructs.

Consider the following examples. First: a reader of *What Car?* magazine writes in defence of the Talbot Horizon, saying, 'I am over six foot and cannot get comfortable in the driving seat of either the Golf or the Escort. No matter how superior the Golf or the Escort may be 'mechanically' that is of no consequence if I find myself permanently uncomfortable in them' (October 1983 issue, p. 19). Perhaps the person in question would act as a neoclassical consumer if the price of the Golf or the Escort were reduced so far as to compensate for any costs of relocating the steering column and driver's seat.

Second: while visiting Perth, Western Australia, I am refused entry to a not-particularly-fancy bar 'because' I am 'wearing a sweatshirt' that bears the slogan 'Theatre Royal: Scottish Opera', despite being generally tidily presented. Obviously, my mistake is that I do not produce a large roll of notes and ask the doorman if I can see the manager. (Interestingly enough, I am not refused the possibility of mingling with the mink-coated Glasgow élite when I turn up to see a performance by the Scottish Opera at the Theatre Royal and am clad in faded denims and an 'animal liberation' sweatshirt—though the subject of dress at the opera often produces some remarkably strong expressions of opinion on the letters page of *Scottish Opera News*.)

Third: a friend who is a strict vegetarian is eating out and discovers that her 'vegetarian curry' has chicken in it. She leaves it aside and refuses to pay. An argument ensues and the hotelier threatens to call the police. Obviously, had she normally be planning to leave a large tip, she could have compensated herself for the inconvenience of eating meat by declining to leave a tip and not losing her temper.

Fourth: I know of a case where the husband of a wealthy hotelier had an affair with one of the chambermaids and was in the space of a few months 'reduced' from driving a Daimler and generally living in style, to being a divorced, unemployed bartender but one who was happy with his new partner. Evidently, he could well have been a sound neoclassical consumer who had weighed up his chances of being caught, after forming subjective probabilities. And, had he offered better performances in respect of husbandly characteristics other than fidelity, he might not have been rejected by his wife 'on the grounds of his adultery'. These are possibilities, sure enough, but not obviously ones that we should believe.

Two things may strike readers as they consider these examples. First, there can come a point when it looks as though attempts to rationalise some modes of behaviour into conformity with the principle of gross substitution do themselves appear to involve adherence to that principle 'at all costs'. Secondly, it is by no means obvious that one needs to adduce information-processing problems as the reason why people choose in ways that are difficult to reconcile with the substitution idea. Certainly passion, like the pressure of a crisis, may cloud one's ability to make overall implicational assessments, while a rule of admittance according to style of dress may be a cost-effective screen against 'riff-raff', especially if potential customers employ a similar means of assessing the atmosphere of social gathering places.

However, if we recall sections 6.2 and 6.6, we can note that many people may adhere to 'principles' even when they can count up the implicational costs of doing so: their construct systems are organised in ways that make them see some events as intrinsic to, or prerequisites for, the maintenance of certain images, even though these constricting channels of construction are their personal creations. To me, it is not obvious that driving a car intrinsically requires one to have a comfortable driving position—but then I am rather shorter than the Talbot Horizon enthusiast. However, like my vegetarian friend, I can see that an intrinsically human obligation is to avoid the killing of other species; I organise my life according to a different (but not *completely* different) code of ethics from the systems employed by my Christian acquaintances, who merrily devour animals and dress in leather because they have not yet had their eyes opened to the broader possible implications of the principle that 'thou shalt no kill'. *Anyone* who is not completely schizophrenic may have some principles which on occasion cause her to disregard opportunity costs that others see as significant.

To see how other theorists might react to these comments about 'principles', we only have to go as far as the work of Elster (1984, pp. 126–7). In discussing lexicographic preferences, he considers how far they fit into orthodox economists' views of 'rational behaviour' and of what constitutes 'economic behaviour'. Elster juxtaposes Becker's (1976, p. 8) claim that the economic approach to choice has a comprehensive range of applicability with the following passage from Borch (1968, p. 22), who argues that, in economics, it is a core assumption that:

some kind of 'trade-off' will always be possible. Formally we can express this by assuming the so-called *axiom of Archimedes*. This means in our example that if we have:
$$(x_1, y_1) \text{ preferred to } (x_2, y_2)$$
we can always reverse the preference by increasing y_2: that is, there exists a $y > y_2$ such that:
$$(x_2, y) \text{ preferred to } (x_1, y_1).$$
This means that a loss of some units of one commodity can always be compensated by a gain of some units of another commodity or, to put it another way, *everything has its price*. It may be tempting to define economics as the science of things which have a price, in a very general sense. Questions of life and death and ethical principles like an absolute aversion to gambling would then be considered as belonging to the more general social sciences (emphasis in the original).

In this quotation from Borch we have a very clear statement

about the central importance of substitution in economics; phenomena that involve behaviour at variance with this notion are, in his way of thinking, not admissible as 'economic' phenomena.

In his own discussion, Elster comes down in favour of the view of Borch, on the philosophical ground that 'when the Archimedean criterion is not satisfied, we are dealing with goods or activities that are in a sense non-comparable and do not lend themselves to the economic approach'. One can, of course, construe the 'economic approach' to choice whichever way one's construct system will admit. My own view is that considerable confusion is liable to result if one insists on arguing that choices involving principles and priorities are 'not within the sphere of economics'. Suppose some buyers in a market are successfully applying compensatory choice heuristics and others are employing non-compensatory ones. From the Borch/Elster standpoint, it is only the behaviour of the former group that should be discussed by a person acting in the role of 'economist'. If policy makers had hired an economist in order to obtain advice on the possible impacts of particular policy options, I doubt if they would be impressed with a report which suggested psychologists and anthropologists would need to be hired for advice on the behaviour of those consumers who brought principles and priorities to bear on choices in the market.

9.6 FUTURE EMPIRICAL WORK

When people with different world-views disagree over how events should be construed, it is quite often the case that empirical work, still less an unsystematic 'appeal to the facts', fails to bring about a change in attitudes on either or both sides. Evidence must be admissible and different systems of thought will admit different kinds of evidence as acceptable. This seems to be so within 'scientific' disciplines, as well as in everyday life. If neoclassical economists cannot bear to face up to evidence that, according to others, refutes their analyses, they can, and probably will, 'carry on regardless' so long as their sheer strength of numbers can determine who gets appointed and what gets taught within the profession (see Feyerabend, 1975, and Eichner, 1983).

But before such evidence exists, they will insist that deviant theorists set about gathering it.

In section 7.7, I noted the possibility of trying to simulate via computer programs the use of contingent sets of choice heuristics. However, I then suggested that it might be more practicable to see how closely consumers approximated in their preferences to predictions derived from various individual heuristics. Here, I wish to consider how the latter kinds of predictions might be generated in relation to characteristic filtering procedures. I would suggest that the researcher might begin by using repertory grid technique to construct impressions of: (1) how subjects construed rival products on their agendas of possibilities, (2) subjects' moulds of tolerance (by asking them each to include a personally imagined 'just about completely adequate' product in their lists of elements), and (3) the areas of tensions where 'mould tightening' might take place in the event of a tie (by asking each subject to include a personally imagined 'ideal' product in her list of elements). To obtain evidence of 'mould-deepening' and/or 'mould-tightening', one might construct repertory grids at an early stage in a decision process, and again around the time of the actual choice: increased numbers of constructs would indicate 'deepening', while 'tightening' would manifest itself in a movement of constructions of 'adequacy' in the direction of the 'ideal'.

To uncover priorities (that orthodox theorists might try to see as importance 'weights'), one could ask subjects to rank their construct adequacy targets in the order in which they would be prepared to *sacrifice* the prospect of meeting them, if forced to do so—one should not ask them to list the order in which they would address the possibility of meeting their various targets, since they might well expect to employ 'short-cut/backtrack' procedures. Such rankings, along with the revealed moulds of tolerance and perceptions of rival products, would enable the researcher to predict individual subjects' preferences; these predictions could then be compared with rankings obtained from each subject by asking her which of the products on her agenda she would prefer, which one she would prefer if the first-preferred option were excluded, which one she would prefer if the first- and second-preferred options were both excluded, and so on.

It would then be interesting to compare the predictive success of this kind of methodology against results obtained by conventional methods for estimating compensatory choice models (see section 2.6). But I would ask researchers to bear in mind the remarks at the end of Chapter 7, before jumping to conclusions about the general validity of any particular model.

In situations where decision makers were facing up to rival self-imagined sequels to particular choices, one could use very much the same techniques to investigate the shapes of moulds of tolerance for uncertain prospects. Having elicited constructs, the researcher could ask the subject whether she was uncertain about how to rate the elements on each construct scale. Given an affirmative answer, the researcher could ask the subject to rate the elements in terms of a five-point potential surprise scale as well as on the (say, seven-point) uncertain construct scale. For each point on the construct scale, the subject could be asked how much of a prospect of surprise she would willingly tolerate (for desired outcomes) or would at least wish to expect (for counter-desired outcomes). It would then be evident which schemes might seem satisfactory gambles. Using a version of the 'which would you prefer if X were impossible?' technique, opportunity costs amongst rival sequels and rival action schemes could be elicited as a means for investigating procedures used for resolving conflicts when no gambles looked entirely satisfactory.

The results of such an investigation of the potential surprise concept could be compared with those from research aimed at testing orthodox views of hazardous choices. This would certainly be a novel line of research. The relative merits of possible means of conducting research to discriminate between rival theories of decision making under uncertainty were considered long ago in Roy's (1954) contribution to a British Association symposium on Shackle's original model. But a decade later, Cyert and March (1963, p. 46) noted that there was still an absence of empirical work on potential surprise. Twenty years after Cyert and March, Ford (1983, p. 187) could still lament the fact that:

Whilst there has been a vast quantity of empirical work surrounding the orthodox model in one form or another..., there has been no such research carried out for the Shackle theory on similar topics. Indeed, there is still a dearth of empirical work on the Shackle theory in any context.

All Ford could point to was some limited use of Shackle's analysis being made by Wray (1957), in her investigation of the women's outerwear industry. (The pertinent part of her book is more easily available as Wray, 1956). Given this prolonged absence of empirical work on potential surprise, John Hey's (1985) recent experimental study is something I heartily welcome even though Hey (p. 84) is driven to conclude that 'the experiment casts doubt on both the conventional wisdom and on Professor Shackle's position, though in my opinion the damage to the latter is the greater'. Hey does admit there are some limitations with his experimental methodology and makes some suggestions for improving it in subsequent experiments. Anyone tempted to do experimental work in this area will be well advised to consult his paper for inspiration. But they might also note Roy's (1954, p. 78) warning that the laboratory may not be the appropriate place for attempting to assess rival theories of choice under uncertainty: it will usually be too expensive to construct a 'brutal' enough choice environment for participants to have an interest in carrying into the laboratory the same procedures that they would use to resolve the dilemmas of everyday life.

If we cannot place much faith in experimental test procedures for investigating choice under uncertainty, we appear to be left either with aggregative statistics, or with a case-study/'protocol analysis' methodology. Roy's (1954, p. 80) case for questioning the former has a similar basis to my objections to 'demand-side' interpretations of hedonic regressions (see section 2.5), as well as anticipating the individuality corollary of Kelly's theory of personality, for he emphasises that 'much economic phenomena is to be explained by the fact that people believe different things about the future and by their attempts to do different things, whatever the similarities of their basic motives'. Such considerations explain my willingness to favour the inelegant and time-consuming methodology of face-to-face research, in which we must be prepared to make greater use of our own powers of judgement as we study real-life decision situations that force our subjects themselves to make judgements. Such an approach to empirical work may not appeal to the typical decision theorist (and the present analysis may help to explain its lack of appeal), but it is important that it should be undertaken. In the next and final chapter, it will be shown that my analysis offers distinctive policy implications of considerable importance for policy makers.

10 Choice Rules and the Competitive Process

10.1 INTRODUCTION

In previous chapters I generally carried out the analysis of decision-making processes as though consumers faced a given set of options which might come to appear on their agendas, and as though they faced a given set of market prices (including the price of labour in various employment slots). Implied in that analysis was a particular set of ideas about how, and why, consumers may behave when confronted with changes in product specifications, availability and market prices. This chapter brings these ideas out into the open and examines their implications for policy makers.

Section 10.2 is concerned with consumer reactions to changes in market environments in situations where it seems possible to compute 'overall implications' of adopting rival courses of action. Section 10.3 examines consumer responses to price changes, as seen from the standpoint of the characteristic filtering analysis. Section 10.4 extends these arguments to encompass 'non-price' aspects of choice in relation to the product lifecycle phenomenon. Section 10.5 draws attention to the implications of these arguments for the product and pricing policies of firms. Section 10.6 adopts an unusual ploy by way of suggesting that these arguments warrant serious consideration even in advance of systematic empirical work aimed at refuting them. It is shown how the theoretical analysis fits in with some motoring journalists' accounts of how they reach verdicts on 'What Car?' to recommend when they have tested a group of close competitors in the ever-changing automotive market. These accounts have not been chosen according to some rigorous sampling procedure, and I make no claim to be conducting what cognitive scientists (for example, Waterman and Newall, 1971, Hunt) 1982, call 'protocol analysis' (since the journalists were not required to describe in order *all* the reasoning stages behind their recommendations). But they might be taken as pointing the way forward to a new kind of empirical work, albeit one that in some ways resembles literary criticism. Sections 10.7 and 10.8 are more obviously addressed to public policy makers and concern, respectively, trade policy and attempts to promote risk-taking behaviour.

10.2 OVERALL IMPLICATIONS OF PRICE AND PRODUCT CHANGES

Increases in prices may be seen by consumers as closing off opportunities for action, whereas price reductions and improvements in products or the appearance of new products may open up hitherto blocked possibilities. However, even if consumers construe that their 'opportunity sets' have changed, they may fail to change their consumption of the goods whose relative prices or non-price performances have changed. This result is a familiar one from conventional models of consumer behaviour as discussed in Chapter 2, where we saw how price and product changes alter the costs of producing particular combinations of characteristics in an efficient manner. *If* consumers could usefully be thought of 'as if' they can compute the overall implications of market changes for their abilities to predict and control events, an analysis of how they might behave in the face of such changes would lead to the usual conclusions about income and substitution effects and consumer surplus. However, an 'implications-based' analysis would not require any restrictive assumptions about continuity of indifference loci and substitution possibilities in characteristics space.

Consider, for example, hypothetical small and large unexpected increases in the price of petrol. Will they lead a consumer to cut her petrol consumption, or will she simply carry on buying petrol as before and make other economies? The question is really one about an appropriate choice of budget: economising on petrol may involve some changes of transport-using lifestyle components (for example, less driving into town in the evenings for entertainment) or changes in one's transport lifestyle (for example, more use of public transport, or the purchase of a more economical, less status-providing vehicle); but a failure to economise will also require some changes (for example, a slower accumulation of savings for new consumer durables, or less 'up-market' leisure expenditure on holidays, eating out and so on). Either way, there will be negative implications for the consumer's way of life, relative to the expectations she previously entertained. These implicational patterns could differ considerably amongst rival budgeting strategies that the consumer considered in each situation (and we would be unwise to imagine that in either situation the consumer would go beyond considering a limited set of discretely separated strategies).

Different consumers who happened to consider identical strategies could attach different patterns of implications to them, which would depend on the extent to which they had built up their lives around the expectation of being able to buy petrol at a particular price and run a particular car (see sections 6.5 and 6.6). If a consumer did not attach any positive implications to any of the strategies she considered relative to her former pattern of expectations, we should expect her to rank the strategies in order of the reverse of their rankings in terms of the total negative implications of adopting them as a preferred option. It is possible that a strategy involving no economising on petrol will come out top—the range of convenience of the consumer's predictive system would thus be reduced by other kinds of cutbacks, but by less than if she sought to economise on petrol. With a large petrol price increase, new more drastic strategies might be considered and one involving some economising on petrol might then seem the least bad option of those evaluated.

Strategies for dealing with such a 'mugging'—whether a small or a large one—might not be without their positive implications relative to the original set of expectations, and these could affect overall rankings by net implications. For example, to change a large 'gas guzzler' for a small, fuel-efficient vehicle might on the one hand seem to have damaging implications for one's self-image, but on the other it might mean that one expected to be more easily able to park in town in rush-hour traffic without embarrassment. On balance, then, the implications for one's self-image might not be all that negative if a switch were made to a smaller car and an implied reduction in petrol consumption.

Where an individual product brand has increased in price, a

consumer who could assess overall implications of rival action schemes would essentially behave in a manner akin to that envisaged in the rather 'neo-Marshallian' version of Lancaster's model proposed by Rosen (1974) (see section 2.4). That is to say, she would examine the implications of buying the brand in preference to its now relatively cheap rivals, and thus of having less money for other things than she would have done had its price not increased. This examination may not involve her in spelling out to herself in detail what she would be giving up if she parted with more money: she might merely correlate her reduced scope for coping with life with the extent of the generalised purchasing power she would have to forgo to purchase an expensive brand, and then subtract this score from the overall implicational tally for the strategy. (Some implications may be all *too* clear. For example, if the consumer had been planning to purchase the brand whose price has increased, she may feel stupid not to have acted sooner; if she resists buying the product now, she avoids the implication that she has let herself be mugged—at least, she does so as long as she has not made public her original plans. This kind of behaviour is entirely in keeping with my Kellian analysis of how people make up their minds, but some readers might also recognise it as fitting in neatly with Festinger's (1957) theory of 'cognitive dissonance'.) To the extent that a consumer seems usually to be more sensitive to spending an extra dollar on a low-value item (for example, a gramophone record) than on a high-value item (for example, a 'hi-fi' system), one might seek to explain this 'diminishing marginal utility of money' in a number of ways: (1) by referring to cognitive psychology literature on 'framing effects' (see Thaler, 1980, for some economic applications of this literature); (2) by arguing that it is a manifestation, in the context of compensatory choices, of what I discuss under the heading of 'rip-off avoidance' in the next section; or (3) by noting that the consumer may attach great significance to spending proportionately a good deal extra in order to obtain a slightly better low-value product (for example, 'people would think I'm crazy if I spend a dollar more on a single bar of soap, even if it does lather better'). There is an obvious need for empirical work to uncover the frequencies of use of these (and any other seemingly possible) modes of thought as devices for appraising the significance of relative price differentials.

With price reductions and product improvements essentially the same 'implicational' arguments apply. For a person to change her behavioural intentions she must be able to see that the change in her market environment has opened up possibilities in respect of which the positive implications of change outnumber the negative ones. For example, a fall in the price of petrol might lead a consumer to contemplate widening the range of her experience by driving out more at weekends to see what she can make of particular places and happenings. However, she might see that to do so would leave her with less time available to 'stop the garden getting out of control'—an event which she might see as implying a lowering of her neighbourhood standing. The net implicational gain for this strategy of change (if indeed there is one) might be less than that from schemes involving the purchase of a more prestigious but thirsty car, or non-petrol-using means of household production, financed by savings from reduced petrol outlays.

10.3 EFFECTS OF PRICE CHANGES ON CHARACTERISTIC FILTERING PROCESSES

Where bounded rationality drives the consumer to employ non-compensatory decision rules as means of approximating choices which might be arrived at by computing overall implications, price changes impact on consumer choices in a somewhat different manner. In characteristic filtering processes, there seem to be six main ways in which realignments of relative prices may provoke changes in consumer behaviour.

First it should be noted that a general change in prices in a particular commodity category, or a change in price for a particular brand that a consumer knows well and uses as a reference point for an entire group, may impact upon this consumer's choice of budgeting strategy. A consumer's preferred budgeting plan may change if a price cut opens up the possibility that, by reallocating expenditure between commodity classes, she may be able to find a cheaper way of meeting aspirations which she would have been able to meet in any case. This saving, in turn, may permit her the prospect of being able to meet priorities which hitherto she has failed properly to attain and/or improve her attainment levels in respect of other goals where past experience had led her to moderate her aspirations. If a price has risen and her money income prospects have not, a budgetary rethink may enable her to reduce the importance of the priorities whose satisfactory attainments she is now forced to forgo. The price effect for the commodity category in question could be positive, zero or negative, depending on her goals and her perceptions of possible technologies of household production. (A 'Giffenesque' example would be as follows: suppose someone makes many short-distance journeys and few long-distance journeys each year, and that the price of petrol falls substantially; she could then end up consuming less petrol, even if she increased her number of journeys somewhat, because the considerable savings on her expenditure on local driving enabled her to afford the luxury of flying on long journeys.)

This price-induced view of changes of strategy differs from the analysis in the previous section since rival budget plans are appraised here as wholes, not in respect of their conjectured overall implications but according to how far they seem likely to allow the consumer to get down her list of priorities without failing to meet a target. As noted earlier (see section 9.5), the consumer may sometimes be able to aggregate the possible implications of the various components of a possible budgeting plan in respect of a single dimension, mindful of scope for synergy, even if she has trouble computing overall implications for such a plan. Thus she may appear willing to make substitutions despite ultimately choosing her plan with the aid of a non-compensatory procedure.

In selecting a particular budgetary plan, the consumer will be defining *price ranges* within which she expects to find schemes of action which will make satisfactory contributions towards meeting her priorities. (Monroe, 1973, offers strong empirical support for the idea that consumers cognitively categorise price by breaking it into ranges; see also Gabor and Granger, 1966, and works cited therein.) Here arises scope for a second effect of price on choice: a product's price, or price per unit, will determine whether or not a consumer will be able to include it on her agenda of possibles if she comes across it. A price 'range' is a device for restricting search efforts, so will usually be a double-sided filter: the consumer sets an upper limit reflecting what she *might have* to spend, and what she can *afford* to spend without jeopardising higher-priority aspirations than those to which the commodity class in question is pertinent; she also sets a lower limit because she believes options priced below this level are not sufficiently likely to fit into the appropriate mould. A product that is outside the price range is debarred from investigation unless the consumer is given admissable reasons why she should take it seriously. (It is quite likely that a consumer would employ such a filter in a non-compensatory manner even if she then proceeded to evaluate the non-excluded brands in a compensatory manner.) Hence a price increase may make a product 'too expensive' to be considered further by some consumers and yet expensive enough to be taken seriously by others. If, in the latter case, the product actually dominated then, for the consumers in question, it would be a Giffen good. Similarly, a price reduction may bring a product out of the 'too expensive' category in the minds of some consumers, and it might then go on to dominate in other tests of adequacy; but a price reduction might also result in other consumers not bothering to evaluate a potentially perfectly adequate product – in which case we would have another 'Giffenesque' example.

Where consumers keep a lower price limit in mind when searching, we can say that information problems are effectively forcing them to judge quality by price (see Scitovsky, 1945, Alcaly and Klevorick, 1970, and Pollak, 1977). The third role of price in the choice process is essentially an extension of this 'judging quality by price' idea: for those products which fall within the consumer's chosen price range, it may well be that, in respect of some dimensions, she allows her conjectures of what they have to offer to be shaped by their prices. A change in price may thus affect, in the same direction, a product's ability to survive some filtering tests.

Fourth, we should note that a change in the price of a product may affect a consumer's assessment of its adequacy in terms of 'value for money' or, in more modern jargon, whether or not she judges it as a 'rip-off'. Here my remarks may be of particular interest to Marxian readers interested in 'value' and 'exploitation'. A consumer may be unable to compute the overall implications to herself of choosing any one of the products on her agenda; yet she may be able to perform a kind of *casual* 'hedonic' assessment of these products, by comparing them with each other in terms of their price and non-price ratings, to see roughly what they *ought* to cost to buy. The consumer might then feel an attempt was being made to exploit her if she concluded that a particular product's actual price exceeded its 'hedonic' price by a considerable margin (see section 2.5 on cost-side interpretations of hedonic equations). I suggest that it would not be unreasonable to expect the consumer to aspire to avoid purchasing products whose actual prices exceeded their estimated 'values' by more than a particular tolerable percentage margin. (The extra margin would make sense, given the roughness of the consumer's estimates of what she ought to have to pay.) Thus although a consumer may be prepared to spend to the limit of her budget, she will not do so if this will involve her in paying an extortionate price—unless all of the options remaining on her agenda at that priority level are felt in some degree to be 'rip-offs', in which case she allows the least bad of these to survive this stage in her filtering process. Such a suggestion would not have seemed outlandish to the businessmen interviewed in the famous study by Hall and Hitch. These authors (1951, p. 113) reported that 'the overwhelming majority of entrepreneurs thought that a price based on full average cost (including and allowance for profit) was the "right" price, the one which "ought" to be charged'. The entrepreneurs did not want to jeopardise their goodwill by appearing to act in an unfair manner.

In advancing this 'value for money' argument about the role of price in the context of a discussion of characteristic filtering processes, I am not suggesting that a lower price helps a product dominate by giving it a higher overall score; rather, a reduction in its price may bring its actual price near enough to what it ought to cost and thereby prevent consumers from ruling it out as 'rip-off'. Bounded rationality is forcing such consumers to treat 'avoidance of paying an unwarranted price' as a separate goal. But one can also envisage the ratio of actual price to 'right' price being included as a separate characteristic score in situations where consumers are able to perform compensatory evaluations and compute overall scorings. Either way, there may seem to be negative implications to finding oneself having to buy something that looks a 'rip-off'. We might expect a 'rip-off avoidance' goal to have quite a high priority (or to carry a non-trivial weight in a compensatory approach to choice), for if one *has* to pay an inflated price, one can hardly claim to be in control in the buying situation, even if one ends up with a useful means towards anticipating and controlling events.

Fifth, and as I have already hinted in the compensatory context, price movements may affect how competent a consumer feels as a decision maker in the market in question. She may feel rather foolish if she buys a product 'too soon after its price has gone up' and consequently may end up adopting a 'sour grapes' attitude to it if she resists it because of this particular problem. This would, of course, be yet another example of what conventional economists would see as an 'irrational' attitude to forgone opportunities (see sections 4.4 and 6.6), but I think we would be unwise not to anticipate that it could be empirically significant. A consumer is also likely to resist buying a product if she judges that its price is 'unduly likely to be reduced in the near future by a significant amount', unless she accords a higher priority to having it right now as a means of household production. If her suspicions are correct, she may not only avoid wasting her money initially; she may also escape losing out due to a fall in the product's second-hand value. These arguments are not without possible significance for firms choosing dynamic pricing strategies through their products' lifecycles—strategies that may embrace introductory 'special offers', subsequent price increases and, later, price reductions aimed at increasing market penetration or warding off competition.

Sixth, and finally, the price dimension may figure in tie-break tests when consumers find that a number of products are adequate in conjunctive terms; hence a change in a product's price may affect whether or not it wins a tie-break. Price is most likely to play this role in contexts where consumers are not connoisseurs and do not approach the evaluation task with a long list of targets in mind and a good idea of how demanding these can be made. The least demanding use of price in a tie-break is simply to 'choose the cheapest' of the tied products. However, as I argued in section 7.6, the 'choose the cheapest' rule might not be employed in choices involving monetary transactions if, during the evaluation process, the consumer has come across additional (new?) product characteristics that seem worth adding to her checklist, or if she attaches positive implications to attainments beyond target levels on her original list of priorities. Here, the consumer is essentially faced with a budgeting question when she thinks of the costs of not adopting the 'choose the cheapest' rule. If she holds back *some* of the money she was *originally quite prepared to spend* on the type of commodity in question, she may be able to meet other aspirations served by other kinds of commodities—aspirations which she might decide to rank more highly than the prospect of obtaining at least some of the newly discovered characteristics.

One of the other aspirations might even be 'to have *ideally* a particular sum of money in reserve', which she had not been expecting originally to meet, yet which was accorded a sufficiently low priority for her to have been prepared to compromise it in working out a budget plan to meet higher-level goals. (A much higher-ranking goal 'to have a particular "bare minimum" of money in reserve' might also have existed *separately* and might not have been compromised in the original plan.) If the number of tied products is small, and if they are deemed identical in many respects, then the consumer may be able (especially if she uses the additive differences procedure) to assess the overall implications of choosing one 'rebudgeting plan'—and hence one product in the class in question—at the expense of its rivals. We would then be back in the world of the previous section, except that the consumer is only focusing on the conjunctively adequate options from the set she evaluated.

10.4 CHARACTERISTIC FILTERING WITH INCOME AND PRODUCT CHANGES

The considerable attention I have just devoted to possible impacts of price changes on non-compensatory choices marks my work out as unusual against the general run of priorities-based choice models. Other priority theorists (most notably Canterbery, 1979, and Pasinetti, 1981, discussed in section 9.2) are less concerned with *brand*-level choices. Instead, they attempt to explain changes in the structure of expenditure at the broad *commodity* level mainly in terms of changes in real income, playing down the significance of substitutions in response to relative price changes. This view accords well with the general findings of Houthakker and Taylor (1970), discussed in section

2.2. However, it ignores the possibility that, wherever a particular want may be served (and/or dis-served) by a variety of kinds of commodities, increases in real income caused by changes in relative prices could result in somewhat different patterns of choice than might be observed if real income increases were produced by rises in money incomes.

Despite raising this qualification to the work of Canterbery and Pasinetti, I feel their reasoning in terms of priorities may provide the basis for a very useful perspective on the relationship between increasing affluence and the product lifecycle phenomenon. A product that serves relatively low-ranking wants may initially be thought of as a luxury because only a small part of the population can afford to purchase it without compromising higher priorities. However, rising affluence may enable the product to acquire a mass market, its sales rising until saturation is reached, whereupon demand falls to replacement levels. Further increases in affluence may result in the product becoming an inferior good for those consumers who are able to revise upwards their budget ranges for the commodity class in question. Higher-grade products/brands thus find places on their agendas and these commodities may enable them to achieve new goals without being unable to meet any of the aspirations served by the product they had hitherto favoured. However, this product may, for a time, later come back into its own as a way of meeting yet-lower-ranking priorities. For example, a consumer may replace a black and white television with a colour one, but later be able to afford a black and white portable for secondary use (see the empirical findings of Hebden and Pickering, 1974, p. 91); in time this, too, may be replaced by a colour set. Whether or not, and when, the product becomes an inferior good at the level of the market as a whole depends on the balance of these saturation/up-market shift/secondary use tendencies.

Products may also enter the decline phases of their sales profiles owing to the new-found ability of acceptably priced, but not necessarily newly launched, brands to dominate in non-price characteristic filtering tests. Here I will note four effects and illustrate them with automotive examples.

First, a product/brand may be introduced within the budget ranges of increasingly sophisticated consumers, offering them the ability to meet new goals. As an example we may note how, in the late 1970s, Chrysler Australia introduced a luxurious 'SE' version of its Australianised Mitsubishi Sigma/Galant and then saw the Sigma range as a whole quickly become the top-selling car in its local segment. As Wright (1985, pp. 88–9) observes, the SE:

attracted many buyers who would never otherwise have contemplated a Japanese four... You could almost lay at the Sigma SE's wheels responsibility for escalating the equipment race. It offered such diverse items as a standard five-speed gearbox, cloth trim, a three-position reclining rear seat squab, an interior boot release, tilt and lumbar adjustment on the driver's seat and rather stylish hubcaps colour-keyed to the exterior. Simply, its specification made everything else look off the pace. It proved Chrysler was serious about the Sigma and undoubtedly helped the sales of the cheaper Sigmas.

A second effect may be ascribed to social interactions amongst consumers (see Bain, 1964, Marris, 1964, Chapter 4, and Ironmonger, 1972). People who initially carry on buying a particular product, because it fails to meet an important priority which newly available rivals fail to attain, may come to rerank their priorities after observing the fortunes of others who have already defected. For example, if quality control standards of domestic products remain irritatingly inadequate and a cause of anxiety, motorists may eventually abandon their patriotic principles and buy an imported model; their friends' experiences with imported vehicles may not merely prove there is no need to tolerate domestic quality levels, they may also make them feel less *guilty* about defecting.

Third, a product which previously has enjoyed healthy sales may lose its position as a result of suffering a lapse in performance in respect of an attribute that many would-be buyers rank highly. In the UK car market in 1971–4, for example, delivery times for many domestically produced models became unacceptably long as a result of the combination of poor productivity levels, industrial disruption and an unprecedented increase in car demand arising from the Heath/Barber reflation (see Dunnett, 1980, pp. 122–7). Thus consumers who, having decided to replace their cars, accorded a high priority to having a new car 'there and then' would have been driven to reject many UK models on the ground of non-availability, regardless of how well they performed in terms of other, lower-priority targets. In fact, a sample of 16,000 new-car buyers in the period mid 1973 to mid 1974 were questioned about the reasons behind their choices and it transpired that 'almost 30 per cent of the people considering buying British cars decided *not* to do so because of unacceptable delivery dates... *Long delivery times rank[ed] second only to price as a reason for not buying a particular model*' (CPRS, 1975, p. 95, emphasis in original).

Fourth, and finally, it is necessary to note another possible instance of the 'mould-tightening' phenomenon. Decision makers may become aware that even if recently introduced rival products in their price range do not offer any extra attributes, they none the less open up possibilities for higher attainments in respect of some existing goals without requiring standards to be compromised elsewhere. For example, executives who have hitherto found Mercedes or BMW luxury saloons entirely adequate are likely to have had their aspiration levels raised in some dimensions if, in August 1983, they happened to read in latest issue of *Car Magazine* the following remarks in a report on the revised Audi 200T:

Passing other cars is merely routine for the 200T in all but rarified 110 mph-plus speeds.

That's the problem with the 200T—you have to redefine the old saloon performance parameters. Previously a car in this class capable of cruising at 120 mph in quiet and comfort was regarded as exceptional, but the lower-priced Audi makes this look easily achievable, even mundane. Mercedes and BMW's next big saloons will have to take 130 mph-plus cruising into their stride and be capable of reaching high into the 140s if they are to top the 200T. Ultimate top speed is still a relevant factor in Germany...but in Britain a 140 mph capability is of academic *[sic]* interest. What *is* important on this island's crowded roads is that the Audi can provide all the performance that's sensible within the bounds of the road conditions, without the slightest strain on itself and with spectacular economy.

In short: product obsolescence may occur because a new rival model *sets new standards* of feasible attainments in respect of existing goals, even though it has nothing fundamentally new to offer in terms of attributes.

10.5 IMPLICATIONS FOR PRICING AND PRODUCT STRATEGIES

The discussions in the previous two sections indicate how important it may be for firms to conduct market research to discover why sales patterns are changing in particular ways. If a product is losing its market share for non-price reasons, a price-based policy may be disastrous, and vice versa. (In Earl, 1984, pp. 145–8, I have discussed how entrepreneurs as shrewd as Henry Ford and William Morris made expensive mistakes of the former kind.) However, we should not forget that it may be possible to use the two competitive weapons in a complementary manner: if price cuts are unprofitable for a particular product, given anticipated demand conditions and the ratio of variable costs to total costs of production, it may be possible to change the situation by removing some of the product attributes not commonly included in consumers' lists of priorities—the impact upon total costs may be less than on sales revenues at lower prices. Such a ploy seems to have been tried by, for example, Ford and Austin Rover in the UK 'super-mini' market in the period 1980–2. When the newly produced Austin Metro base model undercut the basic Ford Fiesta, Ford reacted by offering an even more basic Fiesta, the 'Popular'. Austin Rover then retaliated with the spartanly trimmed 'Metro City'. By keeping the more up-market models in production and/or making the omitted features available as options, companies can seek to make price competition profitable by non-price means without needlessly losing revenue from consumers who would have paid the higher price to get better-equipped models.

Quality-conscious firms may find it hard to face up to the idea of competing in this way when they find the market shares of their relatively expensive products deteriorating. Here we may draw a lesson from Hesselman's (1981) study of the UK market for automatic washing machines. She found that, in the change-over from twin-tub to automatic machines, British firms had lost their market share to imported brands despite the fact that, in terms of a 'hedonic' analysis, their machines offered good value for money. The problem was that British machines offered comparable spin speeds to those available in the dryers of twin-tubs, but could only do so at prices far higher than those of, for example, Italian brands that dried clothes much less effectively. British consumers were increasingly living in centrally heated homes that would permit indoor drying and they therefore opted in droves for the cheaper machines that 'UK manufacturers thought to be more appropriate for sunny Naples than cloudy Birmingham' (Hesselman, 1981, p. 24). The UK manufacturers would have done better had they seen washing machines as components of evolving integrated household production systems and hence realised the need to create cheapened models by 'downgrading' their drying capabilities.

In terms of my characteristic filtering analysis, a firm can be said to be poorly competitive in non-price terms, despite offering its products at 'competitive' prices, if it achieves few sales because its products do not frequently survive far enough down consumer filtering processes for their prices to be brought to bear in their favour as a tie-breaker. Where a firm's market performance is indeed deteriorating for non-price reasons, it has the choice of producing a new model and marketing package, or of making a defensive investment (see Lamfalussy, 1961) in a new sales campaign and/or facelift of the original model. Either kind of investment will be mistaken in this situation if it neither (1) remedies the perceived deficiencies of the product/brand in the eyes of target consumers, (2) brings about a reranking of customer priorities and/or a revision of aspirations conducive to the rejection of the threatening rival products, nor (3) permits a profitable price cut through the repositioning of the product/brand 'down-market' in a lower budget segment where it can dominate in non-price terms. In my earlier (1983c, p. 110) work, I criticised the Citroen and Lancia car companies for their past non-price performances, so it is perhaps appropriate at this juncture to examine from the priority perspective their more recent policies aimed at improving their competitive positions.

In the 1970s, Citroen sold their cars very largely on the basis of innovative styling and suspension systems. The latter made their cars very safe in the event of a 'blow out' and offered an outstanding ride quality. However, partly as a result of the complexity of these systems, the cars acquired a reputation for being very expensive to maintain and this severely affected their trade-in values. Citroen seemed to believe that the merits of their technical achievements could offset their cars' pecuniary penalties.

But, on a priority analysis that noted the high ranking most consumers give to matters of reliability and running costs (see the Cranfield study referred to in section 7.5), I argued that 'unless the Citroen company can succeed with their sales campaigns in persuading people to raise both their safety aspirations and priorities, they would do better to devote their resources to simplifying their cars to make them cheaper to service'. With the Citroen BX, the firm seems at last to have come round to a similar way of thinking, for the BX, as Citroen advertisements have been at pains to point out, 'loves driving, hates garages'. With characteristic ingenuity, Citroen's designers have produced a car with an individual image, and the best ride and handling quality in its class, yet one which requires a mere 108 minutes a year in servicing attention (as the advertisements say: 'such uncomplicated engineering that it spends less time in the service bay than a Ford Sierra').

Lancia's poor reputation, by contrast, has arisen mainly because of very bad rust resistance in its mid-price Beta range (see section 5.2.2), but the firm has enjoyed a high reputation for performance and style. Instead of trying to demonstrate conclusively that it had been able to solve the rust problem (for example, in the way tried by Fiat in the early 1970s, with pictures of its car bodies placed on salt-swept coastlines with and without new rust proofing treatments), the Lancia company initially responded to its collapsing sales by introducing fuel injection and supercharging into its Beta engines and by highlighting its past racing successes. In other words, it emphasised and improved upon its strong points. Its new, slightly less expensive Delta/Prisma range was also sold on driver appeal when first introduced. For example, an advertisement in the *Observer* Colour Supplement (11 September 1983) was built around the slogan 'the new Lancia Prisma: it needs you to make it complete'; nowhere was durability mentioned, despite the fact that the car actually came with a six-year antirust warranty. Lancia's UK market share continued to fall.

From a compensatory standpoint, it would seem not unwise for Lancia to concentrate its efforts where it had a comparative advantage: superb performance could compensate for its credibility gap in respect of durability (and, to a lesser extent, as a result of less well-known yet monumental problems in its up-market Gamma range, in respect of reliability). From a priority-based perspective, however, the strategy could make little sense. If Lancia's cars could not survive high-priority durability tests set by 'typical' customers—in other words, if the 'basics' were inadequate—they would be condemned to appeal to a small minority, with attendant consequences for the firm's unit costs. The majority would remove Lancia cars from their agendas at an early stage, even at the cost of finding themselves with a final choice between cars that were rather uninspiring but expected to be sufficiently reliable and durable. Unless a performance-oriented campaign succeeded in making buyers rerank their priorities and forget the dimensions that were in question, it would amount to little more than a device for reinforcing the opinions of the converted and winning a few sales from its similarly troubled Italian rival, Alfa Romeo.

With its 1984–5 campaigns, Lancia's new UK distributor adopted in some advertisements an eye-catching theme with much more promise in priority terms: 'the 121 mph Tank' (*Car Magazine,* July 1984). No one would normally call a frisky Lancia Delta Turbo a tank—in the car world, the term is usually reserved for durable Volvos! And sure enough, the smaller print tells the reader not merely about superlative performance, but also about 'double-thickness primer cataphoretically bonded to every part of the body', the superior ability of the car to survive a persistent salt-spray test, and '74 lb of corrosion-proofing material distributed round its vulnerable parts'.

The central message of a priority analysis is that the secret to mass-market success is to offer products in which a surfeit of performance in one dimension is not achieved at the cost of what will commonly be regarded as substandard attainments elsewhere. Since the product which gets furthest down customer priority lists dominates, products should not only be at least competent in all major respects, they should be made available with all the characteristics offered by rival brands (a policy which will also work where customers use elimination by aspects). Insofar as it is not possible to offer all the minor features at a price within the target budget range, the sensible policy is to give consumers as many option combinations as possible. That is to say, consumers should be permitted to create products that fit their own particular moulds of tolerance; firms should not presume that compulsory characteristics can compensate for absent ones, or that extra characteristics will always justify a higher price.

10.6 WHAT CAR?—AN ANALYSIS OF SOME RECOMMENDATIONS

Having presented very many motoring examples in this chapter (and elsewhere) by way of illustrating theoretical concepts at work, I feel it may be instructive to examine at least a handful of instances in which expert testers explain their rankings in multiple tests of groups of cars. The question of which decision rules they seem to be employing is one that can make for lively classroom discussions in marketing courses, and it is natural to raise it if one is pursuing a behavioural methodology. In selecting cases for discussion, I have tried to find ones that looked 'short enough' given my self-imposed length budget for this section. It should be noted that they all come from a monthly—*Car Magazine*—which is oriented in favour of the performance-seeking motoring connoisseur. Each case compares models that seem obvious rivals, and this in itself should immediately suggest in readers' minds a preliminary discrimination on non-compensatory lines.

Case 1 ('Giant Test', Car Magazine, May 1983, pp. 106–10) Saloons for Senior Executives
Saab 900 CD Turbo (£14,995); Jaguar XJ3.4 (£14,855); Mercedes Benz 280 SE (£18,602)

The Journalist's Conclusion
Sadly, the easiest of these three to dismiss is the Jaguar. It still does some things superbly. It rides the best, it is the quietest and at the very limit, it handles best too. That is a substantial catalogue of virtues against which must be set its inferior performance *and* economy in this company, and a catalogue of minor drawbacks like the poor heater system, limited luggage space and badly planned minor controls. Together, they are too much to give away to either of the rivals.

The Saab's overwhelming virtues, apart from the excellent and efficient performance conferred by the APC turbo, are those of space and sheer value for money by the standards of this class. In one were truly rational, the Saab would be the one to pick—the CD fully maintains

Saab's image as the thinking man's car. Why, in that case, do we pick the Mercedes as the front-runner?

It is simply that the Mercedes feels so perfectly engineered as an entity. Nothing lets it down. It is rather faster than the Saab and just as economical despite being much heavier. It may not be as roomy, but if you can seat four in genuine comfort, who cares? Most of all, the 280SE impresses with its chassis engineering. Its natural handling balance, the feeling that the car will do *exactly* what was intended, is quite extraordinary. The ride is a superbly chosen compromise for modern European conditions. Then again, there is the visible purity of the design approach. Around the driver, the aim has been utter simplicity rather than showroom appeal. The most expensive of the trio it may be; but it is also the all-round best, as thorough a piece of engineering as ever graced the Mercedes range

Discussion

An orthodox economist would immediately note that the tester's verdict begins with remarks that fall neatly into a compensatory perspective: it is not a single failing that leads to the rejection of the Jaguar but a *catalogue* of relatively poor performances *taken together,* despite it being best in some respects. However, one could also see it as having failed a conjunctive test on a number of counts as a result of the more modern vehicles having set superior standards in respect of acceleration, economy, space and general ergonomics. It is in these areas, not in respect of the high standards of ride, handling and quietness offered by all three vehicles, that the tester's attention is focused.

Precisely why the Saab is rejected looks mysterious at first, for it is not reported as having failed on any particular count, and it is a good deal cheaper than the Mercedes as well as more roomy. The justification for the verdict in favour of the Mercedes seems essentially to turn on the overall excellence of its design; it is as though the tester sees its whole as being 'greater than the sum of its parts', owing to the parts being brilliantly integrated. Clearly, one might argue that this is a compensatory verdict, with superior design quality offsetting the Mercedes' premium price and interior space disadvantages. But in terms of a characteristic filtering analysis, one can also argue that the experience of testing the Mercedes against its rivals seems to have left the journalist with a firm idea of the mould of tolerance into which such a car *should* fit, and that the Mercedes fits this ideal perfectly: 'nothing lets it down'. The new mould is too tight for even the Saab to fit.

Case 2 ('Giant Test,' Car Magazine, July 1983, pp. 110–19)
Up-Market Coupes
Alfa Romeo GTV6 (£10,600); Audi Coupe Fi (£9,592); Ford Sierra XR4i (£9,492)

The Journalist's Conclusion

All three of these cars have a certain appeal; equally, all have certain drawbacks which could be argued more or less convincingly. The Alfa is remarkably quick, with the added benefit of handling which is both safe and easily exploited by the expert up to its very high limit. Against that the GTV6 sacrifices space to the other two—it is certainly the one you would avoid if you wanted a full four seater, for instance, and it suffers from that awful gearchange and driving position. What a shame, we have to say yet again, that a car which gives the keen driver so much on the one hand should take so much away.

Then we have the Sierra: a full and comfortable four seater, just as fast as the Alfa, save for that imperfect handling close to the limit—and a couple of other things. One of those things was that the more we drove it, the more we felt the XR4i styling was too much over the top: people stared at it, certainly, but some seemed to titter and the boy-racer accusation could be seen in some eyes. The other drawback lies in comparing like with like: you have to look at the Ford option list to see what the XR4i really costs. Our test car, for instance, came with central locking, sunroof, electric front windows, headlamp wash, rear-seat sunblinds and tripminder multi-function clock: all desirable, but all extra cost options. A fully specified Sierra would come closer in price to Alfa than Audi.

That leaves the Audi, which is the hardest to argue against and thus turns out the winner. Slowest it may be, but slow is a very relative term in this context. Besides, it offers the compensating advantage of best fuel economy. It may not handle best, but compared with the Alfa we are talking of differences only a skilled driver would appreciate, and then only close to the limit. If you set against that the Audi's relaxed yet wholly competent air, its roominess, the precision of its controls, there is too much going for the German car. In the final analysis, the appeal of the Audi is that it allows its driver to tour sedately or press on elegantly. The Alfa and the Sierra practically *require* their drivers to press on all the time: a tribute to their character in one sense, but hardly a recipe for long-term satisfaction. Any car should be servant, not master, and the Audi's perfectly trained butler is far more liveable-with in the long term than Alfa's eccentric genius or Ford's slightly caddish 'buddy'.

Discussion

Once again, we have a report which begins with 'compensatory-sounding' remarks yet which lends itself to interpretation within the characteristic filtering framework. In terms of handling, the

Alfa dominates over the winning Audi, but both cars handle adequately. But the Alfa has some fatal flaws: the tester would reject it as not being a proper four-seater if he or she sought *that* kind of car; and the gearchange and driving position are both inadequate. Any one of these factors seems sufficient to ensure its rejection.

The Ford is more obviously a 'good all-rounder' than the Alfa, but there are three respects in terms of which its ability to pass tests is somewhat ambiguous, whereas the Audi's capability is not in question. At the limit, the handling of the car is very tail-happy and, as the text of the report notes, 'the result is fairly fast but very spectacular: too much so for most passengers, certainly for anyone coming the other way. For the Sierra, the limit is set not by the roadholding of those wide low-profile tyres, but by the driver's ability to control the beast'. It also seems a source of potential embarrassment due to its styling (and a priori one would expect a self-image aspiration to rank very highly indeed), while it seems open to rejection on grounds of cost—in a pricing tie-break with the Audi, a well-equipped Sierra would lose.

But what sets this report most convincingly in a priority mould is the comment that 'in the final analysis, the appeal of the Audi is that it allows its driver to tour sedately or press on elegantly'. The conventional form of this kind of comparative test forces appraisal against a conjunctive mould, but after considering the good and bad features of the cars in question the tester comes to a conclusion based on a single test—'does the character of the car unduly determine how it seems necessary to drive it?' The comments at the start of the paragraph on the Audi can, of course, be taken in compensatory terms, but the 'final analysis' cannot. The initial compensatory remarks about the Audi reveal that it fails nowhere and can, except in the extremes of performance, set standards which the others, in differing dimensions, cannot match. However, it is the failure of the Audi's two rivals to meet the demand that a car should not make undue demands upon its driver which is sufficient to ensure that the Audi dominates in the mind of the journalist called upon to make the recommendation. If this *single* characteristic filter is enough to reject *both* rivals, it must rank above the other characteristics in terms of which their different shortcomings were analysed. The other characteristics, in terms of which the Audi succeeds where its rivals fail, can be thought of as desired bonuses, but unless they affect the 'servant/master' rating they do not, 'in the final analysis', determine the verdict.

Case 3 'Giant Test,' (Car Magazine, February 1985, pp. 98–109) Executive Cars

Volvo 740GLE (£10,798); Renault 25GTX (£10,395); Rover 2300S (£10,828)

The Journalist's Conclusion

We liked the Rover. It has about it an air of tasteful, opulent luxury that the other two cars lack. Superior refinement and smoothness too, with its six cylinder engine. On top of that, it handles well and is pleasant to drive. Its Achilles heel is the combination of poor performance and heavy fuel consumption. As a company car with someone else paying the bills, we could make a case for the 2300S. For the private buyer we could not.

The four cylinder Volvo lacks the quiet smoothness of the Rover when accelerating, but it cruises very peacefully in overdrive top—a valuable additional gear the Rover badly needs. There is very little wrong with the solid, durable Volvo, and a great deal that's right. It's big, imposing, roomy, well made and agreeably mannered. In this confrontation, though, it's beaten by the Renault 25.

The French car's technical superiority—in particular its light weight and slippery shape—is the clincher. To outperform its two rivals so comfortably, *and* return a better fuel consumption (significantly better than the Rover), is an impressive feat. On top of that, the 25 has on its side fine looks, spaciousness, versatility and ample comfort, even though it is mechanically less refined than the Rover. The dash decor is not to everyone's taste but it's a small price to pay for so many good qualities.

Discussion

This verdict fits very neatly into the characteristic filtering framework. It makes no sense in a compensatory model to single out a particular failing as the Achilles heel of a product and fail it on that ground. Yet this is precisely what we observe in the case of the Rover: it drinks too much petrol for a private buyer and yet offers inadequate (albeit smooth) performance whilst doing so. Interestingly enough, the wording used seems to suggest that, in this test, the journalist is prepared to treat performance and economy as a potentially *compensatory pair* of attributes, the *combined* score for which would be allowed to face a single test of adequacy, *provided* that running costs are not excessive. However, the Renault seems to have demonstrated to the tester that there is no *need* to make a trade-off in this performance/economy dimension; by the end of the test, a new mould of tolerance seemed to have emerged in the person's mind.

The Volvo seems legitimately to be regarded as able to pass a conjunctive test of the form the tester initially had in mind: in the text of the report, the 'little that's wrong' with the Volvo seems to entail points that do not prevent it from meeting aspirations—things such as seats that were rather firm for long journeys (its rivals' seats had different problems and 'on balance' the Rover's were liked best, rather implying a compensatory rule being used within a single dimension in terms of which each car seemed adequate), and an awkwardly high loading lip for its large, deep, well-shaped boot. It seems that the Renault beats it in a tie-break mould-tightening process by setting higher standards in performance and economy due to technical superiority, and because of its more attractive styling and hatchback versatility. However, some readers might wish to argue that the additive differences procedure was used to resolve the choice, since the tester does mention the dash decor of the Renault as a minus point. My reading of the whole text of the report makes me doubt this possibility: in 'summing up', the tester fails to hark back to the other areas where the Volvo beats the Renault (rear cabin space, braking, and driving position); my suspicion is that the dash decor is mentioned because, in terms of overall interior refinement (and particularly in respect of the dashboard), the Renault *barely* came within the 'acceptable' category for this class of car, for the tester describes it as 'brash to the point of being vulgar'.

Case 4 ('Giant Test', Car Magazine, September 1984, pp. 140–7) Decidedly Different Diesels
Citroen BX19RD (£6696 as tested, £6314 without power steering); VW Golf 1.6C Diesel (£6310); Ford Orion 1.6GL Diesel (£6329)

The Journalist's Conclusion
If all these cars were powered by the same diesel engine, the choice would be narrowed down to their widely different style and accommodation. You could then decide if you like the Citroen dynamics more

than the luxury of the Orion GL interior or the proven quality of the Golf. As it stands in a market segment where the engine and the consumption it returns are paramount, the different driving characteristics rule supreme.

Despite its solid feel, undoubted fuel efficiency and very desirable list of good quality fittings, the Orion is the first to be rejected. It fails to appeal because of its primary responses—driving it is too much like hard work.

The simple choice between the Golf and the BX isn't so simple. On price, there's a premium to pay on the Citroen, for without power steering it simply isn't the same car at all. But whichever way you look at it, the BX is far more car than the VW—on size, on comfort, on equipment, on style, especially on performance and, surprisingly on fuel economy. So provided you can live with its quirks, the BX must win.

Discussion

This verdict is particularly interesting. On the one hand, we have the tester in effect saying that, *if* these cars had identical engines, it would be possible to choose in a compensatory manner. But on the other hand, the reality of the situation seen by the tester produces an obviously priorities-based choice: the well-equipped Ford is rejected because it fails to come up to performance aspirations; economy has been achieved at the expense of excessive sluggishness when extensive use is not made of the gearbox. I think we would also be wise to see the remarks about the Citroen's steering as implying that, if power steering were not available, or if one's budget could not stretch to the amount necessary to include it, then the BX would be rejected solely on that ground, letting the VW through to victory. Another tester, in *What Car?* (October 1983), awarded a victory to a petrol-engined BX with unassisted steering but added the proviso that 'the one glaring fault—the appallingly heavy steering for parking —will rule it out of court for any sensible town-bound buyer'. With a heavier diesel engine in the BX, such a problem would be all the more acute.

The choice between the Golf and a BX with power steering can be seen in a variety of ways. From a compensatory standpoint, one could argue that the BX wins because its areas of dominance over the Golf outweigh its price differential and idiosyncracies. However, one can also see this tester as finding both cars able to survive a conjunctive test in non-price terms. The tester does not find the BX's quirks intolerable and elsewhere in the report says that 'if you doesn't [sic] care about a car's character, so long as it goes well and keeps on running reliably, you might choose the Golf from this bunch. There's absolutely no tangible reason to reject it because it does everything so goddam well'. In matters of price, though, the tester then seems to suggest that the Golf is something of a rip-off: 'VW pricing is high, though, which means you only get C level trim for GL money'. Paradoxically, by paying a little extra for the BX with power steering, one avoids paying over the odds and gets a car that fits a tighter mould of tolerance: it looks stupid not to pay the premium for the BX.

Case 5 ('Giant Test', Car Magazine, November 1984, pp. 142–9) Under-1600 cc Family Saloons
Rover 213S (£5999); VW Jetta Formel E CL (£6022); Fiat Regata 85 Super (£6095)

The Journalist's Conclusion
Though the three are close on price, they are way apart on performance, temperament and equipment. Like can't strictly be compared with like anyway, for the economy Regata is nearly £500 less or there is a near £1000 jump to the next model Jetta. VW's choice of small-engined Jettas does seem very curious—there are just the very spartan Jetta C and Formel E—a model that for all its good features is obsessive in the pursuit of economy at the expense of all-round enjoyment. A well-equipped 1.3 Jetta without the economy encumbrances would surely be a very nice car indeed but, as things stand, the Formel E gives up too much drivability for gains in mpg that are not always realised.

Both the Jetta and Regata can teach the Rover lessons in almost every department. Passenger space, luggage space, handling and ride—most of all—are all inferior in the 213. Perhaps its interior is tolerable, though it is all Honda and no Rover. Its ride is not, though, and buyers are best advised to wait and see the outcome of Rover's already-promised suspension revisions. Even with new suspension, it is still hard to reconcile the saloon with the Rover name or traditions. One searches in vain for real class.

The Regata would make no claims to Rover-like status but in its skilful execution it's become something close to what the 213 would like to be. It's enjoyable to drive, thoughtfully finished and good value. It's the car to go for in this bunch.

Discussion
Given that the cars are similarly priced yet very different in non-price terms, one might expect the tester to try to weigh up their advantages and disadvantages. But nothing in this verdict seems

to indicate the use of a compensatory choice heuristic to decide overall scores and hence rankings. Rather, the verdict can be seen as suggesting that neither the Jetta nor the Rover are adequate in conjunctive terms, whereas the Regata is adequate in every respect. The Jetta's problem is that, in trading performance for economy, its designers have produced a product which falls short of the tester's aspirations for drivability. The Jetta that the journalist would like to have tested simply is not available: to get a well-equipped Jetta that goes adequately, one must go outside the price range set for the test (see the end of section 10.5). The Rover, by contrast, is ruled out decisively because of an intolerably bad ride. So, in priority terms, whether or not the Rover beats the Jetta for second place depends on whether drivability is ranked above ride quality. However, it is clear that the Rover would have been trounced by the Regata had things come to a tie-break. The Rover falls behind in terms of space and handling, and its claims to be a small executive-standard car—as opposed to a British-made, badge-engineered Honda Civic saloon—are shown up as pretentious by the Regata which, as the report elsewhere notes, 'also comes with such niceties as electric front windows, central locking and tinted glass, which none of the rest could provide'.

This section has been an exercise in trying rival theoretical templets for their fit on a very restricted set of examples that in no way purports to be a representative sample. Each case can be matched up with the characteristic filtering framework but, in most cases, one can at least partly try to make them compatible with orthodox compensatory ideas. Within the larger reports from which the conclusions have been taken, it is fairly clear that the testers often work out overall rankings for particular dimensions of choice that subsume a variety of characteristics, and that these assessments are often made in compensatory terms. However, when these 'dimensional' performances are brought together in the conclusions, it gets harder to make them fit a compensatory approach. In terms of the orthodox framework, it is difficult to understand why a tester should single out any particular characteristic performance of a product as being *the* reason for its rejection—yet this is precisely what we observe in cases 2 to 5. It is also evident that the cars in question are being asked to meet particular *standards* of sophistication, which differ between categories. The use of such reference standards has no obvious tie-in with the models reviewed in Chapter 2 but, to be fair, one should note that it is not at odds with the 'characteristics cut-offs expectancy value' choice heuristic discussed in section 7.3. I hope that these cases will serve, with Chapter 9, to promote more open-minded attitudes amongst theorists; I am *not* trying to claim that it is impossible to find other cases in similar tests where it is very difficult to make a non-compensatory choice heuristic seem plausible.

10.7 TRADE POLICY WITH NON-COMPENSATORY CHOICE RULES

A priority-based analysis of choice offers a distinctive perspective on policy options that a government might consider when poor performances of domestic firms in international markets arise from poor non-price competitiveness. In this situation, price-based trade policies (devaluations, export subsidies and import tariffs), will only change relative quantities sold in so far as they reduce real incomes in the home market and/or are large enough to enable domestic firms to reposition their products successfully in lower-income segments of export markets where consumers set less-demanding tests of adequacy. Such policies would not work, in a world of predominantly priority-based choices, by changing relative prices within budget ranges where products are presently positioned. Importers whose products were already highly competitive in non-price terms could raise their prices to maintain their profit margins in the face of currency depreciations or tariffs; they would not lose sales unless these increases took their products outside would-be buyers' budget ranges. Domestic firms would be foolish not to follow if uncompetitive in non-price terms; thereby they would improve their profit margins whilst maintaining the price differentials that enable them presently to win sales from the small proportion of customers who make lower non-price demands and use price as a tie-breaker. In the long run, however, the domestic firms' enhanced profit margins might help them develop more competitive products and offer more employment.

This analysis poses some difficulties for the arguments of Cripps and Godley (1978) in favour of a policy package that would combine price-based import controls with a general reflation, as a means of reducing unemployment *without:* (1) further worsening the UK balance of payments; (2) exporting unemployment to the rest of the world by reducing imports, for this would provoke retaliation by other nations; (3) reducing domestic real wages in the course of changing relative prices of imports and exports, for this would provoke retaliation by organised domestic workers; and (4) running into problems of bureaucratic complexity and evasion that one might encounter with non-market-based trade policies. The package rules out a squeeze on real incomes by assumption, so its ability to stop the balance-of-payments haemorrhage is open to question if non-price factors are very often decisive in choice processes.

A rather more promising package (problem (4) aside) would be one which combined reflationary policies with import quotas and 'red tape' (for example, the kinds of official design requirements, relating to emission controls, that Australia uses to protect its environment and its car industry from the impact of imported vehicles). If the physical quantities coming into the economy are restricted, many consumers will find that imported products with superior non-price properties—except, now, in respect of delivery—have effectively been removed from their agendas of possibles. They then have four options: (1) to bid the sought-after imports that *are* available away from other buyers, by offering higher prices; (2) to go without for the present and join appropriate waiting lists; (3) to buy domestic substitutes and fail to meet some of their non-price aspirations; or (4) to use the benefits of any reflation-induced tax reductions to move 'up market' and purchase domestic output that is satisfactory in non-price terms, yet which they previously would have found too expensive. Provided tax cuts and the availability of 'up-market' domestic output are such that, if (1) is unattractive, (4) can be pursued without any need to forgo lower-priority consumption that would otherwise have taken place, the reflation/'non-price import controls' package keeps an increase in demand within the economy without upsetting those workers who were already in employment. However, if the prices of imported up-market substitutes now under controls were marked up, the prices of domestic substitutes might also be increased, and in this case workers would feel disgruntled to find themselves *having* to choose (2) or (3)—though they would have the benefit of any tax reductions to spend on meeting additional, but lower-priority goals. In the event, they might not feel squeezed overall by the policy package, despite the fact that *ex ante* they may act as if the loss of a high-ranking attainment is not compensated for by the gain of several lower attainments.

10.8 INCENTIVES AND RISK TAKING

Having begun this book by noting the hazards of being a consumer in a turbulent world, I feel it is appropriate that my final piece of analysis should concern policies with respect to risk taking. Suppose a person is declining to undertake a particular activity because it seems 'too risky'. In terms of the conventional probabilistic approach to hazardous choices, one can usefully seek to break the person's resistance by highlighting possible desired outcomes or offering a higher gain-side payoff (for example; a higher-interest yield on unsecured finance company stock, which the consumer is considering as an alternative to holding her savings in a bank deposit); it is not necessary to reduce her assessments of downside risks. However, from the standpoint of the analysis in sections 8.3 and 8.5, such a means towards changing behaviour seems potentially futile. In the mind of the consumer, 'too risky' may mean excessive downside risk, as in Blatt's drug-smuggling example, and/or an insufficiently plausible prospect of an adequate gainside outcome. Before offering policy advice, a behavioural theorist would want to know from the decision makers themselves whether they see 'too risky' in the former or latter way, or in both ways. If gainside prospects were seen as entirely adequate, but downside ones were not, it would be pointless to devote resources to improve gainside prospects; what the consumer wants is a better guarantee, more security, not the chance of an extra bonus. (Even as I write, a major local used-car dealer is offering buyers a chance to win a family trip to Disneyland as an extra incentive to buy its products, yet its advertisements make no mention of the terms of warranties, if any, that it offers.)

This non-compensatory view of risk taking suggests that Right-wing policies aimed at raising economic activity by increasing incentives to try to earn high incomes (that is, by cutting direct taxes and by reducing incentives to be unemployed) could be hopelessly misplaced. The policy would look somewhat problematical even from the standpoint of probabilistic views of choice, since higher expected post-tax values on the gainside might be cancelled out by higher expected loss values on the downside. But, in non-compensatory terms, it would be natural to argue that if the previous high tax/'high' safety-net environment was, for many, only just about tolerable on the downside, then the implementation of the Right-wing policy package could easily result in *more* people being inclined to play safe. (Note: downside income-seeking risks need not pertain merely to the loss of one's job or life's savings, or to the prospect of bankruptcy; for many people they should more realistically be thought of as concerning loss of status and easy promotion prospects as a result of attempting to be enterprising—*relative* positions matter.) Such a possibility is made all the easier to believe by the fact that the policy is being implemented against a background of demand-reducing expenditure cuts by the public sector, and by monetary restraint—further core components in Conservative philosophies—that make failures looks less surprising, and conceivable pre-tax returns of a given size look more surprising, in prospect.

The analysis I have proposed is not without relevance to debates in monetary theory between Post Keynesians and neoclassical theorists about the transmission mechanisms of monetary policy. In these debates, one often sees Post Keynesians stressing the significance of possible breaks in the 'chain of substitution' between rival ways of storing wealth (cash, bank deposits, liabilities of non-bank financial intermediaries, short-dated government stock, perpetuities, corporate debentures, equities, durable physical goods). Neoclassical theorists claim that an increase in the money stock will spill over into a demand for all other forms of wealth and hence into a demand for labour. However, some kinds of wealth may look 'too risky' to take on even if yields are falling on other assets with acceptable downside risks: banks may prefer unused lending capacity to consumers that seem altogether too likely to default; and consumers may prefer continued liquidity, despite a reduced interest yield on savings or a reduced cost of borrowing, if they would feel 'too exposed' to downside risks of forced sales of the durable goods they could acquire. Such an analysis would suggest that, at times, there may indeed be breaks in the 'chain of substitution' amongst rival stores of wealth, and that Post Keynesian emphasis on the limited efficacy of an expansionary monetary policy in times of recession could be well founded (see Karacaoglu, 1984).

10.9 CONCLUDING THOUGHTS

The joke about the policy maker who sought to hire a one-armed economist so as to avoid being given advice taking the form 'on the one hand, this; but on the other hand, that' is well known. But whoever was originally responsible for it cannot have been very well acquainted with the economics profession. Economists certainly do disagree amongst themselves, but the kind of open-ended approach to analysis that this book carries over from my (1984) work, to the realm of consumer theory, is very rare. Look around for books by economists on consumer behaviour that emphasise the multiplicity of ways people have for forming expectations—including expectations about what they could, and should, do with their lives—and for ranking rival schemes of action: you will be hard pushed to find very many. But you will find shelves and shelves of books and articles that treat consumers 'as if' they are clones who 'know what they want and know how to get it'. To the lay reader this might well imply that economists—if not policy makers—will be highly receptive to the analysis I have put forward. But I would be surprised to see most economists reacting to it in a positive manner; the vast majority are neoclassical theorists who have never grown more than one theoretical arm and who would never dream of suggesting to policy makers that a variety of models may be useful, in different ways and to different extents, as means towards anticipating and controlling events.

Such theorists are free to construe this book, like any other event, however they wish. I expect that many will seek to ignore inconvenient things that I say about, for example, the significance of psychological inputs and non-compensatory choice heuristics, and will argue that Lifestyle Economics is not relevant or adds nothing to their area of interest. I would not be surprised to find some of them wanting to reach the same conclusion about this book as one reached by a referee of the *Economic Journal* in a negative response to an attempt (Earl, 1985) I made to 'test-market' some of the ideas in a highly compressed form. The referee claimed that 'if we regard the protected core [of constructs] as being a given set of basic tastes, and if positive and negative implications are simply the relative advantages and disadvantages of each commodity in terms of its various characteristics, we would appear to be quite squarely in familiar and orthodox territory'.

I would also expect to see attempts to justify resistance to Lifestyle Economics in which reference is made to my incomplete coverage of 'the literature', notwithstanding the following statement of coverage or the fact that the kind of literature I highlight is largely ignored in orthodox work. I do *not* claim to have referred in the present book to every other deviant theorist whose ideas overlap with my own. (For example, in a longer work, I would certainly have taken up a good deal of space discussing the prescient century-old ideas of Thorstein Veblen, that failed to have enough of an impact to stop marginalist economics from coming to dominate the profession in the way that it has.) Nor do I claim to have referred to absolutely every attempt by an orthodox economist to extend the neoclassical paradigm in a way that tries to confront some of the issues I have sought to address. (For example, I am well aware, from Elster (1984, pp. 76–85), that the (1977) paper by Stigler and Becker on endogenous changes of preferences is by no means the sum total of orthodox thinking in that area; it just happens to be the one that most people seem to mention and as it also has some interface with my own emphasis on the role of competence in choice it is natural that I devote some of my limited space to discussing it at the expense of other contributions.) And I certainly do not intend to suggest that the theoretical ideas and research methods of personal construct psychology comprise the only psychological material that economists might find useful. Constructs in the area of consumer theory, as in life generally, are not costless to collect or make use of, and I have adopted the risky but synergy-rich strategy of exploring and integrating a limited number of them in a rather obsessive manner as a means of dealing with the subject matter.

These closing remarks may sound somewhat tinged with paranoia, but theorists who are not used to working with a variety of tools are to be expected to be hostile to a work that threatens their claims to be going about 'economic science' in *the* right way. So if I succeed in opening the minds of at least a few neoclassical economists, instead of merely satisfying fellow deviants, I shall be well pleased, for even this would come as something of a surprise. But, then, life is full of surprises.

Bibliography

Adams, F. G. (1964) 'Consumer attitudes, buying plans and purchases of durable goods: a principal component times series approach', *Review of Economics and Statistics* **46**, pp. 347–55.

Adams, F. G. and Klein, L. R. (1972) 'Anticipations variables in econometric models', in Strumpel, B., Morgan, J. N. and Zahn, E. (eds.) *Human Behavior in Economic Affairs*, San Francisco, Jossey-Bass.

Adams, J. L. (1980) *Conceptual Blockbusting: A Guide to Better Ideas* (2nd edn.), New York, Norton.

Adams-Webber, J. R. (1970) 'Actual structure and potential chaos', in Bannister, D. (ed.) (1970) *Perspectives in Personal Construct Theory*, London, Academic Press.

— (1979) *Personal Construct Theory: Concepts and Applications*, Chichester, Wiley.

Akaah, I. and Korgoankar, P. K. (1983) 'An empirical comparison of the predictive validity of self-explicated, Huber-hybrid, traditional conjoint and hybrid conjoint models', *Journal of Marketing Research,* **20** (May), pp. 187–97.

Akerlof, G. A. (1970) '"The market for lemons": quality uncertainty and the market mechanism', *Quarterly Journal of Economics,* **84,** (August), pp. 488–500.

Alcaly, R. E. and Klevorick, A. K. (1970) 'Judging quality by price, snob appeal, and the new consumer theory', *Zeitschrift für Nationalökonomie,* **30,** pp. 53–64.

Andrews, P. W. S. (1949) *Manufacturing Business*, London, Macmillan.

Angevine, G. E. (1974) 'Forecasting consumption with a Canadian sentiment measure', *Canadian Journal of Economics,* **7** (May), pp. 273–89.

Bain, A. D. (1964) *The Growth of Television Ownership in the UK: A Lognormal Model,* Cambridge, Cambridge University Press.

Bannister, D. and Fransella, F. (1971) *Inquiring Man* (2nd edn., 1980), Harmondsworth, Penguin Books.

Bannister, D. and Mair, J. M. M. (1968) *The Evaluation of*

Personal Constructs, New York, Academic Press.

Baumol, W. J. and Quandt, R. E. (1964) 'Rules of thumb and optimally imperfect decisions', *American Economic Review,* **54** (March), pp. 23–46.

Bausor, R. (1982) 'Time and economic analysis', *Journal of Post Keynesian Economics,* **5** (Winter), pp. 163–79.

— (1984) 'Towards a historically dynamic economics: examples and illustrations', *Journal of Post Keynesian Economics,* **6** (Spring), pp. 360–76.

Baxter, J. L. (1980) ' A general model of wage determination', *Bulletin of Economic Research,* **32** (May), pp. 3–17.

Beck, A. T., Rush, A. J., Shaw, B. F. and Emery, G. (1979) *Cognitive Therapy of Depression,* New York, Guilford Press.

Becker, G. S. (1962) 'Irrational behavior and economic theory', *Journal of Political Economy,* **70,** pp. 1–13.

— (1965) 'A theory of the allocation of time', *Economic Journal,* **75** (September), pp. 493–517.

— (1974) 'A theory of marriage: part II', *Journal of Political Economy,* **82** (Supplement, March), pp. 11–26.

— (1976) *The Economic Approach to Human Behavior,* Chicago, University of Chicago Press.

Bettman, J. R. (1974) 'Decision-net models of buyer information processing and choice', in Hughes, G. D. and Roy, M. L. (eds.) (1974) *Buyer/Consumer Information Processing,* Chapel Hill, North Carolina, University of North Carolina Press.

Bettman, J. R. (1979) *An Information Processing Theory of Consumer Choice,* Reading, Mass., Addison-Wesley.

Blatt, J. (1983) *Dynamic Economic Systems,* Brighton, Wheatsheaf.

Borch, K. (1968) *The Economics of Uncertainty,* Princeton, Princeton University Press.

Brown, A. and Deaton, A. (1972) 'Surveys in applied economics: models of consumer behaviour', *Economic Journal,* **82** (December), pp. 1145–236.

Bruno, A. V. and Wildt, A. R. (1975) 'Toward understanding attitude structure: a study of the complementarity of multi-attribute attitude models', *Journal of Consumer Research,* **2** (September), pp. 137–45.

Cairncross, A. (1958) 'Economic schizophrenia', *Scottish Journal of Political Economy,* **5** (February), pp. 15–21.

Canterbery, R. (1979) 'Inflation, necessities and distributive efficiency', in Gapinsky, J. H. and Rockwood, C. E., jr (eds.) (1979) *Essays in Post-Keynesian Inflation,* New York, Ballinger.

Carter, C. F. (1954) 'A revised theory of expectations', in Carter, C. F., Meredith, G. P. and Shackle, G. L. S. (eds.) (1954) *Uncertainty and Business Decisions*, Liverpool, Liverpool University Press.

Casson, M. C. (1982) *The Entrepreneur: An Economic Theory*, Oxford, Martin Robertson.

Chandler, A. D. (1962) *Strategy and Structure: Chapters in the History of the American Industrial Enterprise*, Cambridge, Mass., MIT Press.

Chase, W. G. and Simon, H. A. (1973a) 'Skill in chess', *American Scientist*, **61**, pp. 394–403.

— (1973b) 'Perception in chess', *Cognitive Psychology*, **4**, pp. 55–81.

Chick, V. (1983) *Macroeconomics After Keynes*, Deddington, Oxford, Philip Allan.

Coase, R. H. (1937) 'The nature of the firm', *Economica*, **4** (New series) (November), pp. 386–405.

Coddington, A. (1975) 'Creaking semaphore and beyond' (Review of G. L. S. Shackle: *Epistemics and Economics)*, *British Journal for the Philosophy of Science*, **26** (June), pp. 151–63.

— (1982) 'Deficient foresight: a troublesome theme in Keynesian economics', *American Economic Review*, **72** (June), pp. 480–7.

Court, A. T. (1939) 'Hedonic price indexes with automotive examples', pp. 99–117 of *The Dynamics of Automobile Demand*, New York, General Motors Corporation.

Cowling, K. and Cubbin, J. (1971) 'Price, quality and advertising competition: an econometric investigation of the United Kingdom car market', *Economica*, **38** (November), pp. 378–94.

Cowling, K. and Rayner, A. J. (1970) 'Price, quality and market share', *Journal of Political Economy*, **78** (November), pp. 1292–309.

CPRS (Central Policy Review Staff) (1975) *The Future of the British Car Industry*, London, HMSO.

Cripps, T. F. and Godley, W. A. H. (1978) 'Control of imports as a means to full employment and the expansion of world trade: the UK's case', *Cambridge Journal of Economics*, **2** (September), pp. 327–34.

Crockett, W. H. and Meisel, P. (1974) 'Construct connectedness, strength of disconfirmation and impression change', *Journal of Personality*, **42**, pp. 290–9.

Cunningham, M. T. and White, J. G. (1974) 'The behaviour of industrial buyers in their search for suppliers of machine tools', *Journal of Management Studies,* 11 (May), pp. 114–28.

Curry, D. J. and Menasco, M. B. (1979) 'Some effects of differing information processing strategies on husband–wife joint decisions', *Journal of Consumer research,* 6 (September), pp. 192–203.

Cyert, R. M. and March, J. G. (1963) *A Behavioral Theory of the Firm,* Englewood Cliffs, NJ, Prentice-Hall.

Cyert, R. M. and Simon, H. A. (1983) 'The behavioral approach: with emphasis on economics', *Behavioral Science,* **28,** (April), pp. 95–108.

Dash, J. F., Schliffman, L. G. and Berenson, C. (1976) 'Risk and personality-related dimensions of store choice', *Journal of Marketing,* **40,** pp. 32–9.

Davidson, P. (1972) *Money and the Real World,* London, Macmillan.

Day, R. H. (1967) 'Profits, learning and the convergence of satisficing to marginalism', *Quarterly Journal of Economics,* **81,** pp. 302–11.

Deaton, A. and Muellbauer, J. (1980) *Economics and Consumer Behavior,* Cambridge, Cambridge University Press.

Debreu, G. (1959) *Theory of Value,* New York, Wiley.

Douglas, E. J. (1983) *Managerial Economics: Theory, Practice and Problems* (2nd edn.), Englewood Cliffs, NJ, Prentice-Hall.

Dow, S. C. and Earl, P. E. (1982) *Money Matters: A Keynesian Approach to Monetary Economics,* Oxford, Martin Robertson.

Doyle, P. and Fenwick, I. (1975) '"Are goods goods? some further evidence": A Comment', *Applied Economics,* 7 (June), pp. 93–8.

Duck, S. (1983) *Friends, For Life: The Psychology of Close Relationships,* Brighton, Harvester.

Duhem, P. (1906) *The Aim and Structure of Physical Theory,* translated by P. Weiner, Princeton, Princeton University Press.

Dunkelberg, W. C. (1969) 'Forecasting consumer expenditures with measures of attitudes and expectations', Unpublished PhD. Dissertation, University of Michigan.

Dunnett, P. J. S. (1980) *The Decline of the British Motor Industry,* London, Croom Helm.

Earl, P. E. (1983a) 'A behavioral theory of economists' behavior', in Eichner, A.S. (ed.) (1983) *Why Economics is Not Yet a Science,* Armonk, NY, M. E. Sharpe, Inc.

— (1983b) 'The consumer in his/her social setting: a subjectivist view', In Wiseman, J. (ed.) (1983) *Beyond Positive Economics?* London, Macmillan.
— (1983c) *The Economic Imagination: Towards a Behavioural Analysis of Choice,* Brighton, Wheatsheaf (Armonk, NY, M. E. Sharpe, Inc.).
— (1984) *The Corporate Imagination: How Big Companies Make Mistakes,* Brighton, Wheatsheaf (Armonk, NY, M. E. Sharpe, Inc.).
— (1985) 'Expectation formation and resistance to change: a behavioural analysis of demand elasticities', University of Tasmania Economics Discussion Paper No. 85/2.
Earl, P. E. and Kay, N. M. (1985) 'How economists can accept Shackle's critique of economic doctrines without arguing themselves out of their jobs', *Journal of Economic Studies,* **12,** No. 1/2, pp. 34–48.
Edwardes, M. (1983) *Back From the Brink: An Apocalyptic Experience,* London, Collins.
Eichner, A. S. (ed) (1983) *Why Economics is Not Yet a Science,* Armonk, NY, M. E. Sharpe, Inc.
Ellman, M. (1973) *Planning Problems in the USSR,* Cambridge, Cambridge University Press.
Elster, J. (1983) *Sour Grapes: Studies in the Subversion of Rationality,* Cambridge, Cambridge University Press.
— (1984) *Ulysses and the Sirens: Studies in Rationality and Irrationality.* (rev. edn.), Cambridge, Cambridge University Press.
Engel, J. F. and Blackwell, R. D. (1982) *Consumer Behavior* (4th edn.), Hinsdale, Illinois, Dryden Press.
Farley, J. (1964) 'Brand loyalty and the economics of information', *Journal of Business,* **27** (October), pp. 370–81.
Feige, E. L. (1975) 'The consequences of journal editorial policies and a suggestion for revision', *Journal of Political Economy,* **83** (December), pp. 1291–6.
Festinger, L. (1957) *A Theory of Cognitive Dissonance,* New York, Harper & Row.
Feyerabend, P. K. (1975) *Against Method: Outline of an Anarchistic Theory of Knowledge,* London, New Left Books.
Fishbein, M. A. (1963) 'An investigation of the relationships between beliefs about an object and the attitude toward that object', *Human Relations,* **16** (August), pp. 233–9.
Fishbein, M. A. and Ajzen, I. (1975) *Belief, Attitude, Intention and Behavior: An Introduction to Theory and Research,* Reading, Mass., Addison-Wesley.

Fishburn, P. O. (1974) 'Lexicographic orders, utilities and decision rules: a survey', *Management Science*, **20** (July), pp. 1442–71.

Fisher, F. M., Griliches, Z. and Kaysen, C. (1962) 'The costs of automobile model changes since 1949', *Journal of Political Economy*, **70** (October), pp. 433–51.

Ford, J. L. (1983) *Choice, Expectations and Uncertainty*, Oxford, Martin Robertson.

French, M. (1978) *The Women's Room*, London, Sphere Books.

Friedman, M. (1953) 'The methodology of positive economics', in Friedman, M. (ed.) (1953) *Essays in Positive Economics*, Chicago, University of Chicago Press.

Friend, I. and Adams, F. G. (1964) 'The predictive ability of consumer attitudes, stock prices and non-attitudinal variables', *Journal of the American Statistical Association*, **59** (December), pp. 987–1005.

Fryer, D. and Payne, R. L. (1983) 'Unemployed workers' proactivity as a route to understanding psychological effects of unemployment', MRC/SSRC SAPU Memo. 540.

Gabor, A. and Granger, C. W. J. (1966) 'Price as an indicator of quality: report on an inquiry', *Economica*, **33** (February), pp. 43–70.

Galbraith, J. K. (1958) *The Affluent Society*, London, Hamish Hamilton.

— (1975) *Economics and the Public Purpose*, Harmondsworth, Penguin Books.

Gallagher, W. M. (1971) 'The evaluation and control of research and development projects', Unpublished Ph.D. Dissertation, University of Stirling.

Garfinkel, H. (1967) *Studies in Ethnomethodology*, Englewood Cliffs, NJ, Prentice-Hall.

Georgescu-Roegen, N. (1954) 'Choice, expectations and measurability', *Quarterly Journal of Economics*, **68**, pp. 503–34.

Gimpl, M. L. and Dakin, S. R. (1984) 'Management and magic', *California Management Review*, **27** (Fall), pp. 125–36.

Goldstein, M. (1959) 'Relationship Between coping and avoiding behaviour in response to fear-arousing propaganda', *Journal of Abnormal and Social Psychology*, **58**, pp. 247–52.

Gorman, W. M. (1956) 'A possible procedure for analysing the quality differentials in the egg market', Mimeographed.

Grasmick, H. G. and Scott, W. J. (1982) 'Tax evasion and mechanisms of social control: a comparison with grand and

petty theft', *Journal of Economic Psychology* **2,** pp. 213–30.
Green, H. A. J. (1976) *Consumer Theory,* (rev. edn.) London, Macmillan.
Green, P. E. and Srinivasan, V. (1978) 'Conjoint analysis in consumer research: issues and outlook, *Journal of Consumer research,* **5** (September), pp. 103–23.
Green, P. E., Goldberg, S. M. and Montemayor, M. (1981) 'A hybrid utility estimation model for conjoint analysis', *Journal of Marketing,* **45** (Winter), pp. 33–41.
Griliches, Z. (1961) 'Hedonic indexes for automobiles: an econometric analysis of quality change', in *The Price Statistics of the Federal Government,* New York, National Bureau of Economic Research, pp. 173–96.
Griliches, Z. (ed.) (1971) *Price Indexes and Quality Change,* Cambridge, Mass., Harvard University Press.
Gutman, J. (1982) 'A means-end chain model based on consumer categorization processes', *Journal of Marketing,* **46** (Spring), pp. 60–72.
Gutman, J. and Alden, S. D. (1985) 'Adolescents' cognitive structures of retail stores and fashion consumption: a means-end chain analysis of quality', in Jacoby, J. and Olson, J. C. (eds.) (1985) *Perceived Quality,* Lexington, Mass., D. C. Heath (for New York University Institute of Retail Management).
Haines, G. H. jr (1975) 'Commentary on Ratchford, "The new economic theory of consumer behavior: an interpretive essay"', *Journal of Consumer Research* **2** (September), pp. 77–8.
Hall, R. L. and Hitch, C. J. (1951) 'Price theory and business behaviour', in Wilson, T. and Andrews, P. W. S. (eds.) (1951) *Oxford Studies in the Price Mechanism,* Oxford, Oxford University Press (originally in *Oxford Economic Papers* (1939) **2,** pp. 12–45).
Hamouda, O. (1983) 'Time, choice and dynamics in economics', University of Cambridge, mimeographed (November).
Hansen, F. (1976) 'Psychological theories of consumer choice', *Journal of Consumer Research* **3** (December), pp. 117–42.
Harcourt, G. C. (1972) *Some Cambridge Controversies in the Theory of Capital,* Cambridge, Cambridge University Press.
Hart, A. G. (1940) 'Anticipations, uncertainty and dynamic planning' *Journal of Business of the University of Chicago,* **13,** No. 4 (also published separately as a monograph by the University of Chicago Press, Chicago).

— (1942) 'Risk, uncertainty and the unprofitability of compounding probabilities', in Lange, O., McIntyre, F. and Yntema, T. O. (eds.) (1942) *Studies in Mathematical Economics and Econometrics*, Chicago, University of Chicago Press (reprinted in American Economic Association (1946) *Readings in the Theory of Income Distribution*, Philadelphia, A. E. A.).

— (1945) '"Model building" and fiscal policy', *American Economic Review*, **35** (September), pp. 531–58.

— (1947) 'Keynes' analysis of expectations and uncertainty', in Harris, S. E. (ed.) (1947) *The New Economics: Keynes' Influence on Theory and Public Policy*, New York, Knopf.

— (1948) *Money, Debt and Economic Activity*, New York, Prentice-Hall.

Hawkins, D. I., Coney, K. A. and Best, R. J. (1980) *Consumer Behavior: Implications for Marketing Strategy*, Dallas, Business Publications, Inc.

Hebden, J. J. and Pickering, J. F. (1974) 'Patterns of acquisition of consumer durables', *Oxford Bulletin of Economics and Statistics*, **36** (May), pp. 67–92.

Heiner, R. A. (1983) 'The origin of predictable behavior', *American Economic Review*, **73** (September), pp. 560–95.

Henry, H. (1958) *Motivation Research: Its Practice and Uses for Advertising, Marketing, and other Business Purposes*, London, Crosby Lockwood.

Hesselman, L. (1981) 'Non-price factors in the UK washing machine market: a hedonic approach', Economic Working Paper No. 1, NEDO, London.

Hey, J. D. (1983a) 'Towards double negative economics', in Wiseman, J. (ed.) (1983) *Beyond Positive Economics?* London, Macmillan.

— (1983b) 'Whither uncertainty?' *Economic Journal*, **93** (Supplement, March), pp. 129–38.

— (1984) 'Unshackling economics', *Scottish Journal of Political Economy*, **31** (June), pp. 202–8.

— (1985) 'The possibility of possibility', *Journal of Economic Studies*, **12**, No. 1/2, pp. 70–88.

Hicks, J. R. (1937) 'Mr Keynes and the "classics": a suggested interpretation', *Econometrica*, **5** (April), pp. 147–59.

— (1939) *Value and Capital*, Oxford, Oxford University Press.

— (1976) 'Some questions of time in economics', in Tang, A, M., Westfield, F. M. and Worley, J. S. (eds.) (1976) *Evolution, Welfare, and Time in Economics: Essays in Honor*

of Nicholas Georgescu-Roegen, Lexington, Mass., Lexington Books.
— (1980) 'IS-LM: an explanation', *Journal of Post Keynesian Economics*, 3 (Winter), pp. 139–54.
Hinkle, D. N. (1965) 'The change of personal constructs from the viewpoint of a theory of implications', Unpublished Ph.D. Thesis, Ohio State University.
Hirsch, F. (1977) *Social Limits to Growth*, London, Routledge and Kegan Paul.
Hoch, S. J. (1984) 'Hypothesis testing and consumer behavior: "If it works, don't mess with it"', in Kinnear, T. C. (ed.) (1984) *Advances in Consumer Research 11*, Ann Arbor, Association for Consumer Research.
Hoepfl, R. T. and Huber, G. P. (1970) ' A study of self-explicated models', *Behavioral Science*, 15, pp. 408–14.
Hofstadter, D. R. (1979) *Gödel, Escher, Bach: an eternal golden braid*, Hassocks, Sussex, Harvester Press.
Houthakker, H. S. (1952) 'Changes in quantities and qualities consumed', *Review of Economic Studies*, 19 (July), pp. 155–63.
Houthakker, H. S. and Taylor, L. D. (1970) *Consumer Demand in the United States: Analysis and Projections* (2nd edn.), Cambridge, Mass, Harvard University Press.
Huber, G. P., Sahney, V. and Ford, D. L. (1969) ' A study of subjective evaluation models', *Behavioral Science*, 14 (November), pp. 483–9.
Hunt, M. (1982) *The Universe Within*, Brighton, Harvester.
Hutchison, T. W. (1938) *The Significance and Basic Postulates of Economic Theory*, reprinted 1960, New York, Kelley.
— (1977) *Knowledge and Ignorance in Economics*, Oxford, Basil Blackwell.
— (1978) 'Review of subjectivist books by L. M. Lachman, G. P. O'Driscoll, Jr, M. Rothbard, and J. Jewkes', *Economic Journal*, 88 (December), pp. 840–3.
Ironmonger, D. S. (1972) *New Commodities and Consumer Behaviour*, Cambridge, Cambridge University Press.
Jackson, P. R. and Warr, P. B. (1983) 'Age, length of unemployment and other variables associated with men's ill-health during unemployment', MRC/SSRC SAPU Memo. 585.
Jefferson, M. (1983) 'Economic uncertainty and business decision making', in Wiseman, J. (ed.) (1983) *Beyond Positive Economics?*, London, Macmillan.

Johnson, E. J. (1979) 'Deciding how to decide: the effort of making a decision', Discussion Paper, Center for Decision Research, University of Chicago Graduate School of Business.

Kahneman, D. and Tversky, A. (1979) 'Prospect theory: an analysis of decision under risk', *Econometrica,* **47,** pp. 263–91.

Karacaoglu, G. (1984) 'Absence of gross substitution in portfolios and demand for finance: some macroeconomic implications' *Journal of Post Keynesian Economics,* **6** (Summer), pp. 576–89.

Katona, G. (1975) *Psychological Economics,* Amsterdam, Elsevier.

— (1976) 'Consumer investment versus business investment', *Challenge,* January/February.

— (1980) *Essays on Behavioral Economics,* Ann Arbor, University of Michigan Institute for Social Research.

Katzner, D. W. (1970) *Static Demand Theory,* London, Collier-Macmillan.

Kay, H. (1972) 'Do we really know the effects of using "fear" appeals?' *Journal of Marketing,* **36** (April), pp. 55–7.

Kay, N. M. (1979) *The Innovating Firm: A Behavioural Theory of Corporate R & D,* London, Macmillan.

— (1982) *The Evolving Firm,* London, Macmillan.

— (1984) *The Emergent Firm: Knowledge, Ignorance and Surprise in Economic Organisation,* London, Macmillan.

Kelly, G. A. (1955) *The Psychology of Personal Constructs,* New York, Norton.

— (1963) *A Theory of Personality,* New York, Norton.

Keynes, J. M. (1936) *The General Theory of Employment, Interest and Money,* London, Macmillan.

— (1937) 'The general theory of employment', *Quarterly Journal of Economics,* **51,** pp. 209–23.

Koestler, A. (1975) *The Act of Creation,* London, Pan Books.

Kornai, J. (1971) *Anti-Equilibrium,* Amsterdam, North-Holland.

Koutsoyiannis, A. (1982) *Non-Price Decisions: The Firm in a Modern Context,* London, Macmillan.

Kuhn, T. S. (1970) *The Structure of Scientific Revolutions* (2nd edn.) Chicago, University of Chicago Press.

Lakatos, I. (1970) 'Falsification and the methodology of scientific research programmes', in Lakatos, I. and Musgrave, A. (eds.) (1970) *Criticism and the Growth of Knowledge,* London, Cambridge University Press.

Lamfalussy, A. (1961) *Investment and Growth in a Mature Economy: The Case of Belgium,* London, Macmillan.

Lancaster, K. J. (1966a) 'A new approach to consumer theory', *Journal of Political Economy*, **74** (April), pp. 132–57.
— (1966b) 'Change and innovation in the technology of consumption', *American Economic Review*, **56** (May) pp. 14–23.
— (1971) *Consumer Demand: A New Approach*, New York, Columbia University Press.
— (1975) 'Socially optimal product differentiation', *American Economic Review*, **65** (September), pp. 567–85.
— (1979) *Variety Equity and Efficiency: Product Variety in an Industrial Society*, Oxford, Basil Blackwell.
Lea, S. E. G. and Harrison, S. N. (1978) 'Discrimination of polymorphous stimulus sets by pigeons', *Quarterly Journal of Experimental Psychology*, **30**, pp. 521–37.
Leech, D. and Cubbin, J. (1978) 'Import penetration in the UK passenger car market: a cross-section study', *Applied Economics*, **10** (December), pp. 289–304.
Lewis, A. (1982) *The Psychology of Taxation*, Oxford, Martin Robertson.
Linder, M. (1977) *Anti-Samuelson: Volume Two*, New York, Urizen Books.
Lipsey, R. G. and Rosenbluth, G. (1971) 'A contribution to the new theory of demand: a rehabilitation of the Giffen good', *Canadian Journal of Economics*, **4** (May), pp.131–63.
Littlechild, S. C. (1983) 'Subjectivism and method in economics', in Wiseman, J. (ed.) (1983) *Beyond Positive Economics?* London, Macmillan.
Loasby, B. J. (1967) 'Making regional policy work', *Lloyds Bank Review*, January, pp. 34–47.
— (1973) *The Swindon Project*, London, Pitman.
— (1976) *Choice, Complexity and Ignorance*, Cambridge, Cambridge University Press.
— (1978) 'Whatever happened to Marshall's theory of value?' *Scottish Journal of Political Economy*, **25** (February), pp. 1–12.
Loomes, G. and Sugden, R. (1982) 'Regret theory: an alternative theory of rational choice under uncertainty', *Economic Journal*, **92** (December), pp. 805–24.
Lussier, D. A. and Olshavsky, R. W. (1979) 'Task complexity and contingent processing in brand choice', *Journal of Consumer Research*, **6** (September), pp. 154–65.
Lutz, M. A. and Lux, K. (1979) *The Challenge of Humanistic Economics*, Menlo Park, California, Benjamin/Cummings Publishing Company.

Machlup, F. (1946) 'Marginal analysis and empirical research', *American Economic Review*, **36** (September), pp. 519–54.

Mackay, D. (1975) *Clinical Psychology: Theory and Therapy*, London, Methuen.

Maital, S. (1982) *Minds, Markets and Money: Psychological Foundations of Economic Behavior*, New York, Basic Books.

Makhlouf-Norris, F. and Norris, H. (1972) 'The obessive compulsive syndrome as a neurotic device for the reduction of self-uncertainty', *British Journal of Psychiatry*, **121**, pp. 277–88.

Malinvaud, E. (1972) *Lectures on Microeconomic Theory*, Amsterdam, North-Holland.

March, J. G. and Olsen, J. P. (1976) *Ambiguity and Choice in Organizations*, Bergen, Universitetsforlaget.

Marris, R. L. (1964) *The Economic Theory of 'Managerial' Capitalism*, London, Macmillan.

Marschak, J. (1968) 'The economics of inquiring, communicating, deciding', *American Economic Review*, **58** (Supplement, May), pp. 1–18.

Marshall, A. (1920) *Principles of Economics* (8th edn.), London, Macmillan.

Maslow, A. (1970) *Motivation and Personality*, New York, Harper & Row.

Mason, R. S. (1981) *Conspicuous Consumption*, Farnborough, Gower Press.

Menger, K. (1871) *Principles of Economics* (English Translation, 1950, Glencoe, Illinois, Free Press).

Miller, G. A. (1956) 'The magic number seven plus or minus two: some limits on our capacity for processing information', *Psychological Review*, **63** (March), pp. 81–97.

Minsky, H. P. (1975) *John Maynard Keynes*, New York, Columbia University Press.

Mises, L. von (1966) *Human Action* (3rd edn.), Chicago, Henry Regnery & Company.

Mitchell, A. (1985) *The Nine American Lifestyles*, New York, Collier Macmillan.

Monroe, K. B. (1973) 'Buyers' subjective perceptions of price', *Journal of Marketing Research*, **10** (February), pp. 70–80.

Morgenstern, O. (1963) *On the Accuracy of Economic Observations* (2nd edn.), Princeton, NJ, Princeton University Press.

Moritz, M. and Seaman, B. (1981) *Going for Broke: The Chrysler Story*, New York, Doubleday.

Moss, S. (1981) *An Economic Theory of Business Strategy*, Oxford, Martin Robertson.

Muellbauer, J. (1974) 'Household production theory, quality, and the "hedonic technique"', *American Economic Review*, **64** (December), pp. 977–94.

Muth, R. F. (1966) 'Household production and consumer demand functions', *Econometrica*, **34** (July), pp. 699–708.

Nader, R. (1965) *Unsafe at Any Speed*, New York, Grossman.

Nelson, R. and Winter, S. G. (1982) *An Evolutionary Theory of Economic Change*, Cambridge, Mass., Harvard University Press.

Nolan, V. (1981) 'Open to change', *Management Decision*, **19**, No. 2, pp. 1–96.

Olshavsky, R. W. and Granbois, D. H. (1979) 'Consumer decision making—fact or fiction?' *Journal of Consumer Research*, **6** (September), pp. 93–100.

Olson, J. and Reynolds, T. J. (1983) 'Understanding consumers' cognitive structures: implications for advertising strategy', in Percy, L. and Woodside, A. (eds.) (1983) *Advertising and Consumer Psychology*, Lexington, Mass., Lexington Books, D. C. Heath.

Paroush, J. (1965) 'The order of acquisition of consumer durables', *Econometrica*, **33** (January), pp. 225–35.

— (1973) 'Efficient purchasing behaviour and efficient order relations in consumption', *Kyklos* **26**, pp. 91–112.

Pasinetti, L. L. (1981) *Structural Change and Economic Growth*, Cambridge, Cambridge University Press.

Payne, J. W. (1976) 'Task complexity and contingent processing in decision making: an information search and protocol analysis', *Organizational Behavior and Human Performance*, **16**, pp. 336–87.

Payne, R. L., Warr, P. B. and Hartley, J. (1983) 'Social class and the experience of unemployment', MRC/SSRC SAPU Memo. 549.

Penrose, E. T. (1959) *The Theory of the Growth of the Firm*, Oxford, Basil Blackwell.

Pickering, J. F. (1977) *The Acquisition of Consumer Durables: A Cross Sectional Investigation*, London, Associated Business Programmes.

Pickering, J. F., Harrison, J. A., Hebden, J. J., Isherwood, B. C. and Cohen, C. D. (1973) 'Are goods goods? Some empirical evidence', *Applied Economics*, **5**, pp. 1–18.

Pollak, R. A. (1977) 'Price dependent preferences', *American Economic Review*, **67**, pp. 64–75.

— (1985) 'A transactions cost approach to families and households', *Journal of Economic Literature*, **23** (June), pp. 581–608.

Popper, K. (1976) *Unended Quest: An Intellectual Autobiography*, London, Fontana/Collins.

Pyatt, F. G. (1964) *Priority Patterns and the Demand for Household Durable Goods*, Cambridge, Cambridge University Press.

Quine, W. van O. (1951) 'Two dogmas of empiricism', *Philosophical Review*, reprinted in Quine, W. van O. (1961) *From a Logical Point of View*, pp. 20–46, New York, Harper & Row.

Radner, R. (1975) 'A behavioral model of cost reduction', *Bell Journal of Economics*, **6** (Spring), pp. 196–215.

Ratchford, B. T. (1975) 'The new economic theory of consumer behavior: an interpretive essay', *Journal of Consumer Research*, **2** (September), pp. 65–75.

Ray, M. L. and Wilkie, W. L. (1970) 'Fear: the potential of an appeal neglected by marketing', *Journal of Marketing*, **34** (January), pp 54–62.

Reddaway, W. B. (1937) 'Special obstacles to full employment in a wealthy economy', *Economic Journal*, **47** (June), pp. 297–307.

Reilly, M. and Holman, R. (1977) 'Does task complexity or cue intercorrelation affect choice of an information processing strategy? An empirical investigation', in Perreault, W. D. jr (ed.) 1977 *Advances in Consumer Research IV*, Chicago, Association for Consumer Research.

Reilly, M., Holman, R. and Evered, R. (1976) 'Individual differences in information processing: an exploratory report', Working Paper No. 50, College of Business Administration, Pennsylvania State University, November.

Remenyi, J. V. (1979) 'Core demi-core interaction: toward a general theory of disciplinary and subdisciplinary growth', *History of Political Economy*, **11** (Spring), pp. 30–63.

Reynolds, T. J. and Gutman, J. (1983) 'Developing images for services through means-end chain analysis', in Berry L. L., Shostack, G. L. and Upah, G. D. (eds.) (1983) *Emerging Perspectives in Service Marketing*, Chicago, American Marketing Association.

— (1984) 'Laddering: extending the repertory grid methodology to attribute–consequence–value hierarchies', in Pitts, R. E. and Woodside, A. (eds.) (1984) *Personal Values and Consumer Psychology*, Lexington, Mass., D. C. Heath

Reynolds, T. J. and Jamieson, L. F. (1985) 'Image

representations: an analytic framework', in Jacoby, J. and Olson, J. C. (eds.) (1985) *Perceived Quality*, Lexington, Mass., D. C. Heath (for New York University Institute of Retail Management).

Richards, L. (1985) *Having Families: Marriage, Parenthood and Social Pressures in Australia*, (2nd edn.) Ringwood, Victoria, Penguin Books.

Robertson, D. H. (1956) *Economic Commentaries*, London, Macmillan.

Robinson, E. A. G. (1939) '*Oxford Economic Papers*: review', *Economic Journal*, **49** (September), pp. 538–43.

Rosen, S. (1974) 'Hedonic prices and implicit markets', *Journal of Political Economy*, **82** (January), pp. 34–53.

Ross, B. M. and Levy, N. (1958) 'Patterned predictions of chance events by children and adults', *Psychological Reports*, **4**, pp. 87–124.

Roy, A. D. (1952) 'Safety first and the holding of assets', *Econometrica*, **20**, pp. 431–49.

— (1954) 'The possibility of empirical testing of alternative theories of uncertainty', in Carter, C. F., Meredith, G. P. and Shackle, G. L. S. (eds.) (1954) *Uncertainty and Business Decisions*, Liverpool, Liverpool University Press.

Russ, F. A. (1971) 'Consumer evaluation of alternative product models', Unpublished Ph.D. dissertation, Carnegie-Mellon University.

Russo, E. J. and Dosher, B. A. (1983) 'Strategies for multiattribute binary choice', *Journal of Experimental Psychology: Learning, Memory and Cognition*, **9**, pp. 676–96.

Ryan, M. J. and Bonfield, E. H. (1975) 'The Fishbein extended model and consumer behaviour, *Journal of Consumer Research*, **2** (September), pp. 118–36.

Schoemaker, P. J. H. (1982) 'The expected utility model: its variants, purposes, evidence and limitation', *Journal of Economic Literature*, **20**, pp. 529–63.

Schwartz, R. and Orleans, S. (1967) 'On legal sanctions', *University of Chicago Law Review*, **34**, pp. 274–300.

Scitovsky, T. (1945) 'Some consequences of the habit of judging quality by price', *Review of Economic Studies*, **12**, pp. 100–5.

 (1976) *The Joyless Economy*, New York, Oxford University Press.

Selznick, P. (1957) *Leadership in Administration*, Evanston, Illinois, Harper & Row.

Shackle, G. L. S. (1949) *Expectation in Economics*, Cambridge, Cambridge University Press.

— (1955) *Uncertainty in Economics*, London, Cambridge University Press.
— (1958) *Time in Economics*, Amsterdam, North Holland.
— (1961) *Decision, Order and Time in Human Affairs*, Cambridge, Cambridge University Press.
— (1967) *The Years of High Theory: Invention and Tradition in Economic Thought, 1926–1939*, Cambridge, Cambridge University Press.
— (1979) *Imagination and the Nature of Choice*, Edinburgh, Edinburgh University Press.
— (1983) 'The bounds of unknowledge', in Wiseman, J. (ed.) (1983) *Beyond Positive Economics?* London, Macmillan.
— (1984) 'Comment on the papers by Randall Bausor and Malcolm Rutherford' (symposium on uncertainty), *Journal of Post Keynesian Economics*, **6** (Spring), pp. 389–93.
Shapiro, H. T. and Angevine, G. E. (1969) 'Consumer attitudes, buying intentions and expectations: an analysis of the Canadian data', *Canadian Journal of Economics*, **2** (May), pp. 230–49.
Shaw, D. R. A. (1984) 'The hedonic pricing technique applied to the cassette deck market and its relevance to consumer behaviour', Unpublished Honours Dissertation, University of Stirling.
Shibutani, T. (1955) 'Reference groups as perspectives', *American Journal of Sociology*, **60**, pp. 562–9.
Simon, H.A. (1955) 'A behavioral model of rational choice', *Quarterly Journal of Economics*, **69**, pp. 99–118 (reprinted in Simon, 1957).
— (1957) *Models of Man*, New York, Wiley.
— (1959) 'Theories of decision-making in economics and behavioral sciences', *American Economic Review*, **49**, (June), pp. 253–83.
— (1962) 'The architecture of complexity', *Proceedings of the American Philosophical Society*, **106** (December), pp. 467–82.
— (1969) *The Sciences of the Artificial*, Cambridge, Mass., MIT Press.
— (1976) 'From substantive to procedural rationality', in Latsis, S. J. (ed.) (1976) *Method and Appraisal in Economics*, Cambridge, Cambridge University Press.
— (1979) 'Rational decision making in business organizations', *American Economic Review*, **69** (September), pp. 493–513.
Skinner, A. S. (1979) 'Adam Smith: an aspect of modern economics?' *Scottish Journal of Political Economy*, **26** (June), pp. 109–26.

Slater, P. (ed.) (1976) *The Measurement of Intrapersonal Space by Grid Technique: Volume 1, Explorations of Intrapersonal Space*, Chichester, Wiley.
— (1977) *The Measurement of Intrapersonal Space by Grid Technique: Volume 2, Dimensions of Intrapersonal Space*, Chichester, Wiley.
Smith, R. P. (1975) *Consumer Demand for Cars in the USA*, Cambridge, Cambridge University Press.
Steinbruner, J. D. (1974) *The Cybernetic Theory of Decision*, Princeton, Princeton University Press.
Stewart, A. and Stewart, V. (1981) *Business Applications of Repertory Grid Technique*, New York, McGraw-Hill.
Stigler, G. J. and Becker, G. S. (1977) 'De gustibus non est disputandum', *American Economic Review*, 67, pp. 76–90.
Stout, D. K. (1977) *International Price Competitiveness, Non-Price Factors and Export Performance*, London, NEDO.
Streissler, E. W. (1973) 'Menger's theory of money and interest', in Hicks, J. R. and Weber, W. (eds.) *Carl Menger and the Austrian School of Economics*, Oxford, Oxford University Press.
Strotz, R. H. (1957) 'The empirical implications of a utility tree', *Econometrica*, 25 (April), pp. 269–80.
Strumpel, B., Novy, K. and Schwartz, M. A. (1969) 'Consumer attitudes and outlays in Germany and North America', Paper read to the Ciret Conference, 1969.
Svenson, O. (1979) 'Process descriptions of decision making', *Organizational Behavior and Human Performance*, 23, pp. 86–112.
Tarshis, L. (1980) 'Post Keynesian economics: a promise that bounced?' *American Economic Review*, 70 (May), pp. 10–14.
Taylor, J. W. (1974) 'The role of risk in consumer behavior', *Journal of Marketing*, 38 (April), pp. 54–60.
Taylor, L. D. (1975) 'Commentary on Ratchford, "the new economic theory of consumer behavior: an interpretive essay"' *Journal of Consumer Research*, 2 (September), pp. 76–7.
Thaler, R. (1980) 'Toward a positive theory of consumer choice', *Journal of Economic Behavior and Organization*, 1 (March), pp. 39–60.
Thaler, R. and Shefrin, H. M. (1981) 'An economic theory of self control', *Journal of Political Economy*, 89 (April), pp. 396–406.
Thompson, M. (1979) *Rubbish Theory: The Creation and Destruction of Value*, Oxford, Oxford University Press.

Townshend, H. (1937) 'Liquidity premium and the theory of value', *Economic Journal*, **47** (March), pp. 157–69.

Tuck, M. (1976) *How do We Choose?* London, Methuen.

Tversky, A. (1969) 'Intransitivity of preferences', *Psychological Review*, **76** (January), pp. 31–48.

— 'Elimination by aspects: a theory of choice', *Psychological Review*, **79**, pp. 281–99.

Von Neumann, J. and Morgenstern, O. (1947) *The Theory of Games and Economic Behaviour*, Princeton, Princeton University Press.

Warr, P. B. (1983) 'Work, jobs and unemployment', *Bulletin of the British Psychological Society*, **36** (September), pp. 305–11.

Warshaw, P. R. (1980) 'A new model for predicting behavioral intentions: an alternative to Fishbein', *Journal of Marketing*, **17** (May), pp. 153–72.

Waterman, D. A. and Newell, A. (1971) 'Protocol analysis as a task for artificial intelligence', *Artificial Intelligence*, **2**, pp. 285–318.

Watts, M. J. and Gaston N. G. (1982) 'The "reswitching" of consumption bundles: a parallel to the capital controversies', *Journal of Post Keynesian Economics*, **5** (Winter), pp. 281–8.

Weitz, B. and Wright, P. (1979) 'Retrospective self-insight on factors considered in product evaluation', *Journal of Consumer Research*, **6** (December), pp. 280–94.

Wells, W. D. (1975) 'Psychographics: a critical review', *Journal of Marketing Research*, **12** (May), pp. 196–213.

Wheatley, J. J. (1971) 'Marketing and the use of fear- or anxiety-arousing appeals', *Journal of Marketing*, **35** (April), pp. 62–4.

Wilkie, W. L. and Pessemeir, E. A. (1973) 'Issues in marketing's use of multi-attribute attitude models', *Journal of Marketing Research*, **10** (November), pp. 428–41.

Williamson, O. E. (1975) *Markets and Hierarchies: Analysis and Antitrust Implications*, New York, Free Press.

Winter, S. G. jr (1964) 'Economic "natural selection" and the theory of the firm', *Yale Economic Essays*, **4** (Spring), pp. 224–72.

Wolf, C. jr (1970) 'The present value of the past', *Journal of Political Economy*, **78**, pp. 783–92.

— (1973) 'Heresies about time: wasted time, double duty time and past time', *Quarterly Journal of Economics*, **87**, pp. 661–7.

Wood, A. J. B. (1978) *A Theory of Pay*, Cambridge, Cambridge University Press.

Wray, M. (1956) 'Uncertainty, prices, and entrepreneural

expectations', *Journal of Industrial Economics*, **4** (February), pp. 107–28.
— (1957) *The Women's Outerwear Industry*, London, Duckworth.
Wright, J. (1985) 'Mitsubishi milestones', *Wheels*, July, pp. 86–94.
Wright, P. (1975) 'Consumer choice strategies: simplifying vs. optimising', *Journal of Marketing Research*, **12** (February), pp. 60–7.

Index

Adams, F. G., 103
Adams, J. L., 113
Adams-Webber, J. R., xii, 88, 149, 151, 158, 163
Adaptability, 71-2
Advertising, 44-5, 99-100, 200-1, 269-70
Aggregation, 12-13, 46, 74, 177, 212, 219, 235, 243-4, 259
Aggression, 96-7
Ajzen, I., 47
Akaah, I., 47-50
Akerlof, G. A., 62
Alcaly, R. E., 260
Alden, S. D., 153
Allen, R. G. D., 25
Ambiguity, 4, 22, 163-4
Andrews, P. W. S., 97
Angevine, G. E., 103
Animal spirits, xii, 130-1, 148
Anxiety, 31, 96-9, 108, 155, 170-1, 228, 265
Artificial intelligence, xi
Ascendency function, 215-21
Aspirations/targets, 9-10, 45, 79-80, 109, 127, 181-4, 188, 190-1, 194, 196-200, 215, 221-6, 233, 236-7, 244-6, 258, 276-7, 291
Assumptions, 6, 16
Astrology, 112, 228
Attitudes, xi, 3, 99, 149, 153
Austrian economics, 5, 17
Axiom of Archimedes, 249

Bach, J. S., 13-14
Bain, A. D., 265
Bannister, D., 88, 149-50, 163
Bargaining, 83, 100

Baumol, W. J., 9
Bausor, R., 14-15, 63-4
Baxter, J. L., 100
Beck, A. T., 109
Becker, G. S., 6, 29, 59, 65, 86, 108-9, 249, 285
Behavioural economics, ix-x, 4-21 *passim*, 24, 40, 173, 233-7, 245-6, 271
Beliefs, 88, 117, 132, 136-48 *passim*, 163, 214-27 *passim*
Bettman, J. R., 34, 201
Blackwell, R. D., 240-1
Blatt, J., 212-13, 242, 282
Bonfield, E. H., 49
Borch, K., 249-50
Brand loyalty, 33
Brown, A., 27
Bruno, A. V., 206
Budgeting, x, 34-5, 39-40, 66-7, 73, 101-3, 190, 197, 243-4, 256-60, 264, 270, 277, 280-1

Cairncross, A., 65
Cameras, 20, 67-8, 137-45
Canterbery, R., 235, 263-4
Careers, 3, 20, 54, 60, 64, 81, 97, 118-23, 152-4, 244-6, 283
Carter, C. F., 131-2, 220, 225, 229
Casson, M. C., 72, 77
Catch-22, 152
Causality, 11-13
Chance, 112, 220
Chandler, A. D., 163
Characteristic filtering, x, 141, 183-206 *passim*, 213, 221, 233, 236, 242-5, 258-80 *passim*

Index

Characteristics analysis of demand, x, 24-41, 51-2, 127-8, 179-202 *passim*, 235, 239-40
Chick, V., 26
Choice, 1, 53, 83, 92-6, 102-9, 118, 124-5, 129, 153, 169, 257
    crucial, 93, 125, 188, 241
    heuristics, see procedures
    matrix, 175-81, 189-93, 201-2, 205
Clausewitz, C. von, 63-4
Coase, R.H., 76, 80
Coddington, A., 7, 136, 158
Cognitive dissonance, 257
Commonsense, 86, 115, 192
Compatibility, 12
Competence, 1, 82, 88, 101-9, 165, 170, 211, 262, 285
Competition
    amongst consumers, 3, 99, 123
    non-price, 23, 267-81
    price, 23, 267-81
Complementarities, 31, 74-6, 79
Complexity, x, 1, 23, 51, 55, 57-67, 88, 98, 112, 145-7, 190, 212, 218, 233, 236
Confidence, 101-5, 113, 134-5, 230
Conspicuous consumption, 81, 99, 155, 157
Constraints, 4, 38, 102-3
    constrained maximisation, 10-11, 34, 36, 86
Constructs, 88-110, 113, 129, 137-42, 149-59, 165-7, 171-8, 183, 188, 203, 219-22, 237, 248, 251-4, 285
Control, 54-5, 82, 88, 96, 112, 123, 132, 134, 151, 171, 178, 227, 258, 262
Corporations, see firms
Court, A. T., 41
Cowling, K., 44
CPRS (Central Policy Review Staff), 45, 266
Creativity, 24, 113, 129, 135, 148
Cripps, T. F., 281
Crisis, 236-7
Crockett, W. H., 167
Cubbin, J., 44-6
Cunningham, M. T., 58
Curry, D. J., 83
Cyert, R. M., 6, 18, 58, 79, 196, 236, 252

Dakin, S. R., 228
Dash, J. F., 100
Davidson, P., 26
Day, R. H., 10
Deaton, A., 24, 27, 43, 236, 239
Debreu, G., 59
Decomposability, 12, 30, 65, 71-2
Deliberation, 57-8, 67, 116-17, 174, 205
Demand curves, 28, 36-8
Depression, 91, 109
Deviance, 19, 115
Dilemmas, 130, 200, 202, 220-1
Disappointment, 3, 82-8, 102, 106, 109-10, 122, 156, 159, 161, 183, 213
Diversification, 74-6, 101-6, 156, 160-1
Do it yourself, 6, 78-9
Dosher, B. A., 181
Douglas, E. J., 31
Dow, S. C., 26
Doyle, P., 31
Duck, S., 6, 95
Duhem, P., 163
Dunkelberg, W. C., 103
Dunnett, P. J. S., 265

Earl, P. E., ix, 26, 57, 71, 77, 83, 92, 95, 98-9, 103, 106, 163, 173, 199, 221, 226, 240, 242, 267-8, 284-5
Edwards, M., 166
Eichner, A. S., 250
Elasticity (see also resistance to change), xi, 31, 34
Ellman, M., 190
Elster, J., 10, 98, 102, 133, 249-50, 285

Emotions, 96-100
Empirical studies, x-xii, 17-21, 25, 27, 30-1, 41-52, 57, 91-2, 95, 99, 133, 149-55, 158-60, 167, 171-3, 181, 201, 209, 212, 234, 236, 240-1, 250-4, 257, 259
Engel curves, 235
Engel, J. F., 240-1
Entrepreneurship, 54-5, 70, 88, 130, 267, 283
Equilibrium, 11-12, 15, 30, 238
Escher, M., 13-14
Evolution, 12, 68-84, 101-10, 140, 154-62
Expectations, xi, 1, 15, 22-3, 48, 61, 85-90, 97, 102, 107, 110, 118-44 *passim*, 153-74 *passim*, 178, 183, 191, 193, 215-27 *passim*, 256, 284
  rational, 8
Experience, 38, 89, 95, 107, 113, 129, 156, 171, 258, 265
Experimentation, xi, 10, 93-5, 107-8, 113, 158, 171, 188, 193, 214, 253
Exploitation, 260

Farley, J., 33
Fatal flaw, 184, 274
Feige, E. L., 18
Fenwick, I., 31
Festinger, L., 257
Feyerabend, P. K., 98, 228, 250
Firms, viii, 53-84 *passim*, 98, 105, 147, 156, 189, 236
Fishbein, M. A., 47-9, 241
Fishburn, P. O., 233
Fisher, F. M., 43
Flexibility, xi, 70-3, 84, 160
Focusing, 105-7, 215-23
Food, 20, 99, 106, 143, 168-9
Ford, H., 160-1, 267
Ford, J. L., xi, 125, 217-20, 224-5, 252
Fransella, F., 88, 156
French, M., 129
Friedman, M., 6

Friend, I., 103
Fryer, D., 92
Furniture, 20, 71-3

Gabor, A., 259
Galbraith, J. K., 44, 82
Gallagher, W. M., 190
Gambler preference map, 216-20
Garfinkel, H., 115, 138, 148, 151
Gaston, N. G., 35-8
Georgescu-Roegen, N., 238
Giffen goods, 28, 37-8, 259-60
Gimpl, M. L., 228
Godley, W. A. H., 281
Goldstein, M., 100
Gorman, W. M., 29
Granbois, D. H., 58
Granger, C. W. J., 259
Grasmick, H. G., 101
Green, H. A. J., 34, 238
Green, P. E., 50, 241-2
Griliches, Z., 42
Guilt, 99-101, 169-70, 244, 265
Gutman, J., 92-4, 150, 153, 172

Habit, 27-8
Haines, G. H., Jr, 34, 51
Hall, R. L., 261
Hamouda, O., 14-15
Hansen, F., 241
Harcourt, G. C., 36
Harrison, S. N., 182
Hart, A. G., 70-3
Hawkins, D. I., 233-4
Hebden, J. J., 264
Hedging, 7, 74-6, 157-60, 172, 220, 229
Hedonic technique, 25, 41-6, 260-1, 267
Heiner, R. D., 4, 61, 170
Henry, H., 37, 99
Hesselman, L., 267-8
Hey, J. D., 59, 125, 205, 220, 253
Hi-fi equipment, 42, 62, 71-2, 108, 160, 198-9, 201
Hicks, J. R., 25-9, 33, 37, 40-1, 55
Hierarchy, 13-16, 139, 145-7, 174, 177, 238-9

Index

Hinkle, D. N., xi-xii, 150-4, 167, 178
Hirsch, F., 99
Hitch, C. J., 261
Hoch, S. J., 56
Hoepfl, R. T., 48, 50
Hofstadter, D. R., 13-14, 146
Holidays, 20, 60, 75, 95, 125, 168
Holman, R., 240
Hostility, 81, 97-8, 115, 132, 171, 286
Household production theory, xi, 21-43 *passim*, 46, 53, 63, 86, 108, 242
Housing, 3, 20, 65, 78, 95, 176-7, 184-7, 201-3
Houthakker, H. S., 27-9, 51-2, 263
Huber, G. P., 48-50
Human capital, 2, 108
Hunt, M., 254
Hutchison, T. W., 17, 149

Iaccoca, L., 160-1, 167
Ignorance, 23, 57, 132, 196, 229
Imagination, 128, 131, 216, 221, 251-2
Implication grid technique, xii, 150-4, 167, 172
Implications (of choices), 67, 125, 150-71 *passim*, 178-9, 182, 186-8, 199-214 *passim*, 219, 223, 233, 237, 244, 248, 255-9, 263
Impulsiveness, 96, 157, 229
Income, 27, 42, 76, 102, 118-19, 244-6, 263-4, 283
  effects, 26, 235, 264
Indecomposability, 12
Indifference analysis, 24, 27, 86, 145, 178, 215-19, 235, 240, 245
Inducement effect, 105-6
Inertia, 56, 163-9
Inferior good, 235, 264
Infinite regress, 10, 14, 116, 137, 139
Inflation, 1, 80

Information, 8-9, 26, 33, 60, 71, 111-15, 135, 141, 148, 165, 182, 191, 194, 202
  overloading, 56, 59, 180, 183, 185, 201, 212, 224, 244, 248
Insurance, 7, 60-2, 68-9, 77, 165
Interdependence, 3, 170-1
Internalisation theory, 22, 77-9
Intolerance, 40, 241, 246-50
Ironmonger, D. S., 234, 238, 242, 265

Jackson, P. R., 91
Jamieson, L. F., 153
Jefferson, M., 71, 119, 132
Johnson, E. J., 234
Judgement, 17, 21, 39, 54, 110, 138-43, 147, 158, 170, 174-5, 230, 253, 260

Kahneman, D., 209-10, 212
Karakaoglu, G., 284
Katona, G., 6, 103
Katzner, D. W., 34
Kay, H., 100
Kay, N. M., xiii, 11, 54, 63-5, 69, 71, 74, 160
Kelly, G. A., 88-103 *passim*, 109, 139-43, 148-50, 164, 171, 183
Keynes, J. M., xi, 26, 71, 130, 134, 229-30
Klein, L. R., 103
Klevorick, A. K., 260
Koestler, A., 24, 113
Korgoankar, P. K., 47-50
Kornai, J., 194, 220
Koutsoyiannis, A., 29
Kuhn, T. S., 105, 162

Lakatos, I., 164
Lamfalussy, A., 268
Lancaster, K. J., 29-42, 65, 235, 240, 242, 257
Lea, S. E. G., 182
Leech, D., 44-6
Levy, N., 113
Lewis, A., 100, 153

Lexicographic decision making, 233-6, 239-43
Lifestyle, 3-5, 58, 61, 64, 67-79, 110, 129, 153, 159, 168-9, 255
Linder, M., 233
Linkages, 11-13, 64-5, 73-7, 156-62, 167, 170
Lipsey, R. G., 28, 37
Liquidity, 71-4
Littlechild, S. C., 17
Loasby, B. J., 26, 29, 189-90
Loomes, G., 210-11
Lussier, D. A., 241
Lutz, M. A., 238-9
Lux, K., 238-9

Machlup, F., 18
Mackay, D., 96
Macroeconomics, 25-6, 70, 283
Magic, 228-9
Mair, J. M. M., 88, 149, 150, 163
Maital, S., 99, 209, 228
Makhlouf-Norris, F., xiii, 158-9
Malinvaud, E., 236, 239
Management, 53, 228
March, J. G., 58, 79, 196, 236, 252
Market share, 45-6
Marketing, 4, 25, 46-52, 58-9, 99-100, 114, 149, 169, 240-2
Marriage, 6, 59, 67, 77-8, 81-3, 115, 132, 183, 193, 198, 248
Marris, R. L., 230, 265
Marschak, J., 9
Marshall, A., 25-6, 29, 40, 257
Marxian economics, 5, 260
Maslow, A., 239
Mason, R. S., 99
Meisel, P., 167
Menasco, M. B., 83
Menger, K., 238-9
Methodology, 5-22, 93, 108, 113, 214, 240, 252-3, 271
Miller, G. A., 9, 48, 176
Minsky, H. P., 26
Mises, L. von, 17, 70
Mitchell, A., 4

Monroe, K. B., 259
Morgenstern, O., 18, 208
Moritz, M., 160
Moss, S., 105
Motivation, 22, 54, 99, 174, 178, 211
Motoring, 1, 20-1, 43-4, 60, 64, 69, 89-90, 94, 97, 114-16, 149-52, 163-5, 168, 177-8, 192, 195, 204, 237-8, 240, 247-9, 255-79 *passim*
Mould of tolerance, 183, 220-7, 252, 270, 272, 276-8
 reshaping of, 188, 196-203, 251, 266
Muellbauer, J., 24, 42-3, 236, 239
Muth, R. F., 29, 34, 65

Nader, R., 114
Nelson, R., 58
Neoclassical economics, ix, 5-6, 11-14, 17, 21-3, 29, 54-5, 59, 87, 96, 105, 108-9, 175, 217, 238-40, 243-8, 284-5
Newell, A., 254
Nolan, V., 113
Norris, H., xiii, 158-9
Novelty, 67, 103-4

Obsessive behaviour, xi, 156, 164-6, 172
Olsen, J. P., 58
Olshavsky, R. W., 58, 241
Olson, J., 153
Opportunity costs, 59, 65-7, 71, 81, 93, 132, 187, 198, 255
Optimality, 9-10, 36, 53, 179, 188
Organisation, x, 53, 60, 79-83, 89, 139-47, 156-63
Orleans, S., 101

Paradigm, 105, 162, 285
Paroush, J., 235
Pasinetti, L. L., 235, 263-4
Payne, J. W., 181, 201, 234
Payne, R. L., 91-2
Penrose, E. T., 103
Perceptions, x, 15, 70, 77, 80, 86, 99, 108, 170, 242, 251, 259

Index

Personality, 88-9, 91, 148-55, 164
Pessemeir, E. A., 47
Pickering, J. F., 31, 38, 103, 236, 264
Planning
  corporate, 59, 104, 156
  family, 20, 64, 124-5, 129, 222-3, 241
  household, 60-8
  scenario, 71, 132
  Soviet, 190
  strategic, 60-8
Policy making, 6-7, 46, 51, 92, 267-70, 280-4
Pollak, R. A., 76, 78, 83, 260
Popper, K., 17
Possibilities, 7, 61-2, 65, 97, 111-35 *passim*, 137-9, 142, 147-8, 214-27 *passim*, 251
Post Keynesian economics, 5, 26, 234, 283-4
Potential surprise analysis, x, 111, 117-29, 215-27 *passim*, 252-3
Prediction, 7, 88-9, 92-6, 98, 103, 132-4, 148-55, 171, 174, 178, 206, 227, 230, 255-6
Preferences, xi, 4, 33-4, 38, 44, 52, 58, 63, 86, 96, 104, 108, 124, 145, 231, 234-9, 245-6, 251, 285
Prices, 1-2, 11, 20, 27-8, 32-3, 36-8, 40-6, 53, 55, 72, 86, 102, 144, 192, 254-82 *passim*
Principles, 115, 164, 171, 210, 246-50, 265
Priorities, xi, 175, 185-205 *passim*, 232-46 *passim*, 259, 261, 264-82
Probabilities, 2, 111, 123-30, 134, 207-12, 219, 227, 231, 283
Problem solving, 55, 105, 108, 192, 201, 236-7
Procedures for making decisions, xi, 4, 40-1, 45, 165, 230
  additive differences, 180-1, 199, 202-5, 213, 263, 276
  characteristic filtering, see separate entry
  characteristics cut-offs expectancy value, 181, 280
  compensatory, xi, 47-51, 175, 179-82, 193, 197-8, 202-4, 207, 232-3, 241-7, 250-1, 257, 269-79 *passim*, 282
  conjunctive, 159, 182-3, 189, 194-5, 202-4, 241
  contingent, xi, 57, 201-7, 240, 251
  elimination by aspects, 234, 240
  non-compensatory, 46, 182-8, 193-4, 207, 232-53 *passim*, 271-79 *passim*
  polymorphous, 182, 204
  satisficing expectancy value, 179-80
  sequential elimination, 240
  simple averaging, 181-2, 204
Product lifecycle, 21, 171, 254, 262-66
Programmed behaviour, xi, 57, 63, 67, 170
Prospect theory, 209-12
Protocol analysis, 254
Psychographics, 153, 206
Psychology, 9, 17, 22, 85-6, 250
  behavioural, 85
  cognitive, 133, 257
  personal construct theory, x-xi, 85, 88-110 *passim*, 137-45, 285
  physiological, 85
  social, 6
Pyatt, F. G., 236

Quandt, R. E., 9
Quine, W. van O., 163

Radner, R., 166, 236
Random behaviour, 58-9, 117, 194-5, 229
Ratchford, B. T., 31, 38
Rationality, 96-100

bounded, 9-10, 40, 50, 57, 67, 117, 180, 186-8, 194, 233, 258, 261
global, 182
procedural, xi
substantive, xi
Ray, M. L., 100
Rayner, A. J., 44
Recipes for success, 17, 56-7, 84, 227-30
Reddaway, W. B., 103
Reference group, 48, 107, 115, 165
Reference point, 67, 87, 89-90, 109, 178, 180, 209-11
Reference standard, 137, 266, 280
Regret theory, 210-12
Reilly, M., 240
Relationships, 6, 76-83, 87, 105-7, 157, 160, 171
Remenyi, J. V., 164
Repertoire, 57, 90, 109, 137, 151, 180
Repertory grid technique 149-54, 172-3, 176, 251
Research programme, x, 23-4, 164-6, 173
Resistance to change, xi, 22, 85, 99, 160-9, 186, 285
Retirement, 61, 104
Revolutionary change, 24, 81, 232
Reynolds, T. J., 150, 153
Richards, L., 59
Rip-off avoidance, 257, 260-2, 178
Risk
avoidance, 69-70, 211, 230
neutrality, 208
taking, 69-70, 79, 255, 282-4
Robertson, D. H., 166
Robinson, E. A. G., 18
Roles, 81-3
Rosen, S., 39, 257
Rosenbluth, G., 28, 37
Ross, B. M., 113
Routines, 56-60, 84
Roy, A. D., 213, 252-3

Rules (see also procedures for making decisions), 56-7, 137-47, 155-6, 167, 174-231 *passim*, 271-9 *passim*
of thumb, xi, 9
Russ, F. A., 241
Russo, E. J., 181
Ryan, M. J., 49

Safety first, 212-3
Safety margins, 73-4
Satiation, 182, 198-9, 240, 242
Satisficing, x, 9-11, 14, 177-206 *passim*, 221-7
Scenarios, 20, 122-3, 134-6, 237
Schizophrenia, xi, 142, 156-62, 172, 229
Schoemaker, P. J. H., 209
Schwartz, R., 101
Science, 88, 104-5, 109, 162-4, 228-9, 250
Scitovsky, T., 85, 260
Scott, W. J., 101
Seaman, B., 160
Search, 10, 58, 181-3, 189-90, 193, 195, 220
Secondhand value, 54, 72-3, 262
Self-
deception, 134
esteem, 31, 39, 155, 198, 243
image, 94-5, 98-9, 102, 155, 198
Selznick, P., 162
Set-up costs, 86
Settle down, 84
Shackle, G. L. S., xii, 14-15, 98, 111-13, 117-30, 134, 142, 148, 213-27, 252-3
Shapiro, H. T., 103
Shaw, D. R. A., 204
Shefrin, H. M., 102
Shibutani, T., 115
Short cuts, 189-94, 201, 234, 251
Simon, H. A., xi, 2, 6, 9-11, 18, 57, 189
Skills, 1-2, 54
Skinner, A. S., 205
Slack, 73-4, 80, 196-7

Slater, P., 149
Smith, R. P., 103
Specialisation, 81-2, 101-2
Speculation, 1, 3, 70, 102
Spill-overs, 12-13, 156-7, 167-8
Srinivasan, V., 241-2
Standards, 104, 266
Steinbruner, J. D., 58, 131-6, 179, 246
Stewart, A., 149
Stewart, V., 149
Stigler, G. J., 86, 108-9, 285
Stout, D. K., 45
Strange loop, 13-17, 140, 187
Strategies, x, 3, 15, 22, 63-8, 83-5, 101, 256
  corporate, 22, 71, 160
  mental, xiii, 156, 165-72
Streissler, E. W., 72
Stress, 31, 55, 74, 156, 166, 176
Strotz, R. H., 34
Structuralism, 11-13, 63, 148
Strumpel, B., 103
Substitution, xi, 13, 23, 24, 27, 30-34, 43, 53-4, 175, 232, 234-50 *passim*, 255, 263, 283
Subcontracting, 77-9
Subjectivism, 109, 136, 148
Sugden, R., 210-12
Superstition, 228-90
Surprise, 1-2, 7, 10, 55, 57, 62, 73, 84, 87, 117, 141, 155, 286
Svenson, O., 201, 234
Synergy, 74-7, 84, 105, 156, 160, 172, 259, 285

Tactics, 63-7, 84
Tarshis, L., 148
Taxation, 1, 100-1, 153, 282-3
Taylor, D., 195
Taylor, J. W., 100
Taylor, L. D., 27-8, 39, 263
Technological change, 1, 21, 55, 78
Thaler, R., 98, 102, 257
Thompson, M., 237
Threat, 98, 100

Threshold, 98-9, 171, 223
Tie-break, 194-9, 262, 280
Townshend, H., 103
Trade, 280-2
Transaction costs, xii, 44, 68, 77
Trade-offs, 40, 43, 50, 67, 205, 235
Trial and error, 11
Tuck, M., 49
Turbulence, x, 4, 11, 22, 54-5, 68-84 *passim*, 87, 97, 119, 135, 142, 156-62, 170-2, 282
Tversky, A., 209-10, 212, 234, 240

Uncertainty, xii, 1-4, 38, 51, 59, 63, 70-1, 97, 111, 125-31, 153-4, 176, 189, 200, 207-31 *passim*, 252-3
Unemployment, 61, 80, 87, 91-2, 283
Utility, 25, 32, 40, 86-7, 110, 190, 238, 270
  expected, 208-13, 219, 230-1, 242
  tree, 34-6, 55

Value for money, 260-1
Veblen, T., 285
Vegetarianism, 115, 168-9, 248-91
Von Neumann, J., 208

Warr, P. B., 91-2
Warshaw, P. R., 49
Washing Machines, 30, 42, 201, 267-8
Waterman, D. A., 254
Watts, M. J., 35-8
Way of life, see lifestyle
Weitz, B., 240
Wells, W. D., 153
Wheatley, J. J., 100
White, J. G., 58
Wildt, A. R., 206
Wilkie, W. L., 47, 100
Williamson, O. E., 62, 76
Winter, S. G., Jr., 10, 58
Wolf, C., Jr., 165

Women's Movement, 1, 81, 116, 129
Wood, A. J. B., 100
World-view, 90, 93, 140-3, 149-50, 158, 160-1
Wray, M., 253
Wright, J., 265
Wright, P., 240-1